MW01641110

Community Associations: A Guide to Successful Management

Professional Review
Edward H. Boudreau, Jr., CPM®
Robert D. Demson, CPM®
Barbara L. Holland, CPM®

Tulie O'Connor
Editorial Director, Education Publishing

Amanda Hellenthal
Editor, Education Publishing

Markisan Naso
Editorial Assistant

Community Associations: A Guide to Successful Management

Stephen R. Barber, CPM®
Vickie Gaskill, CPM®, ARM®, MPM®

IREM Institute of Real Estate Management

Library of Congress Cataloging-in-Publication Data

Barber, Stephen R., 1946-
Community associations : a guide to successful management / Stephen R. Barber, Vickie Gaskill.
p. cm.
Includes index.
ISBN-13: 978-1-57203-132-6 (hbk.)
ISBN-10: 1-57203-132-8 (hbk.)
1. Common interest ownership community associations—Management. 2. Homeowners' associations—Management. I. Gaskill, Vickie, 1952- II. Title.

HD7287.8.B37 2008
333.33'8—dc22

2007049479

To my father, Melvin, who never got to see me grow up with such wonderful accomplishments and family. Without that drive he instilled in me, I could not have had such a lucky, happy, fulfilling life to share with others. To my lovely, understanding, tall, red-haired Mary, for giving me the space to live such a life. And to our wonderful children: my favorite daughter, Michele, and my special son-in-law, Chuck; my favorite son, Chris; and those happy grandkids, Jordan, Alanna, Drew, and Devon. And, last but not least, to my patient office staff and clients for allowing me the time away from work to complete this book.

S.R.B.

To my mom, who instilled in me a passion for doing the right thing. She never judged me or gave me a "guilt trip," even when I came to her at the ripe old age of 17 and said that I wanted to get married. To my husband, Tim, who doesn't always understand why I do what I do; and to my children, who appear to want to follow me into this crazy business of real estate management.

V.L.G.

To the oftentimes underappreciated, overworked, and underpaid professional manager of community associations. We salute your loyalty and commitment to making the community association environment an enjoyable place to live.

S.R.B. & V.L.G.

Preface

Food, water, and—of course—shelter are the ever-present needs of any existing society, population, community, or life as we know it. Within our communities, we need order and harmony as we share our lives through work and living spaces. With the advent of the community association—or common interest development (CID)—within ever-expanding worldwide population centers, we find the need for order and harmony even greater as these developments continue to evolve into major communities in which more and more individuals choose to live.

As authors of this book, with over 50 years combined working knowledge in residential housing needs and management, we realize the need for an up-to-date transcript of present-day management techniques. Higher density residential communities are becoming the norm rather than the exception in our country today, whether in urban settings or outlying suburban areas. It is important to run our common interest developments with sound guidance and direction.

Here in the Pacific Northwest, where we live and work, the present construction building boom is still toward more owner-occupied homes—and not just single-family lots, but also the popular community associations or CIDs. It is quite evident that the need for community association management will increase due to this growth in housing.

In other areas of the country, in order to meet a city's urban boundary requirements developers are building mixed-use structures that not only contain commercial and retail trade, but also house residential needs. Real estate managers need to have knowledge of all of these uses. Ideally, such properties will employ just one property manager, as it is much more efficient and cost effective. That one manager will need the skills and experience level necessary to preserve harmony among different types of users.

Careers in association or CID management are really just beginning to blossom into some of the most viable occupations for real estate professionals. In writing this book, we could see that, although we covered numerous techniques in specific areas of management, there are still many areas that could make up an entire book on their own—such as management pricing, popular menu-driven contracts, and effective office staffing concepts. The management community is hungry for more formal education on the topic of association management because of the increasing demand for more good managers in this field. IREM sees this need and is beginning to add more education emphasis toward this endeavor.

As authors, we hope this book will get you headed in the proper direction and instill a sound philosophical approach to community association management. There will be much more you will learn when getting into the day-to-day management of a community, but this book should provide you with a level of confidence and reasonable business practices to ensure your association is a successful one.

Acknowledgements

Nothing goes to production without the help of a lot of people. Most of the community association professionals (managers, lawyers, accountants, etc.) are quoted and given their due credit throughout this book. A sincere thank you goes to our mentor, Richard Muhlebach, CPM®, for his inspiration and direction. We would like to thank the IREM staff for all of the assistance and encouragement that they gave us throughout this process. Tulie O'Connor was our rock! In a very kind, supportive way she never let up. Amanda Hellenthal took over editing on this title and made sure that the finished product was of the quality expected from IREM. We'd also like to thank the review team. Their suggestions and insight were greatly appreciated.

About the Authors

Vickie Gaskill, CPM®, ARM®, MPM®, is co-owner/broker for Bell-Anderson & Associates, LLC, AMO®, in Kent, Washington. Ms. Gaskill's professional property management career began in 1986 when she joined Bell-Anderson as a bookkeeper. She and her husband, Tim, purchased Bell-Anderson (founded in 1963) in 2002. Her company manages single-family homes, small multifamily residential properties, and community associations.

Ms. Gaskill has served IREM in many capacities. She has been President of Western Washington Chapter #27, Regional Vice President for Region 12, and has served on many local and national committees. Vickie is a National Faculty Instructor for IREM and has had the opportunity to facilitate the education of hundreds of professional real estate managers.

Ms. Gaskill also volunteers her time and energy to other trade associations representing the real estate management profession, serving as the national Treasurer of NARPM® (the National Association of Residential Property Managers) for 2008. She maintains membership in the National Apartment Association (NAA) and the Community Associations Institute (CAI). Ms. Gaskill has assisted her local community (Kent, Washington) by working to bring in federal grant funds that can be used to enhance the quality of life for its businesses and residents.

Vickie and Tim Gaskill have been married for 38 years. They have two wonderful daughters (Dawn, ARM®, and Carrie, ARM®), two just-as-wonderful sons-in-law (Ross and Scott), and three absolutely fabulous grandchildren (Braden, Cassie, and Tanner).

Stephen R. Barber, CPM®, is founder and president of Invest West Management, LLC, AMO®, a Washington- and Oregon-based full service management brokerage house formed in 1979, specializing in residential, office, and community association (CID) management.

Mr. Barber holds a B.S. degree from Oregon State University. He has an extensive background in the real estate management industry. He has served on numerous trade association committees and directorships. He has been an active member of IREM, participating on both the local Chapter #29 level as a past president and on the national level as Regional Vice President for Region 12. He has spent over 20 years promoting the IREM ethics by facilitating their national ethics classes and serving in all capacities on the IREM national ethics and discipline committees and boards.

Mr. Barber, an avid sailor, has written several articles for the *Journal of Property Management* (*JPM*), has taught real estate investment classes in his community at Clark College, and has spoken at several other community events. He and his lovely wife, Mary, live in Vancouver, Washington.

Contents

1

An Introduction to Community Association Management

INTRODUCTION

Community management is a fast-paced, constantly changing profession, and managers sometimes ask why anyone would want to be in that business. Actually, it offers many rewards and challenges, and competent managers are in demand. Before we delve into the virtues of this much-needed field of expertise, let's consider the phenomena that created it and the types of community associations that currently exist.

THE HISTORY OF ASSOCIATIONS

The *association* is a worldwide living concept that is neither unique to the United States nor a creation of the twenty-first century. Its history goes back to the time of the Roman Empire, when Roman leaders faced with a shortage of land solved their housing dilemma by passing a law permitting Roman citizens to own individual dwelling units in multifamily structures. Questions remain about the details of the Roman law; however, it is generally believed to be the predecessor of the *condominium* concept as we know it today.

This type of higher-density living became popular again in the Middle Ages when many cities in Western Europe feared attack by outside enemies.

This apprehension drove people to live within the confines of defensive walls. With time and population growth, the land within these enclosed cities became increasingly scarce and valuable, thus the evolution of dividing a single building into many separately owned homes.

From the Middle Ages until the early years of the twentieth century, when it was revived in Europe, the condominium concept lay dormant. The concept became an increasingly popular form of home ownership in Belgium, Italy, Spain, Germany, France, and Great Britain. However, the United States did not adopt the condominium idea from the European market.

South America first grasped the concept in 1928, when Brazil became the first South American country to pass a law permitting the sale of *horizontal property*, as condominiums were known there. A few decades later, Puerto Rico, troubled by a booming population, a housing shortage, and scarce buildable property, looked to its South American neighbors and passed its *Horizontal Property Act of 1958*. This act defined the ownership of real property under the condominium concept.

Puerto Rico's legislation set the immediate precedent for the enactment of condominium legislation in the United States. In 1961, the *National Housing Act* was amended to include Section 234, which extended to condominiums the government mortgage insurance provided by the *Federal Housing Administration (FHA)* of the *Department of Housing and Urban Development (HUD)*. While this act did not empower the FHA to lend money, it did permit the FHA to insure loans made by private lenders for the construction, rehabilitation, and/or purchase of single-family or multifamily housing for rent or ownership. The protection of FHA insurance meant developers could more easily obtain loans to build condominiums and buyers could more easily purchase the condos once they were built.

Real estate laws are under the jurisdiction of the individual states. However, following the adoption of Section 234, in 1962 the FHA drew up a condominium statute based on the Puerto Rican Horizontal Property Act. The FHA intended the statute to be a model for states to use in drafting their condominium legislation. By 1968, all states had enacted legislation that enabled the creation and construction of condominiums.

By 1970, this form of ownership became increasingly popular, and condominiums were in demand in many parts of the country. Condominium construction was greatest in ten states—Florida, California, Ohio, Texas, Illinois, Michigan, Arizona, New York, Pennsylvania, and Maryland. According to the HUD Condominium/Cooperative Study in 1975, those ten states accounted for approximately two thirds of the condominium housing in the United States, with Florida and California having the greatest shares.

Currently, the world population's ever-present need for housing, shelter, and communal living necessitates an organized, structured, compatible-living guideline. For the effective implementation of good, sound, social interaction among the participants (the owners), such guidelines frequently require professional management. Most community managers worldwide handle a small number of communities because the properties can be difficult to administer.

CHARACTERISTICS OF COMMUNITY ASSOCIATIONS

What is a *community association*? Also known as a *common interest development (CID)*, this type of housing combines individual ownership of individual dwellings with shared ownership of the *common elements* by the entire group of owners. In other words, the individual owners must share in the decisions affecting those elements of the association that are common to all people (members) in the community. This is a simplistic definition—associations are certainly much more complicated—but it helps to paint the general picture.

The *common elements* can be anything from pools, cabanas, and golf courses to utilities, landscaping, roofing, siding, and roads. The members, as a group, follow a set of rules *(governing documents)* that serve as a guide to the maintenance and financing of the common elements. Membership in the community association is mandatory once an individual purchases property within the association. Living in a community association has perceived advantages and disadvantages.

Advantages

Through assessments, everyone shares in the utility, maintenance, and replacement expenses for the property. In some situations, homeowners don't have to maintain their own yards and common area landscapes. The multiplicity of personalities and profiles allows for diversity of thought in dealing with the operations of the community.

Many people enjoy the social environment provided by living in the community association. Gated communities and the close living situations of many other communities provide a certain amount of safety and security for residents.

Purchasing within a community association allows many people to own real estate who might not otherwise qualify. As land becomes more scarce, community association development allows for intelligent use of the land and its resources.

Disadvantages

Community associations rely heavily on volunteers. Getting the membership to "step up to the plate" and participate in the association's operations is not always easy.

Sometimes very zealous volunteers may consider it their duty to "over enforce" the governing documents for the community. This can create an extreme amount of ill will.

Some members of a community association feel they lose a certain amount of their personal freedom because of the association's governing documents. If some members of the association don't pay their portions of the operations, that puts an undue hardship on the rest of the members to pay the bills.

Numbers

The Community Associations Institute (CAI) (www.CAIonline.org) estimated that in 2006 over 57 million people resided in some 286,000 community associations. This compares to only 2.1 million residents in 10,000 associations in 1970. Zogby International reported the following in a 2005 survey of community association residents:

- The estimated real estate value of all homes in community associations approached $4 trillion, approximately 20% of the value of all U.S. residential real estate.
- The total annual operating revenue for these community associations is more than $41 billion.
- Community association boards also maintain investment accounts of more than $35 billion for the long-term maintenance and replacement of commonly held property.
- More then 1.7 million Americans serve on community association boards, with close to 400,000 participating as committee members. It's estimated that these community leaders dedicate more than 110 million hours of service to their communities every year.

TYPES OF COMMUNITY ASSOCIATIONS

The term *community association* encompasses homeowners associations (HOAs; typically single-family communities), planned unit developments (PUDs), condominiums and townhomes, cooperatives, condo-hotels, mixed-use condominiums, marina condominiums, resort associations, and large-scale planned communities. According to CAI, homeowners associations and other planned communities account for 52 to 55 percent, condominiums for 38 to 42 percent, and cooperatives for 5 to 7 percent of the 286,000 associations discussed previously.

Homeowners Associations and Planned Development Communities

The *homeowners association (HOA)*, also known as *planned development community*, has grown substantially in numbers over the past 30 years. According to CAI, it is estimated that four out of five houses built since the late 1990s are governed by a homeowners association. They are generally made up of single-family residences. The individually owned portion of a homeowners association is called the *lot*; it typically consists of a piece of land and everything on it. Title to the common area is usually held by the association, but the individual owners sometimes hold title to their proportionate shares as "tenants in common."

The primary purpose of the homeowners association is to provide as a whole and at reasonable costs those amenities that real estate purchasers normally wouldn't be able to afford individually. The shared amenities, or common elements, in which all of the members participate, are privately owned streets, recreation facilities (e.g., swimming pools, golf courses, tennis courts, and parks), parking facilities, and groomed landscaping. A secondary purpose of this type of association is to maintain a certain amount of uniformity throughout the community.

Homeowners associations/planned development communities function as small, private governments. Individuals who purchase property within the boundaries of the association/development agree to live by the terms and conditions (governing documents) attached to the parcel of land they purchase. A *lien* can be placed on the property, possibly even leading to foreclosure, if a property owner fails to abide by the regulations governing the association. That means that assessments must be paid and compliance with the rules is very important. Members in homeowners associations elect a volunteer board that often works in conjunction with a professional management organization.

Large-scale planned community associations can have as many as 20,000 units. They operate like small cities and have all of the infrastructure and amenities that many small towns have. They have fire and police departments, schools, and even retail shopping centers within their boundaries.

Many sub-associations in large-scale planned communities operate under a "master" association. The sub-associations elect a representative to sit on the master association's *board of directors*. In such situations, the boards of directors are truly the elected officials for the community. Large-scale planned communities have larger staffs and many more members who volunteer to assist in the operations of the association. They often do not use professional management but hire their own staff to oversee the association's operations.

Condominiums and Townhomes

When individuals purchase condominiums, each buys his or her own unit and an undivided interest in the common elements of the building(s) and/or improvements. The common elements, as mentioned earlier, can be lobbies, cabanas, grounds (including landscaping, parking areas, recreational features), and the building's mechanical operations. Generally speaking, the common elements are anything outside the individually owned units. The interior space within the four walls, floors, and ceilings of each unit is the individually owned portion. Condominium owners frequently also have exclusive use of decks, patios, and assigned parking areas. In most cases, condominium owners acquire title to at least some portion of the common elements within the association. Condominiums are usually stacked units. However, they might also be side-by-side townhomes.

The association is governed by an elected board of directors whose duty is to ensure the enforcement of the community's governing documents. The board is also entrusted to represent the interests of all members of the association when major financial and mechanical decisions are needed.

Cooperatives

Residents of a *cooperative (co-op)* do not actually buy their individual units/apartments; they buy shares in a *cooperative corporation* (also known as an *apartment corporation*). They generally take out a loan to finance the purchase of shares. The shares they purchase are based on factors such as square footage, number of rooms, and location of the unit/apartment within the community. Ownership of the shares entitles the purchaser to a long-term proprietary lease for the unit/apartment. The lease defines the purchaser's rights and obligations with respect to the possession, use, and occupancy of the apartment.

The cooperative corporation owns the building and must pay any mortgages and real estate taxes when due. The corporation pays all other operating costs for the building (payroll, utilities including heat, insurance, etc.). Owners are assessed their portion of the expenses in relation to the number of shares they own in the corporation. Many cooperative corporations hire professional managers to oversee the operations of the building(s).

The co-op is governed by a board of directors that is elected by the owners of the shares of the corporation. The rights, obligations, and responsibilities of the board and its shareholders are spelled out in the corporation's *bylaws*. The bylaws also define the shareholder's rights as they pertain to the proprietary lease. Most co-ops restrict the rights of the tenant shareholders to sell or lease their units/apartments and require other cooperators to approve a new building resident.

Condo-Hotels

The *condo-hotel* is a type of community association that is one of the newest to enter the marketplace. Like traditional condominiums, condo-hotels have a community association and owners pay monthly assessments. However, like traditional hotels, the units are rented to outsiders for a specific amount of time annually. Owners usually are only allowed to occupy their units for specific periods of the year.

In 2006, approximately 250 condo-hotel projects were underway nationwide. This represented almost 10 percent of all hotel rooms in production at that time. Developers seek out these projects because they receive presale monies to build condo-hotels. According to Smith Travel Research (www.SmithTravelResearch.com), most of the condo-hotels being built or converted are in vacation destination cities, such as Las Vegas, Miami, San Diego, New York, and Chicago. The famed Hotel del Coronado in San Diego built 35 condo-hotel rooms to help pay for the expansion and renovation of the 118-year-old hotel.

In the past, the management of hotel-condos was primarily in the hands of the hotel/hospitality industry. In recent years, professional property management companies have entered the field. Mangers are paid via a split in the rental income generated by the hotel. To be successful for both the owners and the manager, the hotel has to work. In other words, all of the characteristics that make hotels great must be seen in condo-hotels. The same strengths: good location and brand, strong management and staff, essential services, and attractive amenities are needed for the successful condo-hotel, according to Greg Hartman of HVS International.[1]

People purchase property in condo-hotels for various reasons:

- They like the prime vacation locations.
- Income from the rents can assist in the payment of mortgages, taxes, and assessments.
- The investment has appreciation potential.
- Interest on the loans may be tax deductible.
- Management handles the maintenance.

Condo-hotel ownership may have some disadvantages:

- Owners often have to make reservations to stay in their own units.
- Owners may not be able to stay in the unit they own.

---

[1] Marilyn Adams, "It's a hotel. It's a condo. No, it's both!" *USA Today*, September 28, 2005.

- The time owners can stay in their units is limited.
- All units are generally furnished alike because it's a hotel.
- Owners may have to contribute additional funds to the operation if the hotel experiences high vacancy rates.

Mixed-Use Condominiums

What do restaurants, bars, offices, movie theaters, retail shops, museums, condos, and apartments have in common? They can all be members of a *mixed-use condominium.* With land prices escalating at unprecedented rates, and in an attempt to stimulate inner-city development, cities are offering more tax incentives for mixed-use facilities, thus the growth of mixed-use condominium developments.

Companies and individuals purchase their particular spaces and become members of the community association. The governing documents for the association may allow only certain types of companies to operate within the facility. Anyone considering purchasing in a mixed-use condominium facility should study the documents thoroughly in advance to make sure that their business aligns with the association's requirements.

The combination of commercial, retail, and residential entities in one facility can offer challenges to association members. The initial design of the project must address the potential effects on the residential units of the parking, noise, and air quality issues that come with restaurants, bars, and movie theaters. As time goes on and all parties are learning to live together, compliance enforcement becomes a major concern. Retail shop owners want exposure and traffic while residential condo owners desire peace and quiet. Both are owners of the common elements, so the professional manager may have a challenge to determine who has authority over what. Well-written governing documents can assist everyone, including the board of directors, in making the right decisions for the community. On a positive note, many people like living and working in a mixed-use environment because they don't have to travel far to take care of day-to-day tasks.

Marina Condominiums

Purchasers in a *marina condominium* buy moorage slips for their boats and pay assessment fees to maintain the common elements. Common elements could be the docks, moorage covers, electrical and sewage hookups, and building facilities. Here again, all of the procedures of operation for the marina condo are outlined in the governing documents and enforced by the elected board of directors.

Some marina condos have some if not all of the ownership in commercial entities such as restaurants and retail shops located within the confines of the property. In this situation, professional association managers should be sure they are well-educated in all aspects of the marina condominium.

Resort Associations

Also known as a timeshare/vacation ownership association, a *resort association* has many similarities to other community associations. Through purchase, individual owners gain some type of interest in the assets of the resort. They own the right to the use of the resort for specific periods. Owners sometimes have 100-percent equity interest in the association's common elements. At other times, the *developer* retains ownership and exclusive control of the common elements, and association members have only the right to use them.

Resort associations, like the other community associations, have governing documents that specify how the association is to be governed. The selection of the board of directors may occur in several ways:

- The membership might elect the board of directors.
- The developer or development entity might have the right to appoint the members of the board.
- The members may have the opportunity to elect the board; however, the developer or development entity retains veto power over the board's decisions.

In resort associations, the member-elected board or the developer/development entity selects the professional management of the association, depending on how the governing documents are written.

The American Resort Development Association (ARDA) is a Washington, D.C.–based professional association representing the vacation ownership and resort development industries. ARDA offers information about timeshare/vacation ownership associations to those interested in purchasing property in or managing such an association.

THE FUTURE OF COMMUNITY ASSOCIATIONS

What is the future of community associations? As mentioned previously, four out of every five housing starts are in some form of community association. The government anticipates that the population of the United States will top 400 million by the year 2040. According to the Center for Environment and Population (www.CEPnet.org), "If the population is going to grow, which it will, we have to find different ways to reside on the land."

Growth management plans will require increased population density in smaller areas. Developers will envision new ways to use the land. They will find competitive advantages in developing communities with a common element that allows many sub-communities to take advantage of shared amenities and services. These smaller private organizations will be able to address many of the functions of local governments, such as parking violations, building restrictions, signage, and storage—to mention a few.

Future generations will live longer, healthier lives, and they will want the conveniences, luxuries, and amenities the community association setting offers. As the population ages, people will want to give up their big houses on many acres and gas-guzzling cars. Empty nesters, baby boomers, and young professionals will want to live in areas that have the greatest appeal. Downtown and urban town centers will be very attractive for these real estate purchasers because of the entertainment, cultural, educational, retail, and medical services provided in such proximity to each other. The mixed-use community will enjoy increasing popularity as the population grows and ages.

WHAT THIS BOOK OFFERS

When we sat down to design this text, we had one paramount goal: to identify just who might benefit from reading a book of this nature. We knew almost immediately that we wanted it to be of value not only to professional managers of community associations but also to association members. Members of community associations are frequently called upon to volunteer personal time and energy to the business operations of their associations, and they need to understand those operations. The information contained within these pages is designed to address both association managers and association members. A brief overview of the subsequent chapters follows.

Chapter 2—Procuring the Association

This chapter specifically addresses the professional community association manager; it presents information necessary to obtain management business. Specific promotional tools for marketing services and suggestions for establishing competitive management fees are included. The chapter gives a complete explanation for developing and creating a management agreement beneficial to both parties. Chapter 2 also contains information essential for beginning a business relationship with a community association client.

Chapter 3—Association Governance

Governing documents establish the community association's rules of operation. This book discusses covenants, conditions, and restrictions (CC&Rs), bylaws, rules and regulations, and other important documents that govern the association. Suggestions are offered as to what constitutes good rules development and what kinds of rules an association may wish to have. Chapter 3 also includes a discussion of some important federal laws that especially affect community associations.

Chapter 4—Board of Directors

The board of directors oversees all association operations—both physical and financial. Board members are entrusted to make good decisions on behalf of all members of the association. Chapter 4 identifies the duties and responsibilities of association officers and gives suggestions for successful meetings.

Chapter 5—Procuring Board and Committee Volunteers

Where does one find willing, capable volunteers to manage the functions of the association? Learn what makes a good community leader and which committees offer the greatest benefit to community association operations. To keep an association running smoothly, providing processes for the continuum of community leadership is imperative. Chapter 5 offers strategies to accomplish that goal.

Chapter 6—Successful Communication

It is said that the biggest misconception about communication is that it has been achieved. Failing to communicate appropriately with the membership and each other is one of the main mistakes professional association managers and boards of directors make. Learn about some highly effective tools for communicating with management, leadership, and membership.

Chapter 7—Managing the Community Association

Depending on their size and needs, community associations must decide who should manage them. The beginning of this chapter presents information about "self-management" and an analysis of volunteerism. The balance of the discussion centers on the staffing and organization of the professional management company and on the role of the professional community association manager.

Chapter 8—Keeping the Books

If we could rank the tasks the leaders of the association and the professional manager perform, the number one task would probably be tracking the flow of money into and out of the association. This chapter starts with financial definitions and moves through the accounting processes. It also discusses creating budgets for the association and maintaining adequate reserve funds for future *capital expenditures*.

Chapter 9—Maintenance Processes

People generally own real estate for its investment potential. However, without proper maintenance, one can see an investment deteriorate in a very short time. Routine site inspections, carefully defined and negotiated maintenance contracts, and emergency preparedness are proactive actions that reduce the potential effects of improper maintenance planning for the community association.

Chapter 10— Legal and Insurance Issues

The degree of liability surrounding community associations and their management is extremely high. In addition, the insurance and legal aspects of a community can be very complicated. We asked two experts to help us with this chapter. One outlines the legal issues that arise within community associations; the other discusses insurance. This chapter describes the types of insurance needed for the association and ways to minimize an individual's risk when sitting on a board of directors or when advising a board as the professional association manager does.

2

Procuring the Association

INTRODUCTION

In the past, a manager could practically hang out a shingle stating "property manager available," and association business might appear. Today, clients are more sophisticated and knowledgeable, and many property management firms have begun to specialize in community association management.

Professional association management requires a broad range of knowledge. The professional community association manager must compete for business, and he or she must demonstrate certain expertise to be successful. This chapter details many of the skills needed to be a true competitor for communities in need of management.

Marketing services, developing promotional tools, determining how much fee is enough, making the presentation, and demonstrating reasons a potential client should choose professional management over self-management are important skills for any successful management firm.

MARKETING ASSOCIATION MANAGEMENT SERVICES

To successfully market your services to community associations, you must first determine the type of association that best fits your firm's capabilities and location. Developing good lead sources is essential to generating prospects for new business. As you prepare to approach potential clients, you should be aware of reasons associations decide to change managers and learn to avoid the pitfalls of association management.

Community Association Type

It is important to target the type of community association that best suits your expertise and your location's sphere of influence. If you step outside these parameters, failure is likely to be the result. So what are the parameters?

Where will your office be located? Perhaps you are on the seaboard, and high-rise beachfront condominiums, marina condos, or even mixed-use developments including commercial, retail, and condo units are potential clients in your area. The closer your office is to the market you choose, the more competitive your cost will be; this could even give you an efficiency edge over other management firms. Chapter 1 illustrates the many different types of condo or homeowner opportunities.

When choosing the type of association to approach, the manager must also evaluate the size of the community. Some firms specialize in communities of a certain size and will not consider associations that vary from their portfolios. This presents opportunities for the newcomer. Many smaller communities may need management, but no existing firm may be tailored to meet their needs. So get creative and solve the problem. One way is to limit the scope of your management services to fit the client's operating budget.

Knowing the advantages and disadvantages of townhouse, condo, planned unit development (PUD), and homeowners association (HOA) management will guide a manager toward the best community type for his or her management expertise. Exhibit 2.1 compares the advantages and disadvantages of managing each type of community.

Acquiring a new community before the transition from the *declarant* (usually the developer) to the association members can present an important potential disadvantage for any manager. If the developer has done a good job and has developed goodwill among the community members, the role of the community manager will be positive after the developer leaves the scene. However, if the developer hires an association manager and then does not perform satisfactorily, the manager may be at a great public relations disadvantage due to the developer's poor performance. Association members may consider the developer and the manager to be the same entity (even though that is usually not the case), and changing that perception may be difficult. One way to avoid negativism in this situation is to be sure a member director is part of the developer's board when the decision to hire a professional manager is made. Once hired, the manager should

Exhibit 2.1

Comparison of Management Demands by Community Type

Advantages	**Disadvantages**
Townhomes	
Townhouses may have fewer physical common assets to maintain.	The manager loses immediate control over the entire community's curb appeal due to lack of control over major exterior improvements.
Townhome associations often do not include direct responsibility for maintaining or assessing common components (such as roofing, exterior siding, and decks) as a board function; each owner must maintain such elements.	More compliance letter implementation is necessary.
Common elements are often limited to the entry areas, any common recreation facilities, roadways, common landscaping, and sidewalks.	More time may be involved for the manager if owners are not timely with responsible exterior maintenance issues.
The manager has less common element maintenance to supervise.	A community room for association meetings is often lacking. The manager may need to provide a meeting place or seek meeting rooms for association business.
Condominiums	
Association declarations provide for the board to have complete maintenance control over all the common and limited common elements.	The manager must spend more time on frequent on-site visits and potentially daily interaction with the board, committee chairs, or homeowners with maintenance or rule compliance issues.
The manager has better control over all physical aspects of the community.	Condominium management requires greater knowledge of property asset management.
More committee volunteerism is usually prevalent than in the other community types.	The manager needs greater budget expertise and additional time to fulfill the responsibility of creating an overall operating budget for all common and limited common components.
Many larger condominiums have common facilities that support a meeting place for association business.	The manager has more common area maintenance to supervise.
Planned Unit Developments and Homeowners Associations	
PUD and HOA management requires the least manager time on the property site; the manager's main function is fiscal or financial implementation and accounting.	The manager may be responsible for facilitating an *architectural control committee (ACC)* and making sure new homeowners' houses meet the community's ACC guidelines.

(continued)

Exhibit 2.1 *(Continued)*

These communities have a minimum of physical common assets to maintain; homeowners are responsible for their entire homes—interior, exterior, and landscaping within their property boundaries. (Sometimes all yards are common; then the association supervises the landscape maintenance of those areas along with any other common elements.)	As with the townhome community, all association meetings usually take place off-site due to the lack of a common facility.
Fewer committees are present than in condominium management.	The volunteer pool for committees is very limited.

make sure the developer performs according to the declarations, bylaws, and rules and regulations.

Geographic Boundaries

When marketing your services, always keep in mind the distance to and from a particular community. This distance dictates the profitability of doing the proper job—for a proper fee. Community manager travel time can be expensive and ineffective if most of his or her time is spent traveling rather than managing.

In a firm's initial years, a manager may occasionally have to compromise this philosophy to create a portfolio, but if the opportunity arises to begin clustering the makeup of the communities he or she manages, the manager should do so. The advantages will be apparent in terms of management office organization, efficiency, and effectiveness. The firm may become the expert in a particular neighborhood, thus creating many referrals for additional business.

Being competitive is difficult when managing from a great distance—unless no other firms are available. Long-distance management relationships may place excessive economic burden on the client's budget. Ways to solve this problem are (1) to acquire a large enough portfolio in the area to develop a satellite office location, and/or (2) to limit the scope of management provided.

Lead Sources

Marketing services to associations requires a unique approach. Associations are run by a committee (the board), and they can be very political. Unless the board appoints an ad hoc committee person, no single owner or entity is available to contact in order to negotiate a *management agreement.* Therefore, acquiring a good lead source is important in finding the property as well as in determining to whom you should direct your request. Too often, the person seeking your services may only be a concerned owner looking for solutions, and he or she may not have official authorization to do so. Much work and planning are needed when approaching an association, and those efforts may all be wasted if the management plan is provided to the wrong person. Always ask what authority the person who approaches you has to inquire about new management.

Typical lead sources include requests from associations. Third-party sources that may be familiar with the property or provide relevant information are accountants, attorneys, community management trade associations, community developers, the yellow pages, and vendors specializing in association needs.

Many property management firms will not handle associations because they appear to be difficult to manage. Get to know the association trade groups. Learn which management firms do not want to engage in community management and turn them into valuable referral resources.

Reasons Associations Change Management Firms

Knowing the reason an association is looking for professional management can be beneficial when developing a management portfolio. The board of directors may be dropping the existing manager for a variety of reasons. Learning the cause of the predecessor's demise may help you determine whether your management style can overcome those issues or whether you might fall into the same dilemma as the present management. The next sections discuss some of the major reasons association boards give for changing management firms.

Compliance Issues. Association boards and members commonly complain that the management company doesn't do enough to enforce association rules. Association governance documents are often limited and unclear concerning compliance issues. This leaves the manager and board open to blame if compliance issues are not resolved.

A good manager will recognize this problem and recommend to the board resolutions or amendments that will improve enforcement of association rules; however, the professional manager can only be as effective as the association's governance and board allow. At times, the board may restrict the manager from performing a compliance process, yet the members expect the manager to enforce compliance as the association's documents direct.

If the board is not fair regarding compliance issues and the management firm does not point out or attempt to change the discriminatory action, both the board members and management may become liable for not implementing the governance as written. If written governance guidelines are vague or nonexistent, a manager must ensure that the board acts in a reasonable and fair manner when invoking its right to bring an offending member into compliance.

Delinquencies. Boards frequently think management companies do not have adequate control of delinquencies. Board members often believe that, in addition to receiving payments, the management firm should collect delinquent assessments. When beginning the management relationship, the manager must clarify the company's position on this issue, or it could destroy the goodwill between the board and the manager when delinquencies occur.

Some states require an agent to be a licensed debt collector to pursue outstanding debts beyond sending a delinquency letter. Debt collection duties are usually turned over to an attorney or a bona fide collection agency. Although most unpaid assessments are automatic liens against a property, delinquent owners can be passive when it comes to paying assessments.

Board members can get frustrated with the time required and the process involved in attempting to collect outstanding debts. Keeping the board informed with timely progress and delinquency reports immensely improves the manager's creditability regarding delinquent assessments.

Financial Reports. Boards often complain that management submits erratic and inaccurate financial reports. Financial statements must be timely and easy to read.

Managers all too frequently send complicated operating statements to the board without any prior explanation. Explaining the differences in cash, modified, or accrual statements is the management company's job. Board members, especially the treasurer, do not want to appear uneducated when reading the financial statement from the board or the management firm. Even so, they sometimes report their opinions concerning alleged inaccuracies as well as their difficulties in reading the reports. By establishing a specific time to explain and illustrate financial statements to the board, the management company can instill confidence and creditability.

If your accounting system is flexible, by all means tailor the association's books to meet the specific needs of the particular property. Specify the date the board will receive the financials, and do not deviate from the schedule without prior notice to all concerned.

Association Management Pitfalls

When considering assuming management of a property, the manager should do extensive due diligence regarding many aspects of the community. Common pitfalls are accepting the management of "sick" associations, failing to make site visits, and failing to establish a minimum fee structure.

Sick Associations. Is this property fiscally or physically considered a *sick association*? Reviewing the current budget in relationship to the association's asset management performance is important. An association with very little working capital and much necessary capital expense is destined to fail. Recognizing this situation prior to contract commencement and determining whether the members are willing to make the necessary financial commitment is crucial to being a successful manager.

No Site Visit. It is extremely important to make a *site visit* before responding to a *request for proposal (RFP)*. The site may require extensive manager supervision due to its physical attributes or detriments. By miscalculating the administrative time involved, the manager risks underbidding a contract that he or she may not be able to fulfill properly.

The RFP presents the association's requirements. The association relies on the professional manager's ability to meet those requirements at a contracted cost that will ensure their implementation. The manager should not project a fee solely by sitting behind a desk. Visit the site.

No Minimum Fee Structure. Previously, managers submitted contract fees that reflected an all-inclusive management service. In those days, the manager was a rather authoritarian agent who made the most of an association's decisions.

In today's market, with the increasing popularity of *common interest developments (CIDs)*, members and directors take a more hands-on approach to governing their associations. Thus the manager's role has changed from that of an authoritarian agent to an advisory agent.

Because present-day relationships with associations are more time-consuming, an increasing number of management contracts are calculated with a reasonable base fee structure. Establishing a minimum fee structure is important. The manager must develop a minimum fee structure that justifiably will compensate the firm for expected and unexpected administration duties. If the minimum fee is too low, the manager may jeopardize good management principles in order to make a profit.

Request for Proposal Traps. Evaluate the RFP for hidden management traps. As cautioned above, make sure to visit the site before completing the

RFP. The RFP may request certain responsibilities that could require extensive management time due to the physical nature of the association. Having seen the entire site will eliminate any shortfalls when projecting costs to administer the contract.

Another potential trouble area might be the number of physical *inspections* requested and the number of meetings per year the manager must attend. Make sure certain on-site services are to be contracted out to third parties—but not at the manager's expense. Payroll of any on-site staffing must be clarified. Will such employees be employees of the association or of the management agent, and if of the agent, who pays for the extra payroll burden and taxes?

Probably the most important trap to avoid is failing to have a clear understanding of the respective duties of the manager and the board. Managers all too often begin their duties only to discover that the board expects more to be done than was expressed in the RFP; boards frequently complain because they expect the manager to be responsible for items not clearly stated in the RFP or management contract. The best way to eliminate this conundrum is for the manager to recognize that such misunderstandings can occur. During the interview process or the RFP completion, the manager should discuss and list the specific tasks for which he or she will and will not be responsible. The manager should question any RFP point that seems vague.

DEVELOPING PROMOTIONAL TOOLS

The tools a management firm uses to present its services can vary. The main importance of such information is first to identify the offered services and then to tailor the services to meet the specific goals and objectives of the community. Today's association clientele are generally well-educated, have strong opinions about their communities, and want the best quality of life within their "kingdoms." Their goals demand a professional firm cognizant of their requirements.

Brochures and Web Sites

Brochures and Web sites must convey a confidence level that community management boards can recognize and trust. They should present materials illustrating the firm's capabilities, education, and successful management experiences.

When promoting your firm, emphasize and illustrate your expertise and ability. The medium used is important because you want to reach your clientele in the manner that is most comfortable for them. If your market involves retirement communities whose occupants are members of the Traditional Generation, use more hard-copy materials, like brochures. Web sites will have more impact on the younger generations—the Baby Boomer, Generation X, or Millennium groups.

The information package should include a brief history of the management firm, the types of properties it manages, its management objectives and goals, testimonials from past and current clients, and descriptions of its employees and their credentials. Pictures of the firm and employees who belong to professional trade associations are beneficial.

Employees determine the success of any business. Constant educating and nurturing of these individuals is imperative to succeed in management. Professional trade associations, such as the *Institute of Real Estate Management (IREM®)* and the *Community Associations Institute (CAI)*, offer courses and professional designations respected in the industry. IREM offers the *CPM® (Certified Property Manager®)*, *ARM® (Accredited Residential Manager®)*, and *AMO® (Accredited Management Organization®)* designations. CAI offers the AMS (Association Management Specialist), the PCAM (Professional Community Association Manager), the AAMC (Accredited Association Management Company), and other designations pertaining to the industry.

Illustrating types of property that you presently manage is also a great confidence builder. (See Chapter 1 for property types.) If the firm is just beginning, this marketing advantage may not be available. However, demonstrating knowledge of a particular type of association governance is a great step toward securing the account.

Informative Checklists

Checklists like the one in Exhibit 2.2 can help you discover the client's goals and objectives and identify the services the firm offers. The manager must know both of these critical aspects when drafting a proposal.

According to William Robinson, CPM, in "Winning the Large Condominium Account" (*Journal of Property Management*, September/October 1999), this can be accomplished through the following:

- Reviewing the documentation to ensure that you fully understand the legal operations of the prospect community.
- Comparing the financial reports to national and local yardsticks. Compare income and expenses to a basis by using IREM's *Income and Expense Analysis for Condominiums.*
- Meeting with colleagues who manage similar properties. Use your network at a local IREM chapter or another trade association.
- Visiting or driving by neighboring condominium and apartment communities.

Exhibit 2.2

Management Screening Checklist

Management Screening Checklist for Great Place Condominiums

All homeowners associations could benefit from professional management. Even the smallest HOA should have professional management when it comes to rules enforcement and collecting money. Here is a checklist of tasks commonly performed by HOA managers to compare services when screening and evaluating proposals.

Date: ___________

Company: **(Your Firm Name Here)**

Contact: Chris Manager

Title: Director of Community Management

Address:

City: Zip:

Phone Fax:

E-mail:

Web site:

❑ **Meetings:** Attends ____12____ board meetings per year plus one annual homeowner meeting included in the basic management fee. Additional meetings carry a charge of $ ____60/hr____

❑ **Meeting Notices:** Prepares and distributes meeting notices and agendas as directed by the board president. Will also assist with procedure at these meetings.

❑ **Property Visits:** Performs general grounds and buildings inspection and follows up on any needed maintenance or problems at least: ❑ weekly ❑ monthly ❑ quarterly

❑ **Maintenance Scheduling:** Orders maintenance on the buildings and grounds according to standard practice or as directed by the board president and follows up to ensure completion. Prepares schedules of regular and extraordinary maintenance and repairs.

❑ **Maintenance Services:**

- ❑ Provides handyman maintenance services at $ _35_/hour during business hours, $ _60_/hour after hours, $ _60_/hour on holidays.
- ❑ Performs larger renovation projects like painting, siding, deck repair, etc. on ❑ bid/proposal basis ❑ time and material basis.

Exhibit 2.2 *(Continued)*

- ❑ **Major Repair Projects:** Assists in the specifications, bid proposals, and project oversight of major repairs. Included in the basic management fee or for an extra charge of: $_____, to be determined by the board and managing agent_______________.

- ❑ **Emergency Response:** Maintains a 24-hour emergency response service to protect the property and safety of the residents.

- ❑ **Purchases:** Negotiates contracts for services, tools, equipment, materials, and supplies for the operation and maintenance of the association's property.

- ❑ **Employees:** Assists in the selection, training, and supervision of any association staff hired to operate and maintain the property.

- ❑ **Insurance Claims:** Processes association insurance claims for

  - ❑ No extra charge
  - ❑ For an extra fee that will be included with the claim

- ❑ **Relations with Owners:** Responds to owner information and maintenance/service requests; records action taken.

- ❑ **Financial Responsibility:** Provides bookkeeping services:

  - ❑ Collects, records, and deposits assessments to the association's bank account in a timely manner.
  - ❑ Pays association bills as authorized by the board in a timely fashion.
  - ❑ Prepares monthly income & expense statements, balance sheets, and delinquency reports in a format usable by the board and auditors. Arranges for audit as directed by board.
  - ❑ Maintains association bank accounts and provides monthly financial statements.
  - ❑ Sends delinquency notices, levies fines, processes liens, and initiates legal action against delinquent owners in accordance with the association collection policy.

- ❑ **Sale Documentation:** Provides sale disclosure information as requested by the seller for a cost of $ ____25–150 (to be paid by seller)____.

- ❑ **Directory:** Maintains current directory of owners/residents, addresses, and phone numbers.

- ❑ **Files & Records:** Maintains current financial, maintenance, and administrative records in an orderly fashion so that they are readily accessible by authorized association representatives.

- ❑ **Insurance:** Arranges insurance as indicated by the governing documents or as directed by the board.

(continued)

Exhibit 2.2 ***(Continued)***

❑ **Operating Budget:** Prepares the draft annual operating budget for board review.

❑ **Reserve Study:** Assists the board or a reserve analyst in the review and update of the association reserve study. (Can also perform the actual reserve study.)

Other:________________________________

Other:________________________________

Other:________________________________

Monthly Management Fee $ ____1,595.87____

Overall Impression: ❑ Excellent ❑ Average ❑ Poor

Provided by Invest West Management, LLC, AMO

- Reviewing your notes of conversations and walking through inspections of the prospect community.

These suggestions could easily be outlined in a checklist when prospecting for new accounts.

Another checklist is the questionnaire format that can inform the prospect community of what to look for when interviewing the management firm. (Yes, by all means, be prepared to be interviewed before a panel of directors when presenting the management contract.)

Exhibit 2.2 is adapted from a trade association Web page: Innovative Homeowner Association Management Strategies, www.regenesis.net. The form has been completed to illustrate its use.

The screening checklist is a great tool in assisting the management firm when making a bid or participating in the initial interview with a community. The form helps the community directors by setting a professional standards platform regarding what to look for when interviewing prospective management firms.

ESTABLISHING FAIR FEES

Solving the mystery of how much fee is enough can be difficult—especially for new firms. Fortunately, resources are available to help managers determine the amount needed to profitably manage an association while offering the client adequate service.

Cost of Adequate Service

What does it cost you to provide adequate service? This does not have to be a mystery. The cost to do business in this management realm can be precisely calculated. IREM resolved the question by creating a format for cost accounting services that all types of property management experts have used for years. Exhibit 2.3 is adapted from the original IREM creation.

When using the cost accounting form in Exhibit 2.3, the manager must know exactly what information is needed to complete each section. Below is a quick summary of the calculations for the example that can serve as a guide to using the format.

- *Top of the form.* The initial section gathers statistical data on the subject property, whether a condominium, homeowners, retail, office, or boat slip association. Be as accurate as possible with all estimated costs. This input will help determine other cost projections listed on the lower portion of the form.
- *Gross costs.* Shown in the box are the gross costs of the management team. The calculations must take into account the employer's payroll burden (wages, taxes, benefits, sick leave, vacation, overtime, and holidays) totaled as a gross cost-per-hour figure. Some firms may have administrative assistants who work with their key management teams, so this staff position was added to the example.
- *Community manager's services.* The topics under this heading are all part of good management practices, and each requires considerable thought. Remember that all of the projections are based on a monthly schedule of events and workload. The following is a brief description of the derivation of each set of numbers in the example.
  - ➢ *Inspection.* This is an in-depth visual visit to the property to check on compliance issues, architectural control, special project reviews, etc. Estimated time was calculated for two times per year at two hours per visit. Thus, the number of monthly visits would be .16 (2 ÷ 12) and the four total hours would be spread out over 12 months. The total hours per month would be .64 (.16 × 4). That figure is then multiplied by the "Gross Community Mgr's Cost," which is listed at $35 per hour, and results in the illustrated "Cost per Month" of $22.

Exhibit 2.3

Association Management Pricing

Community Great Place Condominiums

Homes 100 # Offices ________ # Stores ________ # Boat Slips ________

Age and Present Condition of Property & Improvements Built 2000, Excellent Condition

Miles from Office: 5 Number of Employees: 2
Gross Common Area Budget: $180,000

Gross Community Mgr's Cost:	$35	per Hour
Gross Administrative Asst's Cost:	$20	per Hour
Gross Executive Mgr's Cost:	$50	per Hour
Gross Accounting Cost:	$25	per Hour

COMMUNITY MANAGER'S SERVICES	# per Month	Hours Each	Total Hours	Cost per Month
A. Inspections	0.16	4	0.64	$22
B. Site Visits	1	0.5	0.5	$18
C. Capital Improvement Supervision	0.16	2	0.32	$11
D. Association Meetings	1.08	2	2.16	$76
E. Office Hours per Month	21	0.4	8.4	$294
F. Travel Time: $35 per Hour	2.26	1	2.26	$79
G. Travel Expense: 30 Miles X 0.45 per Mile				$14
TOTAL COST				$513.30

ADMINISTRATIVE ASSISTANT'S SERVICES	# per Month	Hours Each	Total Hours	Cost per Month
A. Inspections	0	0	0	$0
B. Site Visits	1	0.5	0.5	$10
C. Capital Improvement Supervision	0	0	0	$0
D. Association Meetings	1.08	2	2.16	$43
E. Office Hours per Month	11	0.5	5.5	$110
F. Travel Time: $25 per Hour	2.26	1	2.26	$57
G. Travel Expense: 30 Miles X 0.45 per Mile				$14
TOTAL COST				$233.20

Exhibit 2.3 *(Continued)*

EXECUTIVE SERVICES	**# per Month**	**Hours Each**	**Total Hours**	**Cost per Month**
A. Inspections	0.083	2	0.166	$8
B. Site Visits	0.25	0.5	0.125	$6
C. Surveys/Consulting	21	0.16	3.36	$168
D. Association Meetings	0.083	2	0.166	$8
E. Statement Review	1	0.5	0.5	$25
F. Budget Preparation	0.083	2	0.166	$8
G. Travel Time: $ 50 per Hour	0.25	1	0.25	$13
H. Travel Expense: 10 Miles X $0.45 per Mile				$4.50
TOTAL COST				$241.15

ACCOUNTING SERVICES	**# per Month**	**Hours Each**	**Total Hours**	**Cost per Month**
A. Receipts Accounted for __ Days per Month	10	0.25	2.5	$63
B. Disbursements	2	2	4	$100
C. Monthly Billing	1	2	2	$50
D. Payroll: Checks Issued	2	0.25	0.5	$13
E. Assoc. Statement Preparation	1	1	1	$25
F. Resident Statement Preparation	1	1	1	$25
G. Statement Duplication	1	0.25	0.25	$6
H. Director Consultation	2	1	2	$50
TOTAL COST				$331.25

SUBTOTAL BEFORE OVERHEAD AND PROFIT $1,318.90

OVERHEAD AND PROFIT	**Percent of Subtotal Cost**	**Cost per Month**
A. General Overhead	10.00%	$131.89
B. Marketing	1.00%	$13.19
C. Profit & Contingencies	10.00%	$131.89

TOTAL MONTHLY COST $1,595.87

Cost per Unit $15.96

% of Budget 10.64%

Provided by Invest West Management, LLC, AMO
Stephen R. Barber, CPM

- *Site visits.* In the example, this involves one visit per month, taking .5 hour each time for a total of $18. This would be a cursory visit, usually consisting of a drive-through looking only for any obvious association problems or needs. It requires much less time than an inspection as listed above.
- *Capital improvement supervision.* This property requires at least an annual review of any present or proposed capital improvement. This would be a two-hour period.
- *Association meeting.* One per month for a period of two hours. This community requested professional management attendance at all monthly meetings throughout the year.
- *Office hours per month.* An every-weekday projection was made, thus making 21 times per month. At .4 of an hour per day, this calculates to a cost of $294 per month. This time represents telephone calls, compliance issues, maintenance administration, and correspondence.
- *Travel time.* This comprises the amount of travel time per month at the chosen travel cost of $35 per hour. The hourly rate would vary for each staff person.
- *Travel expense.* The figure is derived by multiplying the miles traveled by the cost per mile for staff vehicles.
- *Total cost.* This represents the average calculated management cost for this staff person's time devoted to this community monthly.

• *Administrative assistant's services.* This category may be used for an assistant to the community manager or for another key employee who has association duties, such as a maintenance supervisor, receptionist, etc. The subcategories use the same calculations as the subcategories for the community manager's services.

• *Executive services.* This category is used to account for a community manager's supervisor's time and involvement with the association. The calculations are the same as for the previous two sections—with the exception of items E, "Statement Review" and F, "Budget Preparation." These two items require knowledgeable staff, which usually may be key administrative personnel who work with the community manager. If your community manager's responsibilities cover these two items, add them to this staff line projection in the format.
  - *Items A to D, G, and H.* These items are basically the same calculations as in previous explanations.
  - *Statement review.* This details the time taken to review the fiscal operating report that will be disbursed to the clients (directors and/or homeowners). The accuracy of these reports is very important.

This involves checking for proper chart of account coding, verifying correct vendor payment, reviewing all payables and receivables, etc.

- *Budget preparation*. This item may involve time meeting with the board or a finance committee for projecting the next year's income and expenses. The community manager may also be involved in this process, so be sure to account for that time.

- *Accounting services*. This section accounts for all costs attributed to the fiscal accounting for the community. These staff members probably will not have any travel time or expenses, but instead they may have a regular schedule of meetings in the management office with a director, a treasurer, a finance committee, or all of the above. Therefore, notation of these expenses is included.
  - *Receipts accounted for days per month*. For this, one must determine how many days per month receipts will be forthcoming, recorded, and banked. The example estimated over ten days at .25 hours per day would be required to account for all receipts. This calculated out to an average of 2.5 hours per month for a 100-unit community.
  - *Disbursements*. This category involves payment of all recorded payables. The example illustrates two times per month at two hours per time, or four hours for an average month.
  - *Monthly billing*. This is the time allocated when invoicing the monthly dues to all owners.
  - *Payroll*. This item refers to checks issued. The property in the example had two employees and this time is for the payroll calculations and printing of the payroll checks.
  - *Association statement preparation*. The monthly development of the financial statements is done and discussed with management staff before the final drafts are completed and sent to the clients (i.e., directors and owners).
  - *Resident statement preparation*. This is similar to the above "Monthly Billing," but the work is done prior to the billing. It is a review of the owner's dues ledger to ensure its accuracy on billing and payment receipt prior to the next billing cycle.
  - *Statement duplication*. After the management staff approves the financials, the accounting department makes copies and mails, faxes, or e-mails reports to the clients.
  - *Director consultation*. As stated earlier, this refers to the time staff spends with a director and/or owner explaining any issues or questions about the financials or budget. Budget preparation time spent will also be part of this calculation.

- *Subtotal before overhead and profit.* Calculations beyond this point depend upon your firm's philosophy on overhead and profit strategies. Every competitive management market has established parameters dictating what the market will bear in terms of company profit and overhead. This is subjective and can change with the economic rise and fall within the market.

- *Overhead and profit.* The following calculations are not simply sound economic principles when projecting the complete cost of doing business; the summations derived here can be part of the unknown or contingency costs not accounted for in the above calculations.
  - *General overhead.* According to *Webster's*, *overhead* is "the general operating expenses of a business, as rent, light, heat, taxes, etc."[1] This will be the ratio resulting from dividing the "Subtotal before Overhead and Profit" by your firm's general overhead cost. That is the fixed expense needed to keep the doors open while managing community associations.
  - *Marketing.* This community's share of the firm's overall marketing and promotional costs.
  - *Profit and contingencies.* The *profit* portion, according to *Webster's*, is "the amount of money gained in a business transaction after deducting all the expenses." This is the amount of money attributed to the reason for being in the community association management business. It is a key element in determining the value of your business. *Contingency cost* is the expense to cover any unknown condition, such as an accident, or to cover any unforeseen expense when estimating the above management fees.

- *Total monthly cost.* Congratulations, you have now determined the overall estimated fee needed for a successful, economically sound approach to managing the Great Place Condominiums community.

- *Cost per unit and/or percent of budget.* These are two ways to express your fee structure to a potential client. The *cost per unit* is a nationally recognized way of expressing a fee per month, but the treasurer or finance committee of the community whose business you are seeking might prefer a cost factor that relates directly to its monthly operating budget. In this example, the $15.96 per unit per month fee would equate 10.64% of their fiscal budget.

---

[1] Merriam-Webster, Incorporated, *Merriam-Webster's Collegiate Dictionary*, 11th ed. Springfield, MA: Merriam-Webster, Incorporated, 2003.

Using the cost accounting tool above will help you get your financial goals and needs into perspective. When completing the projected costs for each facet of the firm's operating costs, you will see the depth of thought needed to ensure a reasonable profit. It is imperative to keep labor costs in direct relation to the market wages in your area. Underestimated business expenses here will definitely be a deterrent to a successful management business.

For that reason, the importance of knowing your target market is noted. The extent of management services requested determines the number of employees needed to provide adequate service. Carrying too much labor overhead for too long definitely impacts the profit of a business. This is always a balancing act when a firm is in its infancy.

You will need to readdress the cost-accounting process many times throughout your management tenure. This exercise should be done at least once every couple of years and definitely each year when reviewing the firm's business plan and budget economics.

Importance of Relationships in the Bidding Process

How important is your relationship in the bidding process? "What relationship?" one might ask. Even before commencing a management contract, you must establish a positive relationship with the client. The first meeting with the client is an opportunity to make an impression that will keep you competitive in the bidding process. Be professional, and dress appropriately for that first meeting. Make sure the image you present is exactly what the client will experience when visiting your office.

When you are asked to present your expert analysis of a community and the role of a manager, do not be surprised to learn that some of your local competitors may be there doing the same. This builds real character, and how you handle a potentially awkward situation may be the determining factor as to whether you prevail in the interview. Although the representative of the prospective management firm usually does not explain its methods and management costs in the presence of competitors, you are likely to make presentations before the board of directors and many of the community's interested homeowners.

Be prepared for on-the-spot questions about your firm and ways your management firm would solve certain community issues. Boards have decided to change management companies for many reasons: management brings in contractors to complete projects without first discussing projects with the board; management controls the board and runs the meetings; and management does not bid out projects or, worse yet, management has a relationship with the contractors it selects. Be calm, relaxed, confident, and straightforward with your answers.

Have a list of questions for the board. After all, this is a two-way relationship. Learn what the board believes is being done correctly and what is not, and determine its goals and objectives. Tailor your questions to these specific aspects of the community.

MAKING THE PRESENTATION

When making a presentation to a prospective client, you can use a clear, informative contract as a basis for detailing your services. Be sure to tailor the services you offer to the needs of the specific client and sell the client on your firm's ability to meet those needs.

Use an Informative Contract

The style and content of your management contract can be a priceless tool when maximized. It should be in nontechnical language, thus easy to read, and it should precisely spell out the terms, conditions, and responsibilities of each party to the agreement.

IREM has a standard condominium management agreement that works very well. The agreement is straightforward, and it is designed to serve as the basis for a job description, should your firm be accepted as the new community manager.

Exhibit 2.4 presents the entire agreement, and the authors have added notes addressing specific paragraphs pertaining to the use of the agreement. Note that this agreement should still undergo legal review and be in compliance with any state and/or local laws.

Detail Your Services

This chapter has provided many tools that will assist a firm in detailing the services it will provide. The above management agreement covers many aspects of management that will be included for a particular community.

Some managers use a "menu of services" as an additional exhibit to their management agreement. A *menu of services* illustrates various administrative and/or supervisory capabilities the management firm offers and the cost to the community. This style of agreement allows clients to pick and choose the services they would like to use. Examples of a menu of services and an estimated rates sheet are provided in Exhibits 2.5 and 2.6, courtesy of Invest West Management, LLC, AMO.

(Text continued on p. 48)

Exhibit 2.4

Association Management Agreement

Condominium and Homeowners Association Management Agreement

ASSOCIATION

AGENT

For Property located at
Beginning [ ] 20[ ] Ending [ ] 20[ ]

This agreement (the "Agreement") is made and entered into this [ ] day of [ ], 20[ ], by and between the unit owners' association known as [ ] (the "Association"), which is established in accordance with the laws of the State of [ ] for the property known as [ ] located at [ ] (the "Property"), and [ ] (the "Agent").

> *Note*: In states in which the agent must be licensed, incorporating a reference to the agent's legal qualification (license) to manage the property may be desirable or appropriate.

AUTHORITY OF THE AGREEMENT

The Board of Directors of the Association (the "Board"), on behalf of the Association, hereby appoints Agent to manage the Property, and Agent accepts appointment to manage the Property.

The parties further agree as follows:

Section 1 TERM OF AGREEMENT

The Board appoints Agent exclusively to manage the Property for a period of [ ] year(s), beginning [ ], 20[ ], and thereafter for periods of one year unless this Agreement is terminated as provided in this section or in sections 11 or 12. Either party may terminate this Agreement at the end of the initial term or at the end of any one-year renewal period provided that written notice is given to the other party on or before the sixtieth (60th) day prior to the expiration of the initial term or on or before the sixtieth (60th) day prior to the expiration of such one-year renewal period.

> *Note*: The form and its explanation are silent as to who should initiate "renewal" of the agreement. It is incumbent on the agent to notify the association of the impending expiration of the current term of the agreement to assure continuity of management or, if the arrangement will be terminated, to effect a smooth transition. The agreement calls for 60 days' notice of expiration; requiring equivalent notice of intent to renew may be desirable.

Section 2 SERVICES OF AGENT

Agent shall manage the Property to the extent, for the period, and upon the terms of this Agreement. Agent shall perform the following services in the name of and on behalf of the

(continued)

Exhibit 2.4 *(Continued)*

Association, and the Association hereby gives Agent the authority and powers required to perform these services.

> *Note*: This agreement does not address "analysis of reserve funds," which is required by law in some states, e.g., California and Oregon. It is expected that the agent will negotiate the contract for the conduct of such "reserve studies" by qualified professionals on an annual basis, or as otherwise required by law, with such studies to be performed at the association's expense. If applicable, this would be added as a separate subsection here and would be a consideration in determining the managing agent's compensation.

2.1 COLLECTION OF ASSESSMENTS

Agent shall collect (and give receipts for, if necessary) all monthly and other assessments and other monies that are due the Association with respect to the Property and for all rental or other payments from concessionaires, if any. HOWEVER, Agent shall have no authority or responsibility to collect delinquent assessments or other charges except to send notices of delinquency.

> *Note*: Sections 2 and 3, and especially sections 5 and 13, of this form assume the agent will handle association funds directly. However, if the association has its own accounts, the agent's authorization may be solely to prepare checks drawn against those accounts (but *not* to sign them) and to make deposits to the accounts. Such a different arrangement will require modification of the language in the four sections noted here and may necessitate changes to other sections or subsections of the agreement as well.

2.2 RECORDS OF INCOME AND EXPENDITURES

Agent shall maintain records of all income and expenses relating to the Property, and shall submit to the Association on or before the [ ] day of the following month, a statement of receipts and disbursements for the preceding month, including a statement of the balance in the operating account for the Property.

> *Note*: Subsection 2.2 does not refer specifically to reserve funds. The AICPA Audit and Accounting Guide for Common Interest Realty Associations, issued in August 1991 by the American Institute of Certified Public Accountants, calls for accrual accounting and for separate funds for operating and reserves. Furthermore, *each* association must have its own bank accounts and financial records.

2.3 PREPARATION OF ANNUAL BUDGET

[ ] days prior to the beginning of each fiscal year, which begins on [ ], Agent shall prepare and submit to the Board a recommended Annual Budget for the next year showing anticipated income and expenses for such year.

> *Note*: While subsection 2.2 of the agreement is silent on the issue of budget reconciliation, monthly reports comparing actual income and expenditures to budgeted amounts allow the agent and the board to make better financial decisions on an ongoing basis. It may be desirable to attach an addendum to the agreement stipulating which reports are to be provided, how often, and in what form. Also to be

Exhibit 2.4 ***(Continued)***

considered is whether any extraordinary reporting requirements will necessitate additional compensation to the agent.

2.4 SUBMISSION OF ANNUAL REPORT

Within [ ] days after the end of each fiscal year, Agent shall submit to the Association a summary of all receipts and disbursements relating to the Property for the preceding year. HOWEVER, submission of such annual report shall not be construed to require Agent to supply an audit. Any audit required by the Association shall be prepared at the Association's expense by an auditor(s) of its selection.

2.5 MAINTENANCE OF COMMON ELEMENTS

Subject to the direction of the Board, at the expense of the Association and in accordance with the Association's approved budget, Agent shall cause the common elements of the Property to be maintained according to appropriate standards of maintenance consistent with the character of the Property, including [ ].

2.6 EMPLOYMENT OF PERSONNEL

Agent shall hire, pay, negotiate collective bargaining agreements with (if necessary), supervise, and discharge whatever personnel may be required to maintain and operate the Property on behalf of the Association and in accordance with the budget, job standards, and wage rates previously approved by the Association. All such personnel shall be employees of the Association and not of Agent, and all salaries, taxes, and other expenses payable to or on account of such employees shall be operating expenses of the Property.

Note: Although use of the term *association* should be interpreted to include reference to the board, some agreements may need to specifically reference both entities—i.e., refer to "the Board *or* the Association." This may be particularly useful to clarify the provisions in subsections 2.6, 5.1, 8.2, and 8.3.

2.7 PAYMENT OF EMPLOYMENT TAXES

Agent shall, on behalf of the Association, execute and file all tax and other returns and do and perform all acts required of the Association as an employer under the Federal Insurance Contributions Act, the Federal Unemployment Tax Act, all applicable federal, state, and local income tax laws, and all other laws, regulations, and/or ordinances governing employment and payment of wages. Upon request, the Board shall promptly execute and deliver to Agent all necessary powers of attorney, notices of appointment, and the like. The Association shall supply all funds to pay any taxes.

Note: Subsection 2.7, which requires the agent to file returns and use funds of the association to pay taxes imposed on the association as an *employer*, is *not* intended to address the filing of income tax returns on behalf of the association as a not-for-profit corporation. Such income tax returns should be executed (signed) by an officer of the association, although the agent might be asked to prepare the relevant paperwork. If such a function is to be delegated to the agent, its role and authority should be spelled out in the agreement (in subsection 2.11) and taken into account in setting the agent's compensation.

(continued)

Exhibit 2.4 ***(Continued)***

2.8 UTILITIES AND SERVICES CONTRACTS

Subject to the direction of the Board and on behalf of the Association, Agent shall negotiate contracts for water, electricity, gas, telephone, and such other services as may be necessary or advisable for the common elements of the Property. Agent shall also purchase on behalf of the Association such equipment, tools, appliances, materials, and supplies as are necessary for the proper operation and maintenance of the Property. All such contracts and purchases shall be executed in the name of the Association by its Board of Directors and at its expense.

> *Note*: The documents that establish the condominium should define the common elements of the property; that definition determines the maintenance responsibilities of the agent and its authority to contract for utilities or services on behalf of the association in subsections 2.8 and 2.10.

2.9 PAYMENT OF EXPENSES

From the funds of the Association, Agent shall pay all expenses of the Property, including taxes, building and elevator inspection fees, water rates and other governmental charges, and all other charges or obligations incurred by the Association or by Agent on behalf of the Association with respect to the maintenance or operation of the Property or pursuant to the terms of this Agreement or pursuant to other authority granted by the Board on behalf of the Association.

2.10 RECORDS OF INSURANCE

Agent shall maintain appropriate records of all insurance coverage for the Property carried by the Association as specified in paragraph 10.2. Agent shall cooperate with the Board in investigating and reporting all accidents or claims for damage relating to the ownership, operation, and maintenance of the common elements of the Property, including any damage or destruction to them.

2.11 OTHER SPECIFIC SERVICES OF AGENT

Section 3 LIMITATION ON EXPENDITURES BY AGENT

In discharging its responsibilities under section 2 of this Agreement, Agent shall not make any unbudgeted expenditures or incur any nonrecurring contractual obligation exceeding $[ ], without the prior consent of the Association through the Board. HOWEVER, no such consent shall be required to repay any advances made by Agent under the terms of section 5. Notwithstanding these limitations, Agent may, on behalf of the Association and without prior consent of the Board, expend any amount or incur a contractual obligation in any amount required to deal with emergency conditions that may involve a danger to life or property or that may threaten the safety of the Property or the individual owners and occupants or that may threaten the suspension of any necessary service to the Property.

Section 4 AGENT NOT RESPONSIBLE FOR MAINTENANCE OF INDIVIDUAL UNITS

Agent shall have no authority or responsibility for maintenance or repairs to individual units in the Property. Such maintenance and repairs shall be the sole responsibility of the owners individually.

Exhibit 2.4 ***(Continued)***

Section 5 DISPOSITION OF FUNDS

Agent shall, on behalf of the Association, deposit collections and pay expenses of the Property as stated below.

5.1 DEPOSIT OF COLLECTIONS

Agent shall deposit all monies collected on behalf of the Association in a bank or other financial institution whose deposits are insured by the federal government or such other depository as directed by the Association in writing. The funds of the Association shall at all times be maintained separate and apart from Agent's own funds and from the funds of any others. Agent's designees shall be the only parties authorized to draw upon such accounts. Agent shall not be held liable in the event of bankruptcy or failure of such depository. Such operating account shall not be required to bear interest.

5.2 PAYMENT OF EXPENSES

Agent shall pay all expenses of operation and management of the Property from the Association's funds held in account by Agent. Any amounts owed to Agent by the Association shall also be paid from such account at any time without prior notice to the Association.

5.3 AGENT NOT REQUIRED TO ADVANCE FUNDS

Agent shall have no obligation to advance funds to the Association for any purpose whatsoever. Any funds advanced to the Association by Agent shall be repaid to Agent immediately from the Association's funds. Any sums due Agent under any provision of this Agreement, and not paid within [ ] days after such sums have become due, shall bear interest at the rate of [ ]% per annum.

5.4 BONDING OF EMPLOYEES

All employees of Agent who handle or are responsible for the safekeeping of any monies of the Association shall be covered by a bond protecting the Association. Such bond shall be in an amount and with a company determined by Agent and may be a blanket or umbrella bond. The expense of such bonding shall be paid by [ ].

> *Note*: Sometimes an association will require the agent to acquire fidelity bond coverage in excess of the limits of the agent's usual and customary practice, in which case such additional coverage should be obtained in the agent's name but at the association's expense and so stated in subsection 5.4 of the agreement.

Section 6 ATTENDANCE AT BOARD MEETINGS

Agent, or a designated employee or other representative of Agent, shall attend [ ] regular meeting(s) of the Board each month and the annual meeting of the Association. Upon not less than [ ] hours' notice, Agent or its designated representative shall attend meetings of the Board or of the Association as requested, provided that the Association shall pay Agent $[ ] per hour for that individual's attendance at each meeting. Agent or its representative shall be custodian of the official records of the Board and the Association. HOWEVER, neither Agent nor its representative shall be required to record the minutes of such meetings.

(continued)

Exhibit 2.4 ***(Continued)***

Note: In section 6 of the agreement, it may be desirable to limit the agent's attendance at board meetings to a fixed number of meetings per year (rather than per month) and to stipulate a time limit per meeting (e.g., two hours). Information about the board's scheduling and conduct of its regular meetings should be reviewed so the agent can evaluate the time requirement and state its commitment precisely in the agreement. (This should also be taken into account when determining the agent's compensation.)

Section 7 ONE BOARD MEMBER TO DEAL WITH AGENT

The Board shall designate one of its members who shall be authorized to deal with Agent on any matter relating to the management of the Property. Agent shall not accept directions or instructions with regard to the management of the Property from anyone else. In the absence of any other designation by the Board, the President of the Board shall be deemed to have this authority. Board appoints [ ] as alternate should the President be unavailable. Agent may, but is not required to, submit any matter, direction, instruction, or the like to the Board and shall then follow the direction of the Board.

Note: Because members of the board of directors of a condominium or homeowners association are elected for a specific term of office, references within the body of the agreement to individual board members should be by position rather than by name (e.g., "president of the board" rather than "John Smith") to avoid changing the agreement if there is a change in the board. This applies specifically to designation of specific individuals to deal with the agent (section 7) and delivery of notices per subsection 21.2. [If the agent will be responsible for maintenance inside individual units (and section 4 of the agreement form is modified to accommodate this difference), the agent's relationship with individual unit owners may require definition as an exception to the narrow provision of section 7.]

Section 8 LIMITATION OF AGENT'S AUTHORITY AND RESPONSIBILITY

Agent's authority to act and responsibility for the Property shall be subject to the limitations set forth below.

8.1 STRUCTURAL CHANGES

Agent shall have no authority to make any structural changes in the Property or to make any other major alterations or additions in or to any building or equipment therein, except such emergency repairs as may be required because of danger to life or property or which are immediately necessary for the preservation and safety of the Property or for the safety of the individual owners and occupants or which are required to avoid the suspension of any necessary service to the Property.

8.2 BUILDING COMPLIANCE

Agent shall not be responsible for the compliance of the Property or any of its equipment with the requirements of any building codes or with any statutes, ordinances, laws, rules, or regulations (including those relating to the existence and disposal of solid, liquid, and gaseous wastes, and toxic or hazardous substances) of any city, county, state, or federal governments or agencies, or any public authority or official thereof having jurisdiction over it.

Exhibit 2.4 *(Continued)*

HOWEVER, Agent shall notify the Association promptly or forward to the Association promptly any complaints, warnings, notices, or summonses received by Agent relating to such matters. The Association represents that to the best of its collective knowledge the Property complies with all such requirements, and the Association authorizes Agent to disclose the ownership of the Property to any such officials and agrees to indemnify, defend, and hold Agent, its representatives, servants, and employees, harmless of and from all loss, cost, expense, and liability whatsoever that may be imposed on them by reason of any present or future violation or alleged violation of such laws, ordinances, rules, or regulations.

8.3 AGENT ASSUMES NO LIABILITY

Agent assumes no liability whatsoever for any acts or omissions of the Board or the Association, or any previous boards or current or previous owners of the Property, or any previous management or other agent of either. Agent assumes no liability for any failure of or default by any individual unit owner in the payment of any assessment or other charges due the Association or in the performance of any obligations owed by any individual unit owner to the Association, pursuant to any lease or otherwise. Agent likewise assumes no liability for any failure of or default by concessionaires in any rental or other payments to the Association. Nor does Agent assume any liability for previously unknown violations of environmental or other regulations that may become known during the period this Agreement is in effect. Any such regulatory violations or hazards discovered by Agent shall be brought to the attention of the Association in writing, and the Association shall promptly cure them.

Section 9 AGENT'S COMPENSATION

Agent shall be compensated for specific services as stated below.

9.1 FOR MANAGEMENT SERVICES

The Association shall pay Agent a management fee of $[ ] per month. The management fee shall be paid monthly in advance. The management fee shall be adjusted annually upon approval by the Board of the Annual Budget, which adjustment shall be incorporated into this Agreement by reference. No further charge shall be made by Agent for Agent's services and other services of Agent's professional staff, except as otherwise expressly provided in this Agreement. Any clerical services performed for the Association, such as preparation and circulation of notices and newsletters and general correspondence of the Association, shall be at the Association's expense, including postage and other expenses.

9.2 FOR CONSTRUCTION, REMODELING, OR OTHER CONTRACTING SERVICES

9.3 FOR OTHER SERVICES

Section 10 OBLIGATIONS OF THE ASSOCIATION

The Association shall insure the Property, Agent, and itself against liability and bear the expense of any and all litigation against the Property, Agent, and the Association as stated below. In addition, the Association shall provide for an initial deposit and contingency reserve and, through its Board, approve an Annual Budget for the Property.

(continued)

Exhibit 2.4 ***(Continued)***

10.1 SAVE AGENT HARMLESS FROM LIABILITY SUITS

The Association shall indemnify, defend, and save Agent harmless from all suits or other claims including, but not limited to, those alleging any negligence of Agent or its employees in connection with the Property or the management thereof and from liability for damage to property and injuries to or death of any employee or other person. The Association shall pay all expenses incurred by Agent including, but not limited to, all attorneys' fees, costs, and expenses incurred to represent Agent in regard to any claim, proceeding, or suit involving alleged negligence of Agent or its employees in connection with or arising out of the management of the Property.

10.2 ESTABLISH AND MAINTAIN LIABILITY INSURANCE

The Association shall carry at its own expense public liability, boiler, fire and extended coverage, elevator liability (if elevators are part of the equipment of the Property), and workers' compensation insurance, and such other insurance as may be necessary or appropriate. Such insurance policies shall name both the Association and Agent as insureds, and their coverage shall be adequate to protect the interests of both parties and in form, substance, and amounts reasonably satisfactory to Agent. The Association shall provide Agent with certificates evidencing such insurance or with duplicate copies of such policies within [ ] days from the date of execution of this Agreement; or Agent may, but shall not be obligated to, place said insurance and charge the cost thereof to the account of the Association. Said policies shall provide that notice of default or cancellation shall be sent to Agent as well as to the Association and shall require a minimum of [ ] days' written notice to Agent before any cancellation of or changes to said policies.

10.3 PAY ALL EXPENSES OF ANY LITIGATION

The Association shall pay all expenses incurred by Agent including, but not limited to, Agent's costs and time, any liability, fines, penalties or the like, settlement amounts, and attorneys' fees for counsel employed to represent Agent or the Association in any proceeding or suit involving any alleged or actual violation by Agent or the Association or the Board, or any combination of all of them, of any law or regulation of any governmental body pertaining to environmental protection, fair housing, or fair employment, including, but not limited to, any law prohibiting or making illegal discrimination on the basis of race, sex, creed, color, religion, national origin, family status, or mental or physical handicap. HOWEVER, the Association shall not be responsible to Agent for any such expenses in the event Agent is finally adjudged to have personally, and not in a representative capacity, violated any such law. Nothing contained in this Agreement shall obligate Agent to employ legal counsel to represent the Board or the Association in any such proceeding or suit.

10.4 SAVE AGENT HARMLESS FROM LABOR LAW VIOLATIONS

The Association shall indemnify, defend, and save Agent harmless from all claims, investigations, and suits, or from the Association's or the Board's actions or failures to act, with respect to any alleged or actual violation of state or federal labor laws. The Association's obligation with respect to such violation(s) shall include payment of all settlements, judgments, damages, liquidated damages, penalties, forfeitures, back pay awards, court costs, litigation expenses, and attorneys' fees.

Exhibit 2.4 ***(Continued)***

10.5 PROVIDE FOR INITIAL DEPOSIT AND CONTINGENCY RESERVE

Immediately on commencement of this Agreement, the Association shall remit to Agent the sum of $[ ] to be deposited in the account(s) established for the Association pursuant to paragraph 5.1, such amount representing the estimated disbursements to be made in the first month, plus an additional sum of $[ ] as a contingency reserve. The Association agrees to maintain this contingency reserve amount at all times and shall agree in writing to a new contingency reserve when such is required. The contingency reserve thus established is to enable Agent to pay obligations of the Association as they become due and is an amount separate from the reserve funds that accrue from assessments of individual unit owners.

10.6 APPROVE ANNUAL BUDGET

Within thirty (30) days of receipt of the recommended Annual Budget prepared by Agent, the Board shall either approve the budget as submitted or provide Agent with written notice setting forth those items which are unacceptable to the Board or provide agent with written notice advising Agent what additional information is required. Failure to provide such notice to Agent within said thirty (30)-day period shall be deemed as approval of the Annual Budget by the Board. Upon approval, Agent shall be authorized to operate and manage the Property in accordance with the Annual Budget.

> *Note:* Modification of subsection 10.6 may be necessary to allow for a different (i.e., longer) period for review and approval of the budget by the board and/or the association.

Section 11 TERMINATION BY AGENT FOR CAUSE

Agent shall have the right to cancel this Agreement at any time in the event that any insurance required of the Association is not maintained without any lapse. Agent shall also have the right to cancel this Agreement at any time in the event it is alleged or charged that the Property, or any equipment therein or any act or failure to act by the Board or the Association with respect to the Property or the sale, rental, or other disposition thereof or with respect to the hiring of employees to manage it, fails to comply with or is in violation of any requirement of any constitutional provision, statute, ordinance, law, or regulation of any governmental body or any order or ruling of any public authority or official thereof having or claiming to have jurisdiction over it, and Agent in its sole and absolute discretion considers that the action or position of the Association or the Board with respect thereto may result in damage or liability to Agent, or disciplinary proceeding with respect to Agent's license. Agent shall provide written notice to the Association of its election to terminate this Agreement, in which case termination shall be effective upon the service of such notice.

Section 12 TERMINATION BY THE ASSOCIATION; CANCELLATION FEE

The Association may cancel this Agreement at any time on not less than [ ] days' prior notice to Agent, provided that such notice is accompanied by payment to Agent of a cancellation fee in an amount equal to the total management fee for a period of [ ] months. For this purpose, the monthly management fee shall be presumed to be the same as that of the last month prior to service of the notice of cancellation.

> *Note*: In section 12, the provision for termination of the agreement by the association does not include specific protection for the agent against the association hiring away

(continued)

Exhibit 2.4 ***(Continued)***

the agent's employees. Users may wish to modify the form to provide such protection or, at least, ensure that the agent's employees sign an agreement that prohibits them from accepting employment with an association contracted by the agent while they are employees of the agent or for a specific period after they leave the agent's employ.

Section 13 ASSOCIATION RESPONSIBLE FOR PAYMENTS

Upon termination of or withdrawal from this Agreement by either party, the Association shall assume the obligations of any contract or outstanding bill executed by Agent under this Agreement for and on behalf of the Association and responsibility for payment of all unpaid bills. In addition, the Association shall furnish Agent security, in an amount satisfactory to Agent, against any obligations or liabilities that Agent may have properly incurred on the Association's behalf under this Agreement.

Agent may withhold funds for ninety (90) days after the end of the month in which this Agreement is terminated in order to pay bills previously incurred but not yet invoiced and to close accounts. Agent shall deliver to the Association, within ninety (90) days after the end of the month in which this Agreement is terminated, any balance of monies due the Association that were held by Agent with respect to the Property, as well as a final accounting reflecting the balance of income and expenses with respect to the Property as of the date of termination or withdrawal, and all records, contracts, leases, receipts for deposits, and other papers or documents that pertain to the Property.

Note: Nonfinancial records and those not required for the closeout of payments and accounts by the agent need not be retained by the agent for the full term of 90 days following termination of the agreement (as provided in section 13), but should be returned to the association or transferred to a new managing agent promptly.

Section 14 RELATIONSHIP OF AGENT TO THE ASSOCIATION

The relationship of the parties to this Agreement shall be that of Principal and Agent, and all duties to be performed by Agent under this Agreement shall be for and on behalf of, in the name of and for the account of the Association. In taking any action under this Agreement, Agent shall be acting only as Agent for the Association, and nothing in this Agreement shall be construed as creating a partnership, joint venture, or any other relationship between the parties to this Agreement except that of Principal and Agent, or as requiring Agent to bear any portion of losses arising out of or connected with the ownership or operation of the Property. Nor shall Agent at any time during the period of this Agreement be considered a direct employee of the Association. Neither party shall have the power to bind or obligate the other except as expressly set forth in this Agreement, except that Agent is authorized to act with such additional authority and power as may be necessary to carry out the spirit and intent of this Agreement.

Section 15 INDEMNIFICATION SURVIVES TERMINATION

All representations and warranties of the parties contained herein shall survive the termination of this Agreement. All provisions of this Agreement that require the Association to have insured or to defend, reimburse, or indemnify Agent shall survive any termination; and if Agent is or becomes involved in any proceeding or litigation by reason of having been the Association's Agent, such provisions shall apply as if this Agreement were still in effect.

Exhibit 2.4 ***(Continued)***

Section 16 HEADINGS

All headings and subheadings employed within this Agreement are inserted only for convenience and ease of reference and are not to be considered in the construction or interpretation of any provision of this Agreement.

Section 17 FORCE MAJEURE

Any delays in the performance of any obligation of Agent under this Agreement shall be excused to the extent that such delays are caused by wars, national emergencies, natural disasters, strikes, labor disputes, utility failures, government regulations, riots, adverse weather, and other similar causes not within the control of Agent, and any time periods required for performance shall be extended accordingly.

Section 18 COMPLETE AGREEMENT

This Agreement, including any specified attachments, constitutes the entire agreement between the Association and Agent with respect to the management and operation of the Property and supersedes and replaces any and all previous management agreements entered into or/and negotiated between the Association and Agent relating to the Property covered by this Agreement. No change to this Agreement shall be valid unless made by supplemental written agreement executed and approved by the Association and Agent. Except as otherwise provided herein, any and all amendments, additions, or deletions to this Agreement shall be null and void unless approved by the Association and Agent in writing. Each party to this Agreement hereby acknowledges and agrees that the other party has made no warranties, representations, covenants, or agreements, express or implied, to such party, other than those expressly set forth herein, and that each party, in entering into and executing this Agreement, has relied upon no warranties, representations, covenants, or agreements, express or implied, to such party, other than those expressly set forth herein.

Section 19 RIGHTS CUMULATIVE; NO WAIVER

No right or remedy herein conferred upon or reserved to either of the parties to this Agreement is intended to be exclusive of any other right or remedy, and each and every right and remedy shall be cumulative and in addition to any other right or remedy given under this Agreement or now or hereafter legally existing upon the occurrence of an event of default under this Agreement. The failure of either party to this Agreement to insist at any time upon the strict observance or performance of any of the provisions of this Agreement, or to exercise any right or remedy as provided in this Agreement, shall not impair any such right or remedy or be construed as a waiver or relinquishment of such right or remedy with respect to subsequent defaults. Every right and remedy given by this Agreement to the parties to it may be exercised from time to time and as often as may be deemed expedient by those parties.

Section 20 APPLICABLE LAW AND PARTIAL INVALIDITY

The execution, interpretation, and performance of this Agreement shall in all respects be controlled and governed by the laws of the State of [ ]. If any part of this Agreement shall be declared invalid or unenforceable, Agent shall have the option to terminate this Agreement by notice to the Association.

(continued)

Exhibit 2.4 ***(Continued)***

Section 21 NOTICES

Any notice required or provided for in this Agreement shall be in writing and shall be addressed as indicated below or to such other address as Agent or the Association may specify hereafter in writing.

21.1 TO AGENT

21.2 TO THE ASSOCIATION

President of the Board

DELIVERY OF NOTICES

Notices or other communications between the parties to this Agreement may be mailed by United States registered or certified mail, return receipt requested, postage prepaid, and may be deposited in a United States Post Office or a depository regularly maintained by the post office. Such notices may also be delivered by hand or by any other receipted method or means permitted by law. For purposes of this Agreement, notices shall be deemed to have been "given" or "delivered" upon personal delivery thereof or forty-eight (48) hours after having been deposited in the United States mails as provided herein.

Section 22 AGREEMENT BINDING ON SUCCESSORS AND ASSIGNS

This Agreement shall be binding upon and inure to the benefit of the successors and assigns of Agent and the heirs, administrators, successors, and assigns of the Association. Notwithstanding the preceding sentence, Agent shall not assign its interest under this Agreement except in connection with the sale of all or substantially all of the assets of its business. In the event of such sale, Agent shall be released from all liability under this Agreement upon the express assumption of such liability by its assignee.

SIGNATURES

IN WITNESS WHEREOF, the parties hereto have affixed or caused to be affixed their respective signatures this [ ] day of [ ] 20[ ].

Witnesses:

Board:

Agent:

Firm

By

Submitted by

Exhibit 2.4 *(Continued)*

POWER OF ATTORNEY
KNOW ALL MEN BY THESE PRESENTS, THAT
[(Name)] [(State whether individual, partnership, corporation, etc.)] located at [ ] has made, constituted, and appointed, and, by these presents does hereby make, constitute, and appoint [ ], a resident of the United States, whose address is [ ], (its) true and lawful attorney for (it)(me) in (its)(my) name, place, and stead to execute and to file any Tax Returns due on or after [ ] under the provisions of the Social Security Act, now in force or future amendments thereto.

Dated at [ ] this [ ] day of [ ], 20[ ].

[Signature of Taxpayer]

[Title]

[Signature of Taxpayer]

[Title]

[Signature of Taxpayer]

[Title]

Executed in the presence of:

[Witness]

[Witness]
Acknowledged before me this [ ] day of [ ], 20[ ].

[NOTARIAL SEAL]

Exhibit 2.5
Menu of Services

Good Place Homeowners Association
Monthly Management Services
With Invest West Management, LLC, AMO

All services listed would be included in our standard monthly fee unless otherwise stated.

Board of Director Meetings
Notice of Meeting
Agenda/Packets
Prior Board Meeting Minutes
YTD Financial Statements
Meeting Attendance
Management Report
(See Exhibit 2.4, Section 6)

Annual Association Meeting
Notice of Meeting
Proxy Form
Agenda
Prior Annual Meeting Minutes
YTD Financials
Present Proposed Budget
Quorum Status
Proxy Validation
Registration of Owners
Election/Mailing Certification

Minutes
Duplication
Disbursement to Owners (Mail)
Can Provide Minute-Taker (See Exhibit 2.6)

Property Tours
CC&Rs Compliance Inspections (See Exhibit 2.6)
Enforcement of Governing Documents (CC&Rs)
Fine Assessment
Detailed Onsite Maintenance Inspection (See Exhibit 2.6)

Fiscal Management
Distribution of Welcome Packet
Provide Dues Invoices or Coupons
Late Notices/Fees
Bill Approval/Payment
Financial Statements by 10th of Month
Tax Return Assistance
Annual Corporation Report Filing
Budget Preparation

Collect Assessments (Dues)
Track Delinquencies

Exhibit 2.6

Estimated Rate Sheet (October 2007)

Accounting Services	
Accounting services beyond normal bookkeeping covered in contract	$60/hr
Delinquency/collection letters beyond annual dues billing (billed to owner)	$25 each
Collection fee if using collection agency (bill to be placed on owners account)	$60
Lien filing/releasing (bill to be placed on delinquent account)	$250
Management Services	
Management/accounting rates during business hours	$60/hr
Management representation at board/association meetings	See Exhibit 2.4, Section 6
Minute taker	$40/hr during bus. hrs $60-$80/hr after hours
Compliance inspections (include physical inspection, detailed inspection log e-mailed to board, and initial compliance letters)	$420 (7 hrs allocated)
Additional compliance letters	$25 each
Architectural request processing	$25 each
Detailed maintenance inspection including written report	$480 (8 hrs allocated)
Special projects beyond normal management	TBD
After-hours phone response	$60/hr; $25 minimum per occurrence
Maintenance technician	$35/hr
After hours/holiday maintenance technician rate	$70/hr
Web page and monthly updating	$25/month
Escrow Transactions (Billed to Individual Owner)	
Mortgage/lender inquiries (questionnaires)	$25-$75
Governing documents (CC&Rs, bylaws, articles of inc., and rules)	$25
Product/Supplies	
Postage	Current U.S. Mail rate
Standard photocopies	$.10/page
Color photocopies	$.40/page
Envelopes (#10 or less)	$.20/envelope
Envelopes (above #10)	$.50/envelope
Check stock/MICR ink	$.20/check

The above list is meant to identify services and costs not specifically provided under our management agreement or cost adjustments as allowed per the management contract. There may be some charges incurred by the Association not listed above. Agent will strive to provide cost estimates to the Association prior to commencing additional services not already identified. The above fees may be subject to change with prior written notice to the Association.

Tailor Your Services

A clear knowledge of the community and its workings is essential. A good management agent determines the best type of management for a particular community and tailors the management services to those specifics.

Using a tailored approach instantly gains recognition from a prospective board. The board will realize the uniqueness of your management proposal and recognize that it is not just a "one-size-fits-all" management plan.

Sell Your Services

In an interview with the board, be logical and orderly in presenting your skills and opinions. The board is looking for something different from their past and most recent professional management experiences. Be sure to question the board about its needs, the community, and especially the reason they are changing management firms or going from self-management to professional management. Recognize and acknowledge the efforts of volunteer leadership (the board).

Be honest in your responses; if you cannot answer a question, say so. However, let the interviewer know how you would find the answer. Stress that trust and credibility will develop as management and the association work together.

BEGINNING THE MANAGEMENT TRANSITION

The interview and scrutiny of a potential community management account ends, and your firm is selected. Good news: all of the hard work analyzing the community's needs, the management firm's needs, and cost accounting has brought a positive conclusion. The deal is closed. Now it is time to begin the transition between management companies.

The transition procedures memo (Exhibit 2.7) and the new account checklist (Exhibit 2.8) that follow work well during any management transition. Together, they practically walk a management firm through the initial stages of management.

As the previous managing company sends the documents requested in the transitions procedures memo, check off each item on the checklist in Exhibit 2.8. The checklist helps you track the documents received and follow up on any missing items.

This transition checklist could also be part of the initial management presentation package. It clearly illustrates the manager's expertise and knowledge when transitioning between management firms. It assists in establishing your credibility with the new directors and the community you have just added to your management portfolio.

Exhibit 2.7

Transition Procedures Memo

DATE: August 30, 20XX

TO: ____________Management

CC: ____________________ Homeowners Association, Board of Directors

FROM: Invest West Management has been contracted to perform management services for _____________ Homeowners Association beginning _____________.

In preparation for a seamless transition for ____________ Homeowners Association, we request the following items be made available in the periods referenced.

30 Days Prior to Management Transition (by 09/01/20XX)

Financial: Budget for current year (or future year if current date is in the fourth quarter of the fiscal year); $200.00 to open operation and capital accounts; preliminary direct deposit report; list of unit addresses, unit numbers, and their current assessments

Management: Recorded governing documents (see itemized list attached); tax I.D. number; last annual meeting minutes and board meeting minutes for past 90 days; current contracts for maintenance; current contracts (others)

Operational: Builder and developer contact information; vendor list; board and owner roster

At Transition of Management (10/01/20XX)

Financial: Most recent financial statements, general ledger, and payments ledger (for each homeowner); accounts payable and accounts receivable; historical financial, general ledger, and budget statements; investment information; tax returns; liens and judgments; payment plans; updated direct deposit report

Management: Reserve study; correspondence (pending issues); resolutions; rules and regulations; litigation files and records; maintenance records (pending)

Operational: Committee member roster; updated board and owner roster; utility agreements; insurance policies

Within 60 Days after Management Transition (11/30/20XX)

Financial: Balance of operation funds; final financial statement

Management: Correspondence (historical); maintenance records (historical); meeting minutes (historical)

Operational: As-builts; occupancy permits; elevator permits

After your review of this request, please contact the new Managing Agent, _________, at (___) ___-____ if you foresee any difficulties in meeting the above deadlines. It is our intention to ensure the smoothest transition possible for the homeowners, the board of directors, and both management companies.

Provided by Invest West Management, LLC, AMO
Stephen R. Barber, CPM

Exhibit 2.8

New Account Document and Financial Checklist

New Account Checklist
_______ Homeowners Association

30 Days Prior to Management

1.) Financial Records

- ❒ Budget for current year (or future year if current date is in the fourth quarter of the fiscal year), including supporting documents and budget assumptions
- ❒ $200.00 to open operation account
- ❒ Preliminary direct deposit report
- ❒ Tax ID number
- ❒ Roster of units including address and unit/lot number

2.) Management

a. Recorded governing documents
- ❒ Statutory warranty deeds
- ❒ Legal description—common open space
- ❒ Copy of last annual report
- ❒ Site plan, plot map
- ❒ Landscape plans (drawings)
- ❒ Articles of incorporation
- ❒ Bylaws
  - i. PUD
    - ❒ Deed(s) for common area, if applicable
    - ❒ CC&Rs and amendments
  - ii. Condos
    - ❒ Master deed
    - ❒ Regulatory agreement

b. Meeting information
- ❒ Last annual meeting minutes
- ❒ Board meeting minutes for past 90 days

c. Contracts (current)
- ❒ Maintenance service contracts
- ❒ Other current contracts

3.) Operational

- ❒ Builder and developer contact information
- ❒ Vendor list
- ❒ Board and owner roster
- ❒ Pending architectural approval forms

At Transition of Management

1.) Financial

- ❒ Reserve funds held
- ❒ Completed financial statements, current to within 45 days
- ❒ Payments ledger (for each homeowner)
- ❒ Accounts payable and accounts receivable
- ❒ Historical financial, general ledger, and budget statements
- ❒ Investment information

Exhibit 2.8 ***(Continued)***

- ❒ Tax returns
- ❒ Certified audits (copies of all)
- ❒ Liens and judgments
- ❒ Payment plans
- ❒ Updated direct deposit report

2.) Management

- ❒ Reserve study
- ❒ Copies of all contracts association currently has
- ❒ Correspondence (pending issues)
- ❒ Resolutions
- ❒ Rules and regulations
- ❒ Litigation files and records
- ❒ Maintenance records (pending)
- ❒ All parking permits/key tag records and supplies

3.) Operational

- ❒ Committee member roster
- ❒ Updated board and owner roster
- ❒ Utility agreements
- ❒ Insurance policies and claims history
- ❒ Common area—spec sheets for applicable building materials (e.g., roofing, paint)
- ❒ Equipment warranties, operation manuals, and accompanying software
- ❒ Physical inventory of association property
- ❒ Completed and disapproved architectural requests
- ❒ All tangible association property

Within 60 Days after Transition

1.) Financial

- ❒ Balance of operational funds
- ❒ Final financial statements

2.) Management

- ❒ Correspondence (historical)
- ❒ Maintenance records (historical)
- ❒ Meeting minutes (historical)

3.) Operational

- ❒ As-builts
- ❒ Occupancy permits for common elements
- ❒ Elevator permits

Provided by Invest West Management, LLC, AMO
Stephen R. Barber, CPM

Using tools like the form in Exhibit 2.8 and developing the management skills discussed in this chapter, the professional manager is poised to demonstrate necessary expertise when competing for a potential client's business. After association business has been successfully secured, however, the manager's job is just getting started. There are a myriad of governance issues that the community association manager must be able to address, and we turn to these in the next chapter.

3

Association Governance

INTRODUCTION

Living in a community association is more the rule today than one would have anticipated 30 years ago. Community associations provide amenities and affordability that make property ownership more available to the real estate buyer. However, along with property ownership one purchases the restrictions that come with ownership of a property within the confines of a community association.

Community associations of all types (as discussed in Chapter 1) are designed to function like government entities. They have clearly defined rules of operation as outlined in codes, statutes, or governing documents. Because the community association is responsible for maintaining property values, it is required to make important decisions. It must enforce policies and procedures, collect monies, pay bills, and present financial accounting reports to the association members. For these reasons, the association manager must become familiar with the codes, statutes, and governing documents under which the community association operates.

UNIFORM ACTS AND STATE STATUTES

Looking at the big picture, one cannot consider association governance without first bearing in mind the varied state-to-state statutes as well as the national uniform acts that have been created as guides to developing those statutes.

Uniform Acts

By the late 1960s, almost every state had some form of condominium statute. However, the statutes varied extremely from one state to another. In an effort to bring uniformity to the law, the National Conference of Commissioners on Uniform State Laws proposed model laws in this field. They published the Uniform Condominium Act (UCA) in 1977, the Uniform Planned Community Act (UPCA) in 1980, and the Uniform Common Interest Ownership Act (UCIOA) in 1982 (amended in 1995).

According to the American Bar Association, the Uniform Condominium Act allows flexibility for developers while offering protection, such as requiring extensive disclosure before sale, to consumers. It also covers such matters as endurance, *tort*, and contract liability. As of 2002, approximately 23 states had adopted and/or adapted the UCA. The Uniform Planned Community Act was created with the intent of bringing the issues that the UCA addressed to the planned community environment. The much more encompassing Uniform Common Interest Ownership Act extended its influence to cooperatives as well as condominiums and planned developments. These acts, in and of themselves, are not binding on anyone. They were only designed to serve as models for those entities that were developing their own laws. When questions arise as to how to handle difficult situations, these uniform acts serve as valuable reference material.

State Statutes

Just as common interest ownership has evolved over the years, so have the state statutes governing the ownership type. State condominium laws have existed for many years, but their only emphasis was on the government of condominiums. States have had to enact additional legislation to address the needs of planned unit developments, homeowners associations, and cooperatives. For this reason, numerous acts within the same state may encompass all the different personalities of community associations. In addition, if the association is *incorporated*, it can also fall under the jurisdiction of the state corporation statutes.

For example, the state of Maryland has the Maryland Condominium Act, Maryland Homeowners Association Act, Maryland Cooperative Housing Act, and Maryland Contract Lien Act as well as general Maryland real property and corporate laws that affect community associations. Washington State has the Horizontal Property Regimes Act, Condominium Act, Homeowners Association Act, and Washington Non-Profit Corporation Act. Like Maryland, Washington has numerous additional statutes that come into play with community associations.

Associations may call on their state statutes when the association's governing documents are silent on a particular issue. When reviewing the state statute, association members are advised to defer to the state statute authority on particular situations preceding language like "Except as provided in the association's governing documents...." State law can address such issues as voting procedures, *quorum* requirements, records availability, dissolution of the association, meeting procedures, and disclosure requirements for buying or selling. All board members, professional managers, and legal representatives must familiarize themselves with the state statutes that pertain to the properties they represent.

GOVERNING DOCUMENTS

Much of the organization's governance structure is outlined in the association's *governing documents*—the legally recognized and recorded paperwork that creates and controls the association. Generally speaking, the governing documents are a collection of documents including the plat map, declaration, articles of incorporation, bylaws, rules and regulations, and policies and procedures. Those who purchase property within a community association have no choice but to abide by all of the association's governing documents. This is not voluntary membership and/or voluntary *compliance*. It is mandatory. Living in a community association subjects the owners to covenants and restrictions in order to maintain property values.

Plat Map

The *plat map* is also known as the recorded map, subdivision map, condominium plan, site plan, plan, and parcel map. Whatever the name, it refers to the drawings that illustrate how the property is divided into units or lots. The drawings show the exact location of all property boundaries, unit boundaries, and common area locations.

When an entity decides to develop a piece of land that will eventually become a community association, it uses professionals to survey, plot, and design the community. Once this is accomplished, the drawings are recorded with the county in which the property is located. Sometimes this recorded document is accompanied by the covenants, conditions, and restrictions (discussed below), but these also can be recorded later. The drawings become part of every deed and mortgage, thus making them very difficult to change or alter.

Declaration of Covenants, Conditions, and Restrictions

The *declaration* is to the community association what the Constitution is to the United States. Like the Constitution, it may be the most important document the community association uses to govern itself. Also called the *covenants, conditions, and restrictions (CC&Rs)*, or the *deed of restrictions*, the declaration is the bundle of rights given to all association members; it establishes how everyone and everything is to operate within the organization. The declaration is similar to a deed restriction. It defines the individual ownership rights as well as the association's rights and runs with the land subjecting it to rules of operation.

The declaration is a legally binding contract into which one enters when purchasing a property within a community association. This document cannot be violated. This can be a difficult issue when buyers feel they were misinformed as to the restrictions accompanying the property. Studies have shown that over 30 percent of community association owners learn of the declaration requirements after moving into their homes. The real estate industry must do a better job educating purchasers of property within community associations.

The declaration is designed to give all members the assurance that everyone living in the association has equal rights of stability, compliance, and enforceability. Members can expect that everyone living in their community will abide by the same conditions, covenants, and restrictions. Professional managers of community associations must familiarize themselves with the declaration particular to each association.

Declaration Segments. The declaration of covenants, conditions, and restrictions is the one document that brings everything together and spells out the essential elements of ownership within the association. It creates the framework for the association's operations and defines ownership, responsibility for maintenance, and accountability for all other association issues. No two declarations are exactly alike. However, all cover the same basic concepts discussed in the list below.

- *Description of the property.* The declaration defines the real property that is included within the confines of the association. It provides the legal description as well as the recorded *parcel number(s)* from the plat map.
- *Description of the units.* This section of the declaration provides a lot of essential information. It defines the buildings, including the square footage and boundaries of the units and/or lots. It also includes the definitions of the common area and limited common area (also known as *exclusive common area*). (The next section defines and discusses these terms.) This is vital information because it guides the interpretation of who is responsible for what.
- *Membership.* This section establishes membership in the association and the rights and privileges of membership as well as the organizational structure of the association. It establishes that the affairs of the

association are to be managed by a *board of directors* consisting of a specific number of members who are to serve for a specific period. The association is under the control of the *declarant* (developer) for a defined initial period. Generally speaking, the declarant's authority for overseeing the affairs of the association is mentioned in this section.

- *Use of property.* Here the declaration addresses how the property within the association can be used. Generally, unless it is a *multi-use association* (meaning it has commercial and residential members), the use is for residential purposes only. Timeshares and rental property can also be addressed in this section.
- *Management.* This section gives the board of directors the authority to enter into a contract with a professional management company.
- *Assessments.* The common elements of the association will not take care of themselves. This section defines the specific common elements and gives the association the authority to collect "from time to time" the funds necessary to maintain those elements. It also mandates that the association have a budget to allocate an equal portion of the expense payments to the individual homeowners. Budget ratification, assessment increases from year to year, collection processes, and capital reserve funding are also addressed.
- *Insurance.* The declaration requires the association to obtain and maintain insurance coverage at all times. Generally speaking, the types of coverage required will be property replacement value (casualty), general liability, directors and officers, fidelity bond, and coverage for any personal property owned by the association. The declaration often states the requirement for each individual owner to obtain additional insurance on the homeowner's personal property and any other property that is not otherwise covered by the association's insurance.
- *Maintenance and repair.* This section describes homeowner and association responsibilities for maintenance and repair. The owner is responsible for his or her unit and sometimes for the unit's limited common area. (See the discussion of common and limited common areas in the next section.) The association is responsible for maintaining all of the common elements. The cost is shared among all the unit owners. This section of the declaration also addresses additions, alterations, and improvements to the common area and the limited common area. Many disputes can erupt within the association if members do not have a clear understanding of this portion of the declaration.
- *Protective covenants.* To protect everyone's investment and to ensure a relaxing, coherent environment, covenants are established in the declaration. Issues such as antennas, pets, obnoxious behavior,

vehicle parking, landscaping, architectural control, utilities, etc. can all be addressed in this section.

- *Amending the declaration.* Over time, the association identifies issues that the declaration does not address. For this reason, the declaration may need additions or amendments. This section stipulates the process required.

The above list does not include everything an association's governing documents may address. Additional sections might address *condemnation*, document availability, *easements*, registered agents, liens, damage or destruction, subdivisions, mortgagee protection, dispute resolution, and enforcement. The list is always customized to meet the needs of the particular type of association.

Common and Limited Common Areas. The terms *common area* and *limited common area* have particular importance to the association and its members because those areas often cause disputes between the homeowners and the board.

A *common area* (or element) is that portion of the entire common interest development that is not defined in the declaration as belonging to an association member's individual unit, lot, parcel, or space. The term refers to portions of a building, land, and amenities owned by a planned unit development or the homeowners association of a condominium project; they are used by all of the unit owners, and all owners share the common expenses of their operation and maintenance. Along with the exterior of the buildings, the common area may include swimming pools, tennis courts, recreational facilities, parking areas, driveways in and out of the community, common corridors and lobbies, landscaped areas within the community, and perimeter fencing.

A *limited common area* (or element) is that portion of the common interest development that is defined in the declaration as devoted to the exclusive use of one or more members but not to all of them. One state statute explains, "limited common elements" means a portion of the common elements so designated in the declaration as being reserved for the use of a certain unit or units to the exclusion of other units. The unit owner is entitled to the exclusive use and enjoyment of this area. For that reason, the term *exclusive use common area* is sometimes used to refer to the limited common area. This area may include balconies, patios, exterior doors and their accompanying hardware, windows, shutters, and awnings as well as garages and their doors. It may also include any other fixtures or utilities designated to service a single unit, lot, parcel, or space.

The common area and the limited common area are under the direct control and supervision of the board of directors for the community association. (The board of directors is discussed in Chapter 4.) Because the board makes decisions on the use, maintenance, and repair of all common areas, limited or otherwise, it has the authority to say what can and cannot be done in those areas. Those areas often lead to disagreements between homeowners and the board. Homeowners know that the patios outside their backdoors are for their use only. Conflicts sometime arise when a homeowner uses the area on the patio for something the association's governing documents prohibit. This is when the board has to step in and encourage the homeowner to bring the situation back into compliance with the governing documents. If the board fails to act when a unit is not in compliance, the board members could be in breach of their *fiduciary* duty to maintain the association.

Boards may have the authority to allow homeowners to perform maintenance, repairs, or replacements within their particular limited common area. This is not unqualified homeowner authority. Such authorization is completely subject to board approval and supervision. If a repair or replacement is not performed in the proper manner, the board could require correction of the noncompliant issue.

Articles of Incorporation

The *articles of incorporation* establish the corporate structure for the community association. They bring the business aspect of the association into existence. They also define the purpose and powers of the association.

Not all community associations choose incorporation; however, for the benefit of the members, incorporation is highly recommended. Known as a *mutual benefit corporation*, this nonprofit corporation is formed solely for the benefit of its members. If a dispute arises regarding the operations of the corporation, the members must resolve the dispute because the corporation exists solely to serve the needs of its members. The corporation's responsibility is to serve the interests of its members.

The main reason an association should choose to incorporate is to protect all of the assets of the community and the individuals living within the community. When someone brings a lawsuit against the association, if the association is incorporated, the members of that association don't have to worry about their personal assets being at risk should the person win a large monetary award from the lawsuit.

According to Seattle attorney James L. Strichartz, in his *Community Association Journal* article, "Why Associations Should Incorporate," incorporation has other advantages:

1. The incorporated association can hold title to real property in its own name. This is useful when the association gains title to a parcel of property such as a residential unit.

2. The community association has an easier time opening association accounts with certain banks and vendors and borrowing money when it is incorporated.
3. Corporate law provides another avenue for filling in the gaps in the association's governing documents.

Bylaws

Just as the declaration establishes the "who, what, and where" of the community association, the *bylaws* establish the "how." They set up the procedures, such as the mechanics of administration and management, for operating the association. As soon as the association is incorporated, the bylaws are adopted. Unlike the articles of incorporation and the declaration, the bylaws are often not recorded or filed with any governmental agency. This makes it easier to change or amend the bylaws.

Issues addressed in the bylaws are:

- *Name of the association and location.* This is the property address as established in the declaration.
- *Meeting requirements.* This deals primarily with the process for holding annual and special meetings as well as the definition of "proper notice" for the meetings and the percentage that constitutes a quorum. The processes for voting may also be discussed with meeting information.
- *Board of directors.* Procedures for selecting the board of directors as well as the directors' term of office is defined in this section. The section often reiterates that the board members are not to be compensated for their service. It also addresses the powers and duties of the board. Such duties could include keeping complete records of the business affairs of the association, supervising employees and management, enforcing covenants, maintaining adequate insurance for the association, maintaining the common and limited common areas, adopting an annual budget, and providing resale information to potential buyers. The board is given complete control over all committees, officers, and professional managers, which means it can override the decisions of any of these individuals as long as it does so in agreement with the association's governing documents.
- *Meetings of the directors.* Regular meetings of the board, including special meetings and quorum requirements, are addressed in this section.
- *Officers of the association.* This section of the bylaws defines the officers for the association. This includes a president, vice president,

secretary, treasurer, and members-at-large. Officers vary from association to association and sometimes depend on the size of the association. The duties of the officers are also discussed in this section.

- *Books and records.* Association members have the authority to examine the association's books and records. The procedure for doing so is outlined in this section.
- *Indemnification of officers and directors.* Provision is made in the bylaws to *indemnify* individuals in these positions and reimburse them should they incur expenses in the defense of a claim against them or the association. However, in cases of gross negligence or misconduct, indemnification does not apply.
- *Amendments.* Just as the declaration has a provision for amendment, so do the bylaws. The percentage of members required to pass an amendment to the bylaws is usually smaller than the percentage required to amend the declaration.

Rules and Regulations

Community associations usually adopt *rules and regulations* to give further definition to the declaration and the bylaws. Mind you, however, these rules and regulations cannot contradict or conflict with issues those two documents already address. The declaration and bylaws are designed to protect the physical, visual, operational, and financial aspects of the community. When an association develops rules and regulations for a community, board members must take the intent of these documents into consideration. They must often walk a fine line when trying to create rules and regulations and at the same time to instill harmony for all of the membership. Many a legal battle has been fought over the interpretation of the best interest of the community or the individual member of the association.

The board of directors can develop and adopt the rules and regulations ("regs"). Even though creating or changing the rules and regulations generally does not require membership approval, the board is always wise to include the membership and get people's thoughts and ideas when making such adjustments. One way to get membership involvement is for the board to appoint a committee to produce new rules and regulations for the association—or to analyze and adjust those already in existence. The committee then makes its recommendation to the board for approval.

Rules and Regulations Development Guidelines. Attorney Thomas Hindman wrote the following guidelines for developing good association rules and regulations:

- *Use the KISS approach* (**K**eep **I**t **S**imple, **S**tupid; sorry if anyone's offended!). Remember, most adults read and comprehend at a ninth grade level. When writing rules and regulations, take that into consideration. Leave out the legalese; it is already addressed in the declaration and the bylaws. The rules provide an opportunity to be much more user-friendly.
- *Customize to your community.* Often an association adopts a "boiler plate" set of rules and regulations handed down by the developer. No two associations are exactly alike. Take the time to make sure your association's "rules and regs" are appropriate for the needs of your community.
- *Sell the benefit.* A member is more willing to abide by the rules and regulations if he or she understands "what's in it for me." Using a rule to ridicule or scold someone for what the board interprets as offensive behavior is a good way to lose cooperation. "No walking on the grass" sounds a lot more belligerent than "In order to maintain the beauty of our environment, members and their guests are not to intrude into the landscaped areas."
- *Provide for flexibility and reasonableness.* When analyzing rules and regulations in the cases before them, the courts generally side with the board's decisions if they ascertain that the decisions were reasonable and the board has demonstrated some flexibility in trying to resolve the dispute. The courts have allowed that minor violations of a rule will not result in the loss of ability to enforce the rule in the long term (*Peckham v. Milroy*, Washington Appellate Court; *Pietrowski v. Dufrane*, Wisconsin Court of Appeals).
- *Less is better.* The fewer rules the association establishes, the better. This makes the rules and regulations easier for the membership to keep in mind. In addition, enforcement on the part of the board is less complicated. Remember the "rules and regs" are meant to address the well-being of the community as a whole. Leave the complicated stuff for the municipalities and other government entities.
- *Keep it legal.* Rules must not violate a fundamental constitutional right (e.g., freedom of speech). The rules must be consistent with applicable federal, state, and local statutes (e.g., Civil Rights Act, Americans with Disabilities Act, and Federal Housing Act). Rules cannot prohibit anything that the other legal documents permit.[1]

---

[1] Printed in part with permission from Thomas Hindman, Attorney at Law, Orten & Hindman, P.C., Denver, CO. "The Components of a Good Rule," *Community E-Essentials, The Essential Community Association Law Newsletter*.

Once the board has adopted the new or revised rules and regulations, it must publish and deliver them to the association members. Remember, up to this point the membership has been kept involved and informed during the development process, so the adopted rules and regulations should come as no surprise.

Rules and Regulations Development Outline. An outline for developing rules and regulations for the community association follows.

1. Use and Maintenance of the Common Area (Elements)
    - A. Amenities
        - i. Cabana
        - ii. Pool
        - iii. Sauna
        - iv. Tennis Court
        - v. Playground
    - B. Exterior of Buildings
        - i. Paint Colors
        - ii. Storage
        - iii. Cleanliness
        - iv. Decorations
        - v. Landscaping
        - vi. Signage
    - C. Limited Common Area (Elements)
        - i. Balconies and Patios
        - ii. Garages
        - iii. Entryways
        - iv. Fireplaces/Dryer Vents
        - v. Satellite Dishes
2. Pets
    - A. Breeds
    - B. Size
    - C. Maintenance

3. Parking
   - A. Registration
   - B. Reserved Spaces
   - C. Towing
   - D. Visitor Parking
4. Individual Homes
   - A. Use
   - B. Alteration/Modifications
   - C. Leases
   - D. Insurance
5. Enforcement
   - A. Violation Notification
   - B. Fine Procedures
6. Due Process

Resolutions

From time to time, matters that need clarification may come before the association. These are generally strictly policy or procedural matters. When the declarations, bylaws, or rules and regulations fail to provide specifications on certain issues, the board adopts resolutions. These resolutions further define matters the other governing documents have already addressed.

An example of the need for a specific resolution is in the area of *assessments*. The board, by way of the declaration and the bylaws, has the authority to collect assessments to pay for the operations of the association. These documents may state what can be charged if the assessments aren't collected in a timely manner. However, the documents may be silent as to how the assessments can be collected and what penalties can be assessed. In this situation, the board may adopt a resolution stating the actions it will follow for the collection of delinquent assessments.

A resolution in its formal format is usually presented and discussed at a board meeting, and then a motion is made. By a majority vote of the board, the resolution is adopted. It is highly recommended that resolutions be kept in a notebook containing the historical records and decisions of the community's board of directors. The secretary should maintain the notebook.

Public Offering Statement

New condominium, time-share, and condo/hotel purchasers can often expect to receive a *public offering statement* along with the many other governing documents already discussed. This document is prepared by the declarant for the first sale of each unit. Its purpose is to provide information for new buyers so they can make informed decisions about their purchases. It includes information about the rights and obligations of unit owners. The requirements for public offering statements differ from state to state.

Other Considerations

Getting to know the association's governing documents is essential to understanding the governance of the association. In addition, the board and the association manager must understand the hierarchy among the documents, enforcement of the documents, and amendments to the documents.

Governing Document Hierarchy. Within the community association, the governing documents have a hierarchy of authority:

- *Plat map:* This document describes the location and nature of the common property and the individual lots.
- *Declaration (conditions, covenants, and restrictions):* The declaration provides the rights and obligations of the homeowners within the association.
- *Articles of incorporation:* These create the legal entity.
- *Bylaws:* The bylaws provide the details of operation for the association.
- *Rules and regulations:* These documents more clearly define the CC&Rs and bylaws with enforcement procedures.
- *Resolutions:* The resolutions clarify procedural matters.
- *Public offering statement:* This provides information to new buyers about their rights and obligations.

Enforcement and Due Process. If someone violates the governing documents, what should the board do? Many a board member and professional manager has heard, "This is my home and no one is going to tell me what to do." Does the association fine the violator, fix the situation, call for a meeting with the violator, turn to some sort of arbitration, or just sue the individual? The board must address these issues in a manner that ensures each association member is treated fairly. Some of the most controversial board actions occur in the area of enforcement.

No one likes to be in the position that enforcement demands. To avoid this circumstance, the association must use all available tools to keep its members educated and informed about the operations and functions of the community. The community living environment dictates that one homeowner's action not infringe on the rights of other members; helping each member of the association understand that fact is sometimes difficult. When a member is in a position that involves a violation, there should be no surprises.

The association should keep in mind that not all violations are created equal. Some violations may have little negative consequence on the overall operations of the community, while others may have a much bigger impact. Take for example the flowerpots that one homeowner places at the front door to his or her unit (limited common area) as opposed to the large, aggressive, and sometimes notably dangerous dog that has just moved into one of the units. Obviously, the dog situation would have a much more significant impact on the overall community living conditions than would the flowers at someone's front door. Boards must weigh such issues when developing enforcement procedures.

Associations' stated procedures for assessing fines for violations often delineate different levels (degrees) of violation. For example, as shown in Exhibit 3.1, they may include Level 1 (Minor), Level 2 (Medium), and Level 3 (Serious) violations. Defining the degree of enforcement is helpful when the board attempts to reverse a noncompliant situation. Note that fines should never be established to raise money for the association or to punish the offender. Their purpose is to encourage members to comply with the governing documents. Violators must always be treated with respect and courtesy.

All violation notices should provide homeowners with an opportunity to state their cases in front of their peers. This is called *due process*. Due process is a minimal level of fairness that the courts insist be given to anyone before he or she is punished or fined. A well-defined enforcement policy must include due process procedures. Some state statutes mandate the due process requirement.

Due process includes the following components:

- *Written notice of the violation*. This is the initial warning, and no fines should be assessed at this time.
- *Notice of second violation*. Fines can be assessed. At this time, the board should also outline the process for the offender to be heard and try to encourage a hearing.
- *Hearing process*. The board should inform the offending party that he or she has the right to attend a meeting of a specially appointed

Exhibit 3.1

Sample Rules Violation Schedule

Association Rules Violation Schedule

Each member of the community, whether owner, tenant, or guest, must abide by the community's standards and comply strictly with the declaration, bylaws, and rules to promote the harmony and cooperative purposes of the community. Each owner is fully responsible for the compliance of family members, guests, tenants, and other occupants of the owner's unit while they are within the association boundaries.

Rules violations are classified as follows:

Level 1 (Minor)
- 1st offense = Warning to the owner and occupant
- 2nd offense = $50 Fine
- 3rd and subsequent offenses = $75 Fine

Level 2 (Medium)
- 1st offense = Warning to the owner and occupant
- 2nd offense = $75 Fine
- 3rd and subsequent offenses = $100 Fine

Level 3 (Serious)
- 1st offense = Warning to the owner and occupant
- 2nd offense = $100 Fine
- 3rd and subsequent offenses = $150 Fine

Penalties assessed against an owner or occupant shall be collectable as delinquent assessments.

Fines will be payable to ____________________ within 10 days of notification. A late fee of $15 per month will be assessed against an owner for late payments.

---

hearing board to plead his or her case. The individual can present evidence and have professional representation if desired.

- *Decision*. The hearing board, meeting in closed session, considers all evidence and renders a decision.

Governing Document Amendments

Why amend the governing documents? An attorney for the developer of the community association usually drafts the initial governing documents. At that time, there is no way to predict the issues that may come before the association members and its board of directors. Over the lifetime of the association, laws change, society evolves, and membership profiles change. For these reasons, the association may need to review the existing documents and ascertain if changes are necessary. Most of the time, such changes are one simple amendment clarifying the already existing documents. Sometimes the original documents may be so archaic and out of step with modern situations that the association membership must rewrite and amend the entire set of documents.

How can the association amend the governing documents? The amendment process is as follows:

1. The board of directors and association members recognize a need that the existing documents don't address or address inadequately.
2. The board chooses an attorney specializing in community association law.
3. The attorney analyzes the existing documents and makes recommendations to the board of directors. The attorney either recommends a single issue amendment or an entire new set of documents. (Because obtaining quorum approval to pass amendments is not easy, some attorneys prefer to take the opportunity during the amendment process to clean up all objectionable issues throughout the documents and have the membership vote on the entire newly refined set.)
4. The board reviews the attorney's recommendations and decides either to send them back for more work or to accept the recommendations.
5. Once the board approves the amendment or the newly drafted documents, it should mail them to the membership for review. Following the mailing, a meeting should be set up to discuss any questions and/or concerns the members may have. Sometimes making changes to the governing documents is not a popular decision, so having the attorney on hand at the meeting may be helpful. He or she can answer the questions and alleviate some of the tension.
6. Once everything is in final draft and all questions have been answered, the membership votes to accept or reject the revised documents. When attempting to pass an amendment, the board must observe very specific quorum and percentage requirements.
7. When the amendment passes, the board instructs the attorney to record the new documents with the proper governmental authority.

FEDERAL MATTERS

When a community association considers developing rules and regulations or amending the governing documents already in place, board members should take precautions to avoid breaking any laws. They could be creating documents that are not enforceable because they contradict federal law as well as state and local laws. These laws are far too numerous and complex to include here. For that reason, this text discusses only the federal issues that are most significant to common interest developments.

The three federal issues that have the greatest impact on the community association and that prompt the most litigation are fair housing (which can include the Americans with Disabilities Act), satellite dishes, and sexual predators. Associations and their boards as well as professional management companies may find themselves in the courtroom defending their decisions and actions related to these subjects. For this reason, all parties working in and around community associations must, at a minimum, familiarize themselves with these particular federal matters.

Fair Housing Laws and the Community Association

The *Fair Housing Act* of 1968, also know as Title VIII of the Civil Rights Act, was amended in 1974 and 1988. The act and its amendments prohibit discrimination based on race, color, religion, national origin, sex, disability, and familial status. One may be illegally discriminating in the sale or rental of housing by denying housing based on any of the *protected classes*. Note that state and local laws may add even more protected classes, such as marital status, ancestry, sexual orientation, parental status, source of income, age, etc.

Associations may say, "We're not buying, selling, or renting real estate, so why should the law apply to us?" It applies to the community association because many rules of governance that the association develops and enforces affect the outcome of an individual's ability to buy, sell, or rent housing. When an association allows circumstances to develop that make someone residing in the community feel ostracized because of race, religion, or any other protected class status, the association runs the risk of that individual suing for damages and attorneys' fees.

Because filing a fair housing complaint at www.hud.gov is easy, association members, boards, and professional managers must have knowledge of fair housing at the federal, state, and local levels. If the association's governing documents are old, the board might consider having its attorney analyze the documents for any potential violations. The board should then follow through by making the appropriate changes and/or amendments. Common areas of potential liability are discussed below.

Children. A rule that states, "Children cannot play in the common area," or "No children riding their bikes or skateboards in the driveways," can be interpreted as discriminating on the basis of the protected "familial status" class.

Neighbor-to-Neighbor Discrimination. The courts have ruled that an association can be liable for violating the Fair Housing Law if it knows of discriminatory behavior by one neighbor against another and does nothing to stop it. In the case of *Reeves v. Carrollsburg Condominium Unit Owners Association*, a former president of a community association—who happened to be an African American female—was continually harassed by a white neighbor. The harassment took the form of stalking, threatening to rape and kill her, and screaming racial and sexual epithets. Ms. Reeves asked the board for help. The board did send a few letters; however, it did not fine or sanction the offender, which was within its authority per the association's governing documents. Part of the suit Ms. Reeves filed claimed that the association perpetuated a hostile housing environment in violation of federal fair housing laws. The association settled the suit before trial by agreeing to buy her unit and pay her an additional $550,000.

Another suit filed in U.S. District Court for the State of Maryland involved a couple being racially harassed by their neighbor *(Doka v. Greencastle Lakes Community Association Inc.)*. For more than a year, Mr. and Mrs. Doka, an African American couple and homeowners in the Greencastle Lakes Community in Burtonsville, Maryland, were harassed and threatened by their neighbor, John Tuma. It was found that on at least 16 separate occasions, Mr. Tuma dumped debris and dead animals, including dead crows, squirrels, and mice; razor blades; shards of broken glass; nails; and empty beer and vodka bottles, on the Dokas' property. The couple complained that the association did nothing in spite of repeated requests to stop the harassment. The board of directors and the management company maintained this was a dispute between neighbors and refused to take any action. The Dokas filed suit against both the board and the management company, as well as the homeowner, Mr. Tuma, stating they all fostered a racially hostile environment in violation of the Fair Housing Act.

Florida attorney and former CAI national president Ellen Hirsh de Haan, Esq. has outlined the following steps to take in member-to-member abusive/harassment behavior situations:

1. *Verify the complaint.* Make sure the complaint is credible. Seek out witnesses. Document findings. If there is evidence, move on to steps 2–4.

2. *Meet with the abusive member.* If the situation is nonviolent, the board should attempt to meet with the abusive member to point out potential violations of the governing documents. Be very specific in

the conversations with the abusive member about the dates and times of the violations. Document all meetings with the abusive member and attempt to have a meeting with all parties to the incident(s).

3. *Send warning letter(s).* If step 2 does not work, put everything in writing, including the dates and times of all incidents and violations of the governing documents. Warn the offender of potential fines, suspensions, suspension of privileges, and legal action.
4. *Take further action.* If all efforts to stop the behavior fail, seek legal advice as to how to proceed. In some situations, the police might be of assistance.

Members with Disabilities. On occasion, a disabled resident may petition the board to make a "reasonable accommodation." Examples of reasonable accommodation requests include (1) asking for an assigned parking place closer to a residence, (2) installing a wheelchair ramp to a dwelling, and (3) using a motorized scooter in the common area in order to move about the community.

Federal laws define *disabled*:

> An individual is disabled if he or she has a physical or mental impairment that substantially limits one or more major life activities, has a record of such impairment, or is regarded as having such impairment. *Major life activities* include caring for oneself, performing manual tasks, walking, seeing, hearing, speaking, breathing, learning, and working. The term *physical or mental impairment* includes impairments to vision, speech, and mobility as well as diseases and conditions such as epilepsy, cancer, heart disease, diabetes, HIV infection, and alcoholism. This definition does not include an individual who is a drug addict and who is currently using illegal drugs or an alcoholic who poses a direct threat to the property or safety of others due to alcohol use.

The law contains provisions to follow in order to make such accommodation requests. It allows the association to ask for verification from the member's health care provider or other professional such as a social worker or therapist. With the assistance of the professional association manager, the association's board of directors must develop policies and procedures for its members who request reasonable accommodation. However, community associations must be careful not to unreasonably deny such requests, because serious consequences may arise if a member's request is refused (such as in the case of *Karlsrud v. Pell Revocable Trust*).

According to Goff & DeWalt, LLP (http://www.GoffDeWalt.com; accessed May 27, 2007), "The verification does not need to require the health care provider to provide any particular medical information, the health care provider should only be required to state whether the requesting party is disabled as defined under federal law and whether the accommodation is necessary." Exhibit 3.2 provides a sample of the reasonable accommodation request forms.

Many associations have rules against animals in their communities. Individuals with disabilities often require the assistance of a service animal to accomplish their daily routines. If the association applies its regular pet rules to service animals, it could find itself in violation of the Fair Housing Law. Note that the state of California has a law giving owners in common interest developments the right to keep at least one pet, regardless of whether the resident has a disability. The law applies to any governing documents that a common interest development adopts, amends, or modifies after January 1, 2001.

Satellite Dishes and the Community Association

In 1996, the Federal Communications Commission adopted the *Over-the-Air Reception Devices* rule concerning governmental and nongovernmental restrictions on viewers' ability to receive video programming signals from direct broadcast satellites, broadband radio service providers, and television broadcast stations. This rule prohibits restrictions that impair the installation, maintenance, or use of antennas to receive video programming. It applies to video antennas, including direct-to-home satellite dishes that are less than one meter in diameter, TV antennas, and wireless cable antennas. The rule was amended in 1999 and again in 2000.

Satellite dishes have become very popular in the past ten years. Community associations are often concerned about the dishes' unattractiveness and their effect on property values—probably rightly so. Improperly installed dishes can cause extensive damage to the building structure. Satellite dishes installed on rooftops, chimney chases, railings, and exterior siding can cause water penetration problems.

So what can the association do? First, if the satellite dish or antenna is one meter or less in diameter and is being installed completely within a unit, the association will not have any say in the situation. In fact, trying to enforce any rules on a resident/owner under these circumstances would probably get the association into trouble.

Exceptions. There are some exceptions to the rule. The association does have some say in the realm of common and limited common areas. The common area is under the control of the community association. One could reasonably argue that the limited common area, even though

Exhibit 3.2

Reasonable Accommodation Request Forms

REASONABLE ACCOMMODATION
REQUEST FORM

(To be submitted by member with signed Medical Information Authorization)

The ______________________ Association will consider all requests for reasonable accommodations due to disability. The Association must verify that the requesting member qualifies as disabled under federal law and requires the requested accommodation in order to have an equal opportunity to enjoy the use of his or her home and the common area and/or limited common area of the Association. Under federal law, an individual is disabled if he or she has a physical or mental impairment that substantially limits one or more major life activities; has a record of such an impairment; or is regarded as having such an impairment.

Member's Name: ______________________________

Address: ______________________________

____

Phone: ______________________________

The undersigned member requests that the ______________________ Association provide a reasonable accommodation as follows:

(Please describe the type of accommodation, how it will assist you, and other details, which you believe, are relevant to your request)

____

____

____

My specific functional limitation is:

____

____

____

______________________________ ______________

Member's Signature Date

(continued)

Exhibit 3.2 *(Continued)*

MEDICAL INFORMATION AUTHORIZATION

(To be provided to health care provider with Reasonable Accommodation Request — Health Care Provider Verification)

The undersigned has requested a reasonable accommodation due to disability. Additional medical information is needed to provide the accommodation I have requested. Therefore, I, ________________ hereby authorize:

____
Physician's Name

____
Street Address

____
City/State/Zip

____
Phone

I hereby authorize the release of medical information pertinent to the accommodation requested on the Reasonable Accommodation Request Form to the ________________ Association, its agents, attorneys, and/or representatives. Information obtained under this release shall be limited to information necessary to verify the reasonableness of the request for accommodation, and to information up to five years old.

______________________________ ____________
Member's Signature Date

Exhibit 3.2 ***(Continued)***

REASONABLE ACCOMMODATION FOR DISABILITY REQUEST
HEALTH CARE PROVIDER VERIFICATION

Health Care Provider: ______________________________

Address: ______________________________
____

Community Association: ______________________________

Address: ______________________________
____

REQUEST FOR ACCOMMODATION:

Member's Name: ______________________________

Address: ______________________________
____

The above named member has requested that our community association provide a reasonable accommodation due to disability as follows (*state nature of accommodation request*):

____
____
____
____

Under normal circumstances, this request may have been denied pursuant the governing documents of the Association. However, if an individual with disabilities requests a reasonable accommodation to that disability, the Association will consider the request. To aid the Association in considering the request, it must verify that the individual is disabled and requires the accommodation in order to enjoy the use of his or her home and the common elements of the Association. The Association requests that you provide it with the information requested below. A signed copy of the release of medical information is attached for your records, consenting to the release of this information.

DEFINITION OF "DISABLED":

An individual is disabled if he or she has a physical or mental impairment that substantially limits one or more major life activities; has a record of such impairment; or is regarded as having such impairment. Major life activities include such activities as caring for oneself, performing manual tasks, walking, seeing, hearing, speaking, breathing, learning or working. The term "physical or mental impairment" includes impairments to vision, speech and mobility, and includes diseases and conditions such as epilepsy, cancer, heart disease, diabetes, HIV infection and alcoholism. This definition does not include an individual who is a drug addict and who is currently using illegal drugs, or an alcoholic who poses a direct threat to the property or safety of others due to alcohol use.

1. Is the individual named above disabled as defined above? Yes No
2. In your professional opinion, does the individual named above require the requested accommodation in order to have the same opportunity as a non-disabled individual to use and enjoy his or her home and/or the common elements of the Association? Yes No
3. If you answered, "Yes" to Question 1, can the individual's condition be otherwise treated to prevent any substantial limits on his or her major life activities? Yes No

(continued)

Exhibit 3.2 *(Continued)*

4. Would you be willing to testify under oath as to the necessity of the requested accommodation? Yes No

Name & Title: ______________________________

Signature: ______________________________ Date: ______________

meant for the exclusive use of the homeowner, is also under the control of the association. If the installation and maintenance of the satellite dish is found to compromise public safety or interfere with the historic preservation of the property, the association may be permitted to restrict such installations. In some instances, the community association may have a central or common antenna available.

Each exception to the rule is extremely complicated because each has specific parameters to be met in order to qualify as an exception. Regardless of the exceptions, associations are not allowed to enforce rules that unreasonably inhibit a member's satellite dish installation and maintenance. As associations develop their rules and regulations for dish installation, they should have an attorney review the documents. Remember, nothing is enforceable if it takes away a right already conferred by law.

Satellite Rule Creation. What can the association do when creating satellite dish rules?

- *Deny installation in the common area (elements).* Depending on the governing document's definition of the common area, the association can deny satellite dish installation there. This could mean forbidding installation of personal satellite dishes on exterior walls, rooftops, walkways, hallways, stairwells, fencing, and cabana facilities.
- *Deny installation of any dish over one meter in diameter.*
- *Control installations in the limited common area (elements).* Generally speaking, this area is under the member's exclusive control and use. Balconies and patios attached to the unit are examples of "exclusive control" elements. When the association is writing rules for the limited common area, the board must be extremely careful not to unfairly inhibit any member's use of a satellite dish. If the rule makes dish installation too difficult or too expensive and hinders reception, the member may be in a good position to question the legitimacy of the rule.

- *Restrict installation due to genuine safety concerns.* If placement and use of the satellite dish will compromise any fire safety matters (i.e., block fire lanes or fire exits), intrude on or into any electrical wire or panel installations, or inhibit utility service for the association, rules can be designed to enforce safety concerns.
- *Require member responsibility for individual dishes.* Satellite dishes need maintenance and repair. The association can require members to maintain their dishes. It can also make the member responsible for any damages to property or person that the dish may cause to another member, tenant, or guest.
- *Make provisions for historic preservation.* If the building structures are included in or eligible for inclusion in the *National Register of Historic Places*, restrictions may be made in the rules and regulations to preserve the site from the installation of satellite dishes. This situation is rare, and the restrictions must be no more burdensome than necessary to accomplish the goal of preservation.

Associations interested in regulating satellite dishes in their communities should be aware of the federal laws pertaining to them. For more information and a copy of the rules, contact the Federal Communications Commission at 202-418-7096 or toll free at 888-CALLFCC (888-225-5322). For answers to frequently asked questions, go to http://www.fcc.gov/cgb/satellite. Some suggestions are: (1) familiarize yourself with the federal rules, (2) design your association's rules, (3) have the association's attorney review the rules, and (4) publish and implement your rules.

Sexual Predators and the Community Association

The third area of federal law that has particularly strong implications for community association policy is the treatment of known sexual offenders.

Megan's Law. In 1994, seven-year-old Megan Kanka was brutally raped and murdered by her neighbor. The neighbor had been convicted of sexual offenses involving children prior to the attack, but no one in the neighborhood—including Megan's parents—knew that. Studies have shown that sexual predators statistically tend to be repeat offenders. For this reason, in 1996, the federal government enacted legislation that has come to be known as *Megan's Law*. The law mandates that every state must provide some level of community notification when a sex offender moves to a new address.

The majority of states have since adopted statutes of their own that further define the actions of government and law enforcement. Most states use a three-tier system, such as the one shown in Exhibit 3.3, when classifying sexual offenders.

Exhibit 3.3

Three-Tier Sexual Offender Classification

Level	Description
One	Low risk to the community. These individuals are presumed to be at the lowest risk to re-offend. They do not normally exhibit predatory characteristics.
Two	Moderate risk to the community. These sexual offenders are at higher risk to re-offend because of the nature of their previous crime(s) and lifestyle.
Three	High risk to the community. These individuals are a threat to re-offend if given opportunity. Most of these offenders have prior sex crime and other convictions. They live lifestyles that give them a propensity to re-offend.

Megan's Law and the state laws that followed it serve to protect the public from known sex offenders by making certain funding contingent on state agencies notifying local residents of known sex offenders. This is where problems may arise. To what degree do local jurisdictions and community associations have to inform their constituents? At present, legislators and litigators are seeking answers to this question through ongoing debates and the judicial process.

Many states have no requirement that local jurisdictions physically notify their constituents when an offender moves into the neighborhood. Local jurisdictions only have to make the information available. In the meantime, however, community associations cannot choose to ignore this law.

Association Policy and Megan's Law. Association leaders must educate themselves concerning where to find the appropriate information. This information can usually be found on two Web sites. The National Sex Offender Public Registry, http://www.nsopr.gov, is a site maintained as a result of Megan's Law. To learn if your state has a sexual offender Web site, visit KlaasKids Foundation at www.KlaasKids.org/pg-legmeg.htm. The KlaasKids Foundation was established as a result of another horrific incident in which a child was abducted, raped, and murdered by a known sexual offender.

Informing the association membership of a sexual offender living among them is not as easy as phoning the membership or creating a notice and posting or mailing it to the membership. Be cautioned that notices or postings may be considered harassment if done to threaten or intimidate the individual; civil rights attorneys will step in to ensure the individual's rights are protected. As mentioned, the association should research the issue (i.e., check out available Web sites and talk to local law enforcement officers) and then, with the help of the association's attorney, draft and adopt a policy stating how it will keep members informed if the situation arises.

What will this policy look like? Parts of it should establish procedures to verify information as well as procedures to inform the membership. According to author Molly Brennan, in a *Common Ground* article from September/October 2005, the best way to inform your residents is to use the indirect approach. Statements like, "We've received information that a Megan's Law registrant resides in our community. Information concerning this can be obtained on this Web site," are much better than giving the name and address of the specific offender. Using this procedure, the members must then take it upon themselves to become more fully informed. The association's policy should also have some element of police and/or law enforcement cooperation. These groups can be used to speak directly to the membership regarding very specific sexual offender issues. State and local laws require police and law enforcement officers to give information that the association's leaders cannot give.

Megan's Law and its complexities have many legal ramifications for the community association. Designing policies and procedures for handling sexual offender issues is just a start. Common interest projects are being developed that have language in their governing documents banning sexual offenders from even living in the community. Whether such language is enforceable is yet to be seen; however, because of the common interest element of a shared living environment, the community association will be an integral entity in developing legislation related to sexual offenders.

TROUBLESHOOTING

The governing documents address just about every situation and circumstance that comes before a community association. However, the language in the documents as well as in state statutes can be unclear, confusing, and vague. This can be upsetting to the board of directors, the association members, and the professional manager when they can't find answers. When problems arise, everyone wants resolution.

You've investigated all the relevant documents, state statutes, legal authorities, and historical references. Now what should you do? Should you walk away hoping that no one ever broaches the subject again? Should you make arbitrary, opinionated decisions? Not exactly. Just "sweeping it under the rug" can be very risky.

Take, for example, a situation in which the board is confronted with what they believe to be a "dangerous" dog in the community. The dog has cornered a few of the homeowners, bitten a child, and terrified anyone coming close to the unit. The CC&Rs, bylaws, and rules and regulations don't define what constitutes a "dangerous" dog. So what does the association do about the dog? The city code and the state statute have very vague verbiage identifying a "dangerous" dog. The attorney won't take any action on behalf of the association because the offended parties will not put anything in writing for fear of retaliation. The attorney also tells you that the city, county, and state ordinances really do not support the board in taking any legitimate action.

Now what does the board do? If the board members decide to do nothing, there could be terrible consequences. The best choice would be to study all possible options, interpret the available information, and write a policy to address the situation. The professional manager who works with the board might have additional material to assist in the decision-making process. Professional organizations such as the Community Associations Institute (www.CAIonline.org) and the Institute of Real Estate Management (www.irem.org) may have recommendations for managing the situation.

The board must also consider the entire community. A survey given to the association's members might provide some insight as to how the board should proceed. After doing their homework and exhausting all references, the board members should write a formal policy, present it as a motion, vote on it, record it, and take action if necessary. In this way, the board takes reasonable steps to address a situation that the governing documents and state statutes do not address.

The board of directors, entrusted with carrying out governance responsibilities for the entire association, is discussed in more detail in the next chapter.

4

Board of Directors

INTRODUCTION

Just as the governing documents discussed in Chapter 3 are the road map for the governance of the association, the board of directors is its driver. The *board of directors* is responsible for carrying out the duties and responsibilities of the association. As the leader of the organization, the board interprets, enforces, and initiates policy for the association and its members. The job is not always glamorous, but the association's members elect the board members to make the important decisions.

Corporate America provides the model that association boards follow when making decisions for their communities. It has shown us that the board must operate in a spirit of cohesion and consistency. Corporate America has also taught us the importance of keeping the members of the organization well-informed and hiding nothing from them.

Board members should possess certain characteristics, and they must accept serious responsibilities. Titles and job descriptions given to board officers vary from association to association; the most common are discussed below. The end of this chapter includes suggestions for holding effective board meetings and increasing the board's productivity.

BOARD MEMBERS

Board members may have different personal qualities and skills; however, they must all be willing to devote the time necessary to make good decisions for the community and to maintain or improve property values. In addition, like corporate leaders, board members assume an important *fiduciary* responsibility.

Personal Qualities

Most association members have the potential to be good board members. Well-organized associations maintain lists of all members that detail their interests and specialties. Having gleaned this information from surveys and personal contact, boards can identify members who can be useful to their communities. Unfortunately, some board members are ineffective for a variety of reasons, and the board must be aware of potential problems with those members.

Effective Board Members. Successful members of the board of directors for homeowners associations possess important personal qualities. Because the board oversees personal and financial information for the organization, honesty and integrity are essential hallmarks of the board's members. They must know how to communicate and how to use common sense. They must be courageous. The board of directors is sometimes charged with making decisions that aren't popular—such as raising association dues. Even though board members are also affected by the dues increase, some members of the association may look on the board as the "enemy." Board members must be brave and fearless in helping the entire membership understand the decisions they make.

Members of the association look to the board of directors for leadership. Individuals can direct other members to amazing accomplishments simply by developing good leadership qualities. *The Leadership Challenge* by James Kouzes and Barry Posner is a compilation of years of research regarding effective leadership. The authors describe five fundamental practices of exemplary leaders:

- *Challenge the process.* Leaders are willing to take risks and find new and better ways of doing things. They listen to others.
- *Inspire a shared vision.* Leaders have a desire to make things happen. They inspire commitment.
- *Enable others to act.* Leadership is a team effort. Very good leaders enlist the support and assistance of all those who must make the system work.

- *Model the way.* Behavior wins respect. Leaders set the example.
- *Encourage the heart.* Volunteers often become exhausted, frustrated, and disenchanted. Leaders encourage the heart to carry on.

Other qualities and skills can also benefit the association's board of directors. Certified public accountants (CPAs), bookkeepers, investors, and bankers make good association treasurers. They are accustomed to looking at numbers, and they can explain those numbers to the members in understandable terms. Lawyers, consultants, engineers, doctors, teachers, and human resource specialists all make good board candidates. Those who have experience dealing with the public likely have developed good "people skills" and might make great leaders for the community. Home-based workers, entrepreneurs, and retired individuals have been major assets in the operations of homeowners associations across the nation. The list goes on and on.

Ineffective Board Members. Not all volunteers make good board members. Exhibit 4.1 compares the behavior of effective and ineffective board members.

Exhibit 4.1

Comparison of Effective and Ineffective Board Members

Effective Board Member	Ineffective Board Member
• Is familiar with the association's governing documents • Is consistent and dependable when making decisions • Considers the entire scheme of things • Allows all members to have an opportunity to participate in the operations of the association • Respects the rights and privileges of others • Works in a spirit of cooperation • Fulfills assignments in a thorough and timely manner • Is well prepared and productive at all meetings • Seeks the advice of professionals*	• Regularly misses meetings • Does not accept or complete tasks • Is motivated by personal agendas • Monopolizes discussion or never participates in discussion—except after the meeting • Treats peers disrespectfully or is not a team player • Betrays confidentiality • Does not disclose conflicts of interest • Does not understand when to retire and leave a place for others to carry the torch**

* Courtesy of Vickie Gaskill, CPM®, ARM®, MPM®, RMP®.

** Courtesy of BoardSource, www.BoardSource.org (accessed December 19, 2006).

Some individuals have personal characteristics or agendas that can undermine the board's work.

- *Personal agendas.* Members of the association may volunteer to be on the board because they have a personal agenda. They may believe that by being on the board they'll be able to control certain outcomes in their favor. This motivation may not always be bad, but if a volunteer's personal agenda starts to dominate the association's agendas and board meetings, it may become a problem.
- *Micromanagers.* Some volunteers assume they have to know absolutely everything that happens. Take, for example, a volunteer who is appointed association treasurer but, instead of overseeing just the association's financial operations, checks up on the landscaper, calls a contractor on a bid, calls the management company daily to see if certain assignments from the last board meeting are getting done, walks the property and notes noncompliance issues, and so on. This can be extremely frustrating to other volunteers in the organization who want to do their assigned jobs. It is especially annoying to the professional manager because the manager may have to do double duty: report to the assigned volunteer *and* to the micromanaging volunteer. This also opens up the possibility something will be left out because the manager thought he or she had already given the report to the appropriate party. To avoid such issues, professional managers must firmly establish to whom and how they report.
- *Harassment and intimidation.* Some board members take their assignments too far. As board members, they see themselves in a position of control and authority. When taken too far, their behavior can become intimidation and can even be considered harassment by those at whom it is directed. The other board members and the professional manager should not tolerate such behavior. The best approach is for the parties to meet and discuss the situation in private. Tell the offender just how his or her behavior is inhibiting the operations of the association's business. Also, let the individual know how he or she makes others feel. If this process doesn't work, the board should remove the volunteer from office. Board members can also take steps, usually through the special meeting process, to remove the volunteer from the board.

Commitment

Being a member of the board of directors requires commitment to making good decisions for the entire association, maintaining property value, and devoting time to the operations of the organization.

Making Good Decisions. Members expect their leaders to operate in the best interests of the association as a whole. That is, they are expected to take reasonable care and incorporate due diligence in all decisions emanating from the board of directors. The governing documents provide the direction for the association. The directors must familiarize themselves with those documents in order to make sound business decisions for the community.

Sustaining or Improving Property Values. Board members should be committed to retaining or improving the value of the real estate with which they are entrusted. Collection of the *assessments* in a timely manner, competitive contract bidding, and funding of the reserves for future capital replacement all contribute to sustained or improved real estate values. The directors should pay close attention to these issues.

Devoting Time. Board members understand that they must spend additional time overseeing the operations of the association. They must prepare for and attend committee, board, and annual meetings. They may be requested to conduct site inspections and to meet with site contractors. A well-managed, well-organized board of directors addresses all such issues.

Some board members say they only commit to three or four hours a month. However, if many items are before the board, the time commitment may double or even triple.

Fiduciary Responsibility

The board of directors of any corporation, including nonprofit homeowners associations, has a *fiduciary relationship* with its members; that is, the board holds a position of trust. The fact that the organization is nonprofit and its board members are volunteers does not excuse or relieve the board from the responsibility of making good decisions for the association. Court cases have decided that ignorance and inexperience are no excuse. The members of the association have put the directors into their respective positions because the members believe those individuals will act responsibly and will not harm the association's interests.

What interests are we talking about? Directors are responsible for preserving property values, maintaining the property, establishing house rules and regulations, overseeing the organization's finances (including collecting assessments), maintaining appropriate insurance coverage for common area liability and property damage, and keeping the members informed.

Members of the board must be careful not to involve their personal agendas when making decisions for the association. Individuals often run for an elected position on the board simply because they don't like something that affects them personally. They are upset with the dues increase; they want a maintenance issue in a unit addressed; they don't like pets so they want to try to get pets banned from the association; or they may even want to keep a certain group of individuals from moving into the community. Such individuals see membership on the board as a means of getting their way. However, this is contrary to the board's fiduciary responsibility. Personal agendas must be set aside. Directors are required to protect the best interests of the entire body of association members.

Board members, especially new ones, often do not understand the concept of fiduciary responsibility, so the professional association manager must assist in educating them. Along with information on various board responsibilities, the manager might provide an explanation of fiduciary responsibility and a code of behavior for new board members to help them avoid compromising the trust of the membership. According to the 2005 Vendome Group report (Report Document 3C: 20–23), the following principles can be shared with all board members:

- Board members should always act in good faith and the best interests of the association.
- Board members should seek the advice of experts.
- Board members should act within the scope of their authority.
- Board members should avoid the following four mistakes:
  - Taking personal advantage of personal business opportunities
  - Disclosing any affiliation the board member has with businesses working for the association
  - Giving friends or supporters preferential treatment
  - Accepting gifts or kick-backs from vendors

TITLES AND JOB DESCRIPTIONS

Every successful business organization, whether profit or nonprofit, must have an organizational structure to accomplish its affairs. As already established, homeowners associations are nonprofit corporations, and the board of directors is charged with overseeing the corporation's operations. The board accomplishes its responsibilities through officers it elects or appoints. The board of directors makes policies for the association; the officers carry out the policies and oversee the association's administrative functions. The board of directors serves as the governing body for the association. It is ultimately responsible for the association's decisions. The officers ensure that the board's decisions are carried out and enforced.

The board and the officers may be the same individuals. Unless stated otherwise in a statute or governing document, the selection process is that the members of the association elect the board, and the board elects the officers.

The officers for the association are typically a president, secretary, and treasurer. Occasionally, the governing documents allow for additional appointments such as a vice president or members-at-large. Unless prohibited in the bylaws, the board may appoint other officers to assist in carrying out the corporation's duties. Committees also assist the board in conducting its work.

President

Every corporation needs a chief executive officer (CEO). The CEO of the nonprofit corporation (the homeowners association) is the president. To be successful, the president must have a good working knowledge of the association's governing documents, the laws governing associations in the state, and the previous board policies and procedures. The basic duties of the association president are to provide meeting agendas, preside over meetings, appoint committees, execute contracts, serve as the association's spokesperson, and oversee its day-to-day administration.

The association president's job description follows:

- *Prepare meeting agendas.* Without a prepared agenda, meetings lack organization and structure. The president is responsible for providing an agenda for all meetings for which he or she has oversight. Most of the association's work is done between meetings. The purpose of the agenda should be to allow a steady flow of information regarding day-to-day operations of the association that were accomplished since the last meeting.
- *Preside over meetings.* The purpose of association meetings is to conduct the business of the association and make decisions; the president of the association is responsible for seeing that this is achieved. He or she must have a working knowledge of *parliamentary procedure. Robert's Rules of Order* is a good guide for conducting timely, orderly meetings.
- *Appoint committees.* Committees can assist the board in carrying out its duties to the membership. The president has the authority to appoint committee chairs. Committees need direction, so the president's job is to ensure that the committee chair and members know what is expected of them and when their task is to be completed. When giving directions to committee members, the president should let them know to which officer they report.
- *Execute contracts.* The president has the authority and responsibility to sign contracts that involve the association. This should never be

done without the consent and approval of the rest of the board members.

- *Perform day-to-day administration.* Generally speaking, the president is the liaison to the association's hired professionals such as the management company, contractors working on the property, financial consultants, and legal professionals. Once again, the president should always work in accordance with the decisions of the rest of the board.
- *Act as spokesperson for the association.* As CEO of the association, the president is the source of information for outside organizations. The president must be mindful of the authority to which he or she is speaking and always consider the best interests of the association's membership.

Secretary

The secretary is responsible for maintaining and preserving the official records of the association. The *official records* can include notices of mailings, meeting minutes, membership lists, association correspondence, and association history. The duties of the secretary are outlined in a state statute or in the governing documents.

The secretary's job description follows:

- *Maintain membership lists.* The secretary maintains the list of homeowners living in the association. Included in the list may be names, addresses, assigned parking stalls, makes and models of cars, and pets. Every list should be customized to the association's needs. The only data on the membership list should be information needed to conduct association business. Nothing maintained on the list should have any potential to be interpreted as discriminatory.
- *Give notice of mailings.* Most bylaws require the secretary to oversee all mailings and to verify that the mailings have taken place. This can be accomplished by way of a *proof of notice affidavit*—a document the secretary signs verifying that the mailing went out on a given date through the U.S. Post Office. Even when using professional management services, the secretary must oversee that association mailings take place using proper procedures.
- *Keep meeting minutes. Minutes* document the operations of the association's board meetings, annual meetings, or special meetings. The secretary is responsible for overseeing the recording and writing of minutes. The secretary need not do this personally. He or she may ask another member of the association or even an outside source to

accomplish this task. However, the secretary must review the written minutes, make corrections, and submit them to the board for acceptance. When required, the secretary ensures that the minutes are distributed to association members.

- *Maintain association correspondence.* The board mails a lot of information to the membership. The secretary maintains files of such correspondence. Often with the assistance of an outside source, such as a professional management company, the secretary must oversee that association correspondence is filed and maintained in an organized manner. The secretary is responsible for ensuring access to this correspondence and other association records.
- *Preserve association history.* In conducting the business affairs of the association, the board accumulates a lot of information. It is the responsibility of the secretary to ensure that all historical data is preserved for documentation and future reference. Important documents to retain in an organized manner are minutes for board meetings, annual meetings, and special meetings; board resolutions; financial reports; contracts; governing documents and any amendments to them; annual reports; and employee information. The secretary develops procedures and policies for retention of these valuable records.

Treasurer

The treasurer is overseer of the financial operations for the association. This individual is the guardian of the association's funds, securities, and all financial records. The treasurer should have a reasonable understanding of financial accounting methods. He or she ensures that the bills are paid, deposits are made, and financial statements are prepared in a timely manner. The annual budget preparation is also a function of the treasurer. The treasurer supervises the association's tax filings and annual audits when required to do so. Occasionally, the treasurer may be asked to investigate investment strategies for reserve funds. Like the other officer positions, the duties of the treasurer are outlined in the association's bylaws and/or the state statute.

The treasurer's job description follows:

- *Understand financial accounting.* Financial reporting terms are very specific to the accounting process (see Chapter 8). The treasurer must be familiar with the terms as well as their definitions and applications. Understanding the basic components of financial statements assists the treasurer in making reports to the board and association members.

- *Review financial statements.* Very few association treasurers are responsible for the direct production of the financial statements. Bookkeepers, accountants, and professional management firms provide this function. The treasurer must ensure that the information provided is accurate. In reviewing the financial statements, he or she must be sure the association's funds are collected in a timely manner, bills are paid, and money is set aside for future capital reserve replacement items.
- *Prepare budgets.* The *annual budget* is the financial plan of operation that the association adopts. The budget determines assessments, purchases, and savings strategies. It is also a tool for measuring financial performance. The treasurer ensures the development of the annual operating budget as well as subsequent capital reserve budgets and long-term budgets for the association. He or she may accomplish this by working closely with a budget committee and/or with the association's professional management firm.
- *Develop investment strategies. Capital replacement reserves* are monies set aside in an investment tool for future major expenses (e.g., roof replacement, painting, asphalt sealing). The treasurer's duties are to investigate and recommend to the board investment policies structured to provide safety, liquidity, and growth of the association's funds. This, like budget preparation, can be done with the help of a committee appointed by the board president.
- *Oversee tax filings and annual audits.* The annual *audit* is an independent look at the association's financial records. CPAs analyze the association's financial statements and provide assurance they are presented in accordance with generally accepted accounting principles. The treasurer should make a recommendation to the board regarding the appropriate accounting firm to hire for the annual audit. Ideally, this should be neither a personal friend, the CPA of a board member, nor a member of the association. The association needs an independent, neutral firm to review its financial operations. The same firm can usually handle the tax filings.
- *Report on the financial condition of the association.* At board meetings and, most important, the association's annual meeting, the treasurer reports on the association's financial condition. Exhibit 4.2 provides a template most treasurers can customize to their association's needs.

Vice President

Overall, the vice president of the homeowners association has all the responsibilities of the president whenever the president is unable to fulfill those duties. The vice presidency is a rather simple position to hold;

Exhibit 4.2

Treasurer's Report

Treasurer's Report for XYZ Association
June 30, 20XX

Cash Balance	$ 25,000
Association's Maintenance Reserve	$ 100,000
Association's Insurance Reserve	$ 50,000
Association's CD/Money Market Accounts	$ 200,000
Accounts Receivable	$ 10,000
Accounts Payable	$ 1,000
Delinquencies	$ 7,500

Note: As the treasurer reports on each category, he or she provides the details that may affect that particular category for the timeframe the report covers.

however, it is an important position. Whenever the president must step aside or is unable to attend and oversee meetings, the vice president assumes the president's duties. Should the president refuse to act or resign the position, the vice president steps in. The vice president should understand meeting protocol. He or she should attend all association meetings and functions in order to be ready to step in for the president at any time.

The bylaws or the board of directors may empower the vice president with other duties such as committee work, employee oversight, or other association activities. Some governing documents allow for more than one vice president, with each assigned a specific specialty (e.g., finance, maintenance, human resources). In such situations, the order of ascension to the presidency is outlined in the association's bylaws.

Members-at-Large and Additional Officers

The association's bylaws may provide for a *member-at-large* position. If the bylaws don't specifically prohibit such action, the board may appoint *additional officers* and grant them duties and responsibilities it feels would benefit the operations of the association. In either case, these individuals may have such assignments as assistant secretary, assistant treasurer, committee chairperson, and board liaison to the management company. Using members-at-large and additional officers allows the board to divide its responsibilities into manageable segments. The board should have specific, written job descriptions for each of these additional officers that explain the scope of their authority as well as their duties and responsibilities.

Committee Chairs

The board determines which committees the association needs and appoints a chairperson to lead each. The governing documents mandate some committees (e.g., architectural control committee, finance committee). The chairperson leads the committee and presents committee decisions, recommendations, and *motions* to the board of directors for approval. Committees do not supplant the board's responsibility. Committees require job descriptions written and authorized by the board. Each job description must be relative to the specific committee assignment. Committees are discussed in Chapter 5.

BOARD MEETINGS

An association's business is conducted at meetings. The official actions of the association occur at the monthly, quarterly, annual, and special meetings. Individual association articles of incorporation and bylaws mandate how meetings are to be conducted. In some cases, the state law stipulates as to why, when, and how meetings of the members are to take place—especially if the association falls within the jurisdiction of the corporate laws of the state.

The board of directors facilitates association meetings. How well the board performs this task is a good indication to the members of how well it addresses the association's affairs. Well-planned, organized meetings indicate that the leadership is managing business in an effective, efficient manner.

Large corporations like Intel have recognized the importance of "meeting discipline" to make meetings work for the organization. Michael Fors, corporate training manager at Intel University, was quoted in a *Fast Company* article by Eric Matson ("The Seven Sins of Deadly Meetings," April/May 1996) as saying, "It isn't complicated. It's doing the basics well: structured agendas, clear goals, paths that you're going to follow...." Walk into a conference room at any Intel factory or office in the world, and you will see on the wall a poster with a series of simple questions about the meetings that take place there: Do you know the purpose of the meeting? Do you have an agenda? Do you know your role? Do you follow the rules for good minutes? Homeowners associations can once again take lessons from the corporate world.

Meetings must be productive; otherwise they can be a waste of everyone's time and energy. At the end of many meetings, one can hear comments such as, "That meeting was way too long," and "I don't think that we accomplished a thing in the past two hours," from those filing out of the meeting. Other times, meetings have been known to get completely out of control, and figuring out who is in charge can be difficult. Meetings are most fruitful when they have a written agenda, a system of procedural protocol, member participation, and time limits.

The president organizes, conducts, and concludes the meetings. As the leader, the president must maintain order and keep control of the meeting. For this reason, he or she should be familiar with writing agendas, using parliamentary procedures, and ensuring that everyone has the opportunity to participate in the process. The president should also make sure that the meetings accomplish their intent. To facilitate this, all board members should have access to *Robert's Rules of Order for Parliamentary Procedure* or another guide specific to parliamentary procedure.

Parliamentary Procedure

Yes, *parliamentary* is a big word, but don't let it scare you. In order for meetings to run smoothly and productively, there must be a guide to follow. Having a good understanding of parliamentary procedure provides association boards great success at their meetings. Some states and some associations' governing documents require the use of parliamentary procedure in association meetings.

The following list includes some fundamentals of parliamentary procedure that the presiding officer (usually the president of the association) and the board must know.

- *Quorum*: Attendance requirements for the association and the type of meeting being conducted. Business cannot be conducted at a meeting unless a quorum is present.
- *Agenda*: The outline or plan for the meeting. Have it in writing, stick to it, and have it timed if necessary.
- *Methods of voting*: Unanimous consent, voice, show of hands, roll call, and ballots are commonly used voting methods.
- *Handling a motion*:

  1. Business is only brought before a meeting by motion or resolution.
  2. While a motion is before the assembly, no other business of a different nature may intervene, except "questions of a higher privilege" and motions that "aid in or dispose of the main question."
  3. The motion is stated, seconded, and then restated by the chair. After that, it is the property of the assembly, which means the person who originally made the motion cannot change it without permission from the assembly.

4. The motion is debated.
5. The assembly votes on the motion.
6. The chair announces the results, which the secretary records.

- *Making a meeting productive*:

1. Follow the Golden Rule of civility.
2. Start and end on time.
3. Allow opportunities for, but set rules reasonably limiting, owner input.
4. Be prepared.
5. Know and use parliamentary procedure.

- *Managing debate*:

1. No debate takes place unless a motion is on the floor.
2. The chair recognizes only one speaker at a time, in order.
3. No one may speak a second time until everyone else who wishes to speak has spoken.
4. No one may speak a third time without permission from the assembly or the chair.
5. Time for speaking may be limited (e.g., two to three minutes).

The procedures used at various association meetings should fit the purpose of the particular meeting. According to Jim Slaughter, JD and expert on parliamentary procedures (www.JimSlaughter.com; accessed December 19, 2006), smaller board and committee meetings may sometimes take a more informal approach to the meeting than would be allowed at an annual meeting of the entire association membership.

Some less formal guidelines are as follows:

- Members are not required to obtain the floor and can make motions or speak while seated.
- Motions need not be seconded.
- There is no limit to the number of times a member can speak to a question.
- Motions to close or limit debate generally should not be entertained, unless there is an adopted rule to the contrary.

- The chair need not rise while putting questions to the vote.
- The chair may speak in discussion without rising or leaving his or her seat and, subject to custom, the chair usually may make motions and vote on all questions.

More formal procedures include the following:

- Strict rules of debate are followed so there is no perception of showing favoritism.
- Formal votes are made to avoid legal challenges.
- Limits on the debate are set to keep the meeting on time.

Whether the board elects to adopt formal or informal protocol, two keys words are *fair* and *consistent*. The board and the presiding officer must ensure that they treat all participants fairly and that the decisions they make are consistent with the governing documents and previous board decisions.

Agendas

The well-prepared meeting agenda has many purposes. It communicates the intention of the meeting, itemizes the topics for discussion, and sometimes gives the allotted time for each discussion. The agenda serves as an outline for the meeting and ensures that all of the pertinent business is addressed. It provides focus and direction. Exhibit 4.3 is an example of an agenda.

The board president develops and implements the agenda. However, if the association has a professional management firm, the firm sometimes prepares the preliminary agenda, and the president then reviews and finalizes it. The steps for preparing an agenda follow:

- *Gather information.* E-mailing or phoning the meeting participants about one to two weeks before the meeting is a good idea. Meeting participants can include the board of directors, contractors, the association manager, and homeowners. This is the time to find out if anyone has anything to be discussed at the meeting. The president decides how much time to allot for each discussion point and which meeting participant will be responsible for it.
- *Develop the agenda.* In order for the meeting to achieve its purpose, each agenda item must be titled. Arrange the items in the sequence in which they are to be discussed. Identify the discussion points, the

Exhibit 4.3

Sample Meeting Agenda

Agenda

Establish quorum

Call the meeting to order

Approval of minutes from the previous meeting

*Homeowners' forum

Officers' reports

Committee reports

Manager's report

Unfinished business

New business

*Homeowners' forum

Adjournment

*There are two schools of thought regarding the location of the homeowners' forum on the agenda. Some believe the homeowners should have a chance to speak before the business items of the association are addressed. Others think the homeowners should have an opportunity to hear the business items and make their comments accordingly. Either way, at an open meeting of the board of directors, time must be set aside to allow the homeowners to speak and be heard.

person responsible for them, and the action that must take place as a result of the discussion.

- *Determine timing.* Plan the time allocations for each agenda item. Don't try to do too much in one meeting. Be realistic. The meeting participants expect to meet, make decisions, and go home to have dinner or spend time with their families. Lack of preparation and timing is a quick way to lose volunteers. A timed agenda keeps the meeting focused.
- *Publish the agenda prior to the meeting.* Send the completed agenda to the participants at least one day before the meeting. This will give them one last chance to review the discussion points and prepare for those that have been assigned to them. In addition, if they recognize any needed changes to the agenda, they can contact the president

ahead of the meeting. (Note that there should be no changes to an agenda once the meeting has begun.)

- *Implement the agenda at the meeting.* The president or another assigned officer is responsible for conducting the meeting. There should be little or no variation from the original agenda. Only items specifically on the agenda should be discussed and acted upon by the group. The president may recognize that progress is being made on a specific discussion item and that with a little more time, the item can come to resolution. He or she should have some leeway on the time allocations, but the decision is exclusively the president's.

Meeting Minutes

To have good records of the association's business, the board is charged with the responsibility of keeping minutes at its meetings. As mentioned in the "Secretary" section above, the *minutes* are an official record of a meeting's proceedings. They document the decisions made and provide a public record for present and future association members. The association secretary is generally responsible for recording the minutes. However, that assignment may be given to an outside party or even another member of the association. In such cases, the secretary is responsible for reviewing the other party's minutes, making additions and corrections as needed, and presenting the minutes to the board for final approval.

Taking a little time in preparation before the meeting helps the secretary ensure that he or she is ready to record the meeting's events. The agenda is the roadmap for the meeting. Making an outline of the agenda and leaving enough space to write notes allows the recorder to follow the discussion easily. Acceptable ways to record the minutes include pen and notebook, tape recorder, or laptop computer. The choice should be one that works easily for the person taking the notes. A combination of recording tools might be used to have backup for transcribing the meeting information into the formal meeting minutes. However, don't make the recording process too cumbersome, because frustration can easily set in.

All meeting minutes should include a minimum of the following information:

- Date, place, and start time of the meeting
- Purpose of the meeting (e.g., association board meeting, annual meeting)
- Name of the person conducting the meeting

- Attendees at the meeting
- Assigned action items
- Decisions made
- Ending time of the meeting
- Signature of the person recording the minutes
- Date of approval of the minutes

Meeting minutes should not be an exact replica of the meeting; they are a synopsis of the main events. Do not try to write down every word. Many are intimidated by the act of writing the association's minutes. This is generally because they think they have to record everything word for word. That is not the case. Focus on action items (the motions), define the decisions, and record who will follow up and when. Remember this is a business document; stay away from "creative writing." Avoid adjectives and personal opinions when describing the events of the meeting. If additional documents are distributed, be sure to attach them as appendixes to the minutes.

As soon as the meeting is over—and no more than 24 to 48 hours after the meeting—the secretary should review his or her notes, add any brief additional comments, and write out the *draft* minutes. The more time that passes between taking notes and writing the minutes, the greater the potential for omitting information. The draft should be given to all parties involved to facilitate the work to be done before the next meeting. Upon approval by the board at a subsequent board meeting or by the membership at an annual meeting, the secretary should mark the minutes "approved," sign them, and place copies in the association's minute book.

Annual Meetings

At the *annual meeting*, the board gives its annual report to the members and presents the new budget for ratification, if necessary. This is the one meeting of the year for which the membership is expected to come together to elect new directors for the upcoming year.

Boards should use the annual meeting as a time to build community in the association. It should be an event—something to which the membership looks forward. It should be a time for celebrating the community. As with any celebration, good planning is necessary.

Preparation. The declaration or the bylaws generally set the date, time, place, and agenda for the annual meeting as well as the lead time required to give the membership notice of the meeting. Along with the meeting notice, the board might include the new budget, an election ballot, a *proxy*, the annual meeting minutes from the previous year, and the agenda for the meeting. The board may consult the previous year's mailings to determine what to mail to the members. Exhibit 4.4 shows an example of a checklist used to prepare for an annual meeting.

Once the time and date of the meeting are established, the marketing begins. The main rule of thumb in marketing is to promote early and often. The objective is to get the members of the association together and to do it in a way that promotes a positive feeling about living in the community.

If the community has a social committee, the board should enlist its help. The committee can plan the social aspects of the gathering as well as make personal phone calls inviting the members to the meeting. If members can see a value to their attendance, they will come. The board's job is to create that value by explaining the benefits of attending the annual meeting. This is the one meeting for which the board might consider serving refreshments and giving door prizes.

Members too often view this time as an opportunity to vent their frustrations with and complaints about the board and managing agent. Here again, with good preparation and planning, the board should be able to circumvent any potential problems.

The Meeting. After everyone has signed in and before the meeting can begin, the president of the board verifies that a quorum is present. He or she then welcomes everyone and introduces the board, the managing agent, and any special guests. Following introductions and the announcement of a quorum, the president explains the purpose of the meeting. This establishes the ground rules. Then the president asks for a motion and a second to approve the minutes of the previous year's annual meeting.

The directors' reports are next. Among them are the president's and treasurer's reports and the budget presentation. This might also be the time to hear from the property manager.

Next is the election of directors. The president may wish to give the nominees the opportunity to say something about themselves before the actual counting of the ballots.

Following the election, an acknowledgement and thank you should be given to those directors who will be leaving the board. Without any further business to discuss, the president should thank everyone for coming and request a motion, second, and vote to adjourn the annual meeting.

Effective Board Meetings

The basics of a good board of directors' meeting have been discussed. All meetings need a well-planned agenda, good minutes, and enforceable

Exhibit 4.4

Annual Meeting Checklist

Somewhere Estates

ANNUAL MEETING APRIL 22, 2007

ITEMS	CHECKLIST	PROPERTY MANAGER	DATE OF MEETING	MAILING DATE
Notice Mailed	3/31/07	Mary Manager	April 22, 2007	3/31/07
Proxy Mailed	"			"
Budget Mailed	"			"
ITEMS FOR ANNUAL MEETING				
Notice	x			
Agenda	x			
Ballot				
Proxy	x			
Budget	x			
Sign-in Sheet	x			
Previous Annual Meeting Minutes	x			
Election Spreadsheet	x			
Signature Cards for Banking				
Adding Machine				
Pens				
Manager's Approval & Initials				

parliamentary procedure. Additional tips to keep the board meeting running smoothly follow:

1. *Give the meeting participants as much information ahead of time as possible.* For example: If the upcoming year's budget is up for

discussion, make sure everyone has a copy of the proposed budget as well as the financial spreadsheet for the previous 12 months. If the board is going to consider a new contract proposal, each participant should have a copy of the contract specifications and copies of the proposals under consideration.

2. *Use committees effectively*. Everyone in a community association is a volunteer, and sometimes sufficient free time is not available for all the business that must be accomplished. Assigning a committee to a specific task spreads the responsibility throughout the membership. Remember, however, that committees need direction. Make sure they receive specific plans of action for their assignments. If a committee is asked to make a recommendation to the board, the chairperson should come to the board meeting with the recommendation written in the form of a motion to present at the end of the report.

3. *Control the audience*. The president needs to know when to stop discussion and call for the vote. A member may only speak twice to a motion; the member's second chance comes only after everyone who wants to speak has had that opportunity at least once. This keeps any one individual from dominating the discussion.

4. *Enforce ground rules*. For example, use courtesy, let one person speak at a time, allow no interruptions, and have no ridiculing of another person's opinion. Members frequently show up at meetings simply because they have a passion for one particular issue. If the president has established some basic ground rules at the beginning of the meeting, he or she will have the support of the majority of the participants when the time comes to intercede and close the discussion.

5. *Find ways to shorten the meeting*. For example, in some board meetings, requiring a motion for approval on an action taken is not always necessary. If no one objects to the action, the president simply states that the action is approved, and the secretary records it in the minutes. This is called *unanimous consent* or *general consent*. The president asks, "Is there any objection?" If not, he or she may then say, "Hearing none, the action is approved."

6. *Consider having conference-call board meetings*. They might help the board conduct business more easily—particularly if board members have to travel great distances to meet. This is especially true for vacation communities. If one member can't attend a meeting but others can, consider having everyone gather around a speakerphone so the distant member can participate. You may want to check with your attorney to confirm whether this can be done at your

association board meetings. Teleconferencing sometimes calls for an amendment to the association's bylaws.

EFFECTIVE BOARDS

In a *Harvard Business Review* article from September 2002, "What Makes Great Boards Great," Jeffrey A. Sonnenfeld offers suggestions for building an effective board. An adaptation of that article follows.

- *Create a climate of trust and candor.* Share important information with your board in time for them to read and digest it. Rotate board positions so that everyone understands each other's roles and has the opportunity to work with others.
- *Foster a culture of open dissent.* Don't punish mavericks or dissenters, even if they are sometimes nuisances. Dissent is not the same thing as disloyalty. Use your own resistance as an opportunity to learn. Probe silent board members for their opinions, and ask them to justify their positions. If asked to join a board, say no if you detect pressure to conform to the majority. Leave a board if the president expects obedience.
- *Utilize a fluid portfolio of roles.* Don't allow board members to be trapped in rigid, typecast positions. Push them to challenge their own roles and assumptions. Do the same for yourself.
- *Ensure individual accountability.* Give board members tasks that require them to work outside the executive environment. This includes cultivating links to other members of your association.
- *Evaluate the board's performance.* Examine the board's confidence in the integrity of the group, the quality of the discussions at the board meetings, the credibility of reports, the use of constructive professional conflict, the level of interpersonal cohesion, and the degree of knowledge used. Go beyond reputations, résumés, and skills to look at initiative, roles, participation in discussions, and energy levels.

PRODUCTIVE BOARDS

The board of directors of a homeowners association is accountable to its members as outlined in the governing documents. The board must be sure it is operating within the criminal and civil laws of the land. If any one member of the association feels that the board has breached its duty, that member could take steps to remove the offending board member(s) or even to file a formal lawsuit against the board. The board must therefore take every precaution to govern the association with trustworthiness and accountability.

Code of Behavior

Most societies, groups, and associations agree that certain behaviors are acceptable within a particular organization. A *code of behavior* is a set of principles describing the behaviors that are commonly recognized and used to govern an organization. These behaviors are frequently outlined in a specific ethical code or a code of conduct for the members of the organization to follow. Such codes exist to guide interactions between individuals or within the group.

When conducting the association's business affairs, board members refer to an established code to determine acceptable behavior. The board of directors for every association should establish a specific behavioral code. Ongoing business can only be conducted between individuals who understand, share, and follow similar codes of behavior. Established within the code should be tools of enforcement for use when violations occur.

Guidelines to include in a board of directors' code of behavior are:

- Treat everyone with dignity and respect;
- Be honest and open-minded;
- Work in the best interests of your fellow members;
- Do your homework;
- Behave professionally;
- Comply with all governing documents; and
- Respect the rights of others.

If your board needs ideas for writing a code of behavior, board members can look to the Community Association Institute's "Rights and Responsibilities for Better Communities" (available free of charge at www.CAIonline.org). In addition, the March 2005 issue of *Community Association Management Insider* contains a model code of conduct for boards of directors.

Business Judgment Rule

The board of directors is sometimes responsible for making serious and controversial decisions for the association. If faced with the potential of a lawsuit over an unpopular decision, the directors may be able to rely on the *business judgment rule*. Simply stated, when the board has acted in good faith, exercised honest judgment, and acted in the best interests of the association, the courts will tend to treat the board the same as they would any other corporate director making a business decision for an organization. The business judgment rule serves to protect the decisions of the board when those decisions are not arbitrary or illogical.

When making decisions for the association, the board of directors should take the following actions:

- *Stay informed*. Board members often do not have the background or training to completely understand the complexities of an issue. Relying on experts such as attorneys, professional property managers, and contractors will assist them in making informed decisions.
- *Consider alternatives*. The courts like to see that, before the final decision was made, the board members contemplated all the options and chose what they believed to be the best solution.
- *Document everything*. As the board makes decisions, board members should provide and write down the reasons for these decisions. This is usually accomplished through the meeting minutes; however, even when something may appear to be incidental, a short written note can serve as a reminder in the future.
- *Establish good hearing and due process procedures*. Everyone deserves an opportunity to be heard. The board should have a policy and procedure in place to hear all sides of an issue—even when the confrontation might be difficult.

In 1997, the Washington Supreme Court summarized the law on the business judgment rule in *Riss v. Angel*.[1] To paraphrase the court:

1. Directors will not be held liable for honest mistakes.
2. Condominium directors have a fiduciary duty to exercise ordinary care.
3. The decisions of the homeowners association must be reasonable.
4. The court will not substitute its judgment for that of corporate directors unless there is evidence of fraud, dishonesty, or incompetence.
5. A director must act with such care as a reasonable, prudent person in a like position would.

---

[1] *Riss v. Angel*, 934 P.2d 669, 131 Wash. 2d 612,632.

Similar court decisions have been made in New York (*Levandusky v. One Fifth Avenue Apartment Corporation*), California (*Lamden v. La Jolla Shores Condominium Association*), and Colorado (*Colorado Homes, Ltd. v. Loerch-Wilson*).

Strategic Planning

To do a good job for the association and its members, the board of directors must develop and implement a strategic plan. *Strategic planning* determines where an organization is going over the next one to ten years, how it will get there, and how it will know if it gets there. The board uses the strategic plan as a road map to the community's future.

As soon after the annual meeting as board members can meet, the new board should convene, analyze the current strategic plan, and develop its own strategic plan for the upcoming year. Included in the overall strategic plan should be the association's purpose as well as realistic goals and objectives the plan will be designed to meet.

Components of the board's strategic plan should include a statement of the association's vision for the future, its mission statement, and its goals. A well-designed strategic plan contains action items that describe how the association will meet its goals.

The association's *vision* describes where the members want to see themselves in a specified time. The board benefits from envisioning the future. If board members see a need for more technology, capital improvements, and better communication to the members in the association's future, they should visualize how all of that can be accomplished.

The *mission statement* identifies the association's purpose. Statements that begin "To improve and protect the quality of life..." or "In order to maintain property values..." are examples of mission statements.

The *goals* are a plan of action to accomplish the vision. If the board sees a need for capital improvements, one of the strategic planning goals could be to have a professional reserve study analysis done for the association.

Boards should put the strategic plan in writing, share it with their members, monitor it, make adjustments, and update it periodically throughout each year of implementation. Board members can refer to it when developing the annual budget, when considering new members for the board, and when implementing programs and procedures for the association. The board should keep the strategic plan simple so others will understand and embrace it.

A community association's strategic plan provides direction and assistance to the management professional. Everyone from the board to the committee members to the manager and site staff (if any) should be focused on the organization's priorities. The strategic plan is the association's guide. The professional manager uses the plan to assist the board in staying focused on the "big picture." In addition, the professional manager can develop a personal accountability to the board's strategic plan if he or she has a clear and concise understanding of it.

Conflicts of Interest

A *conflict of interest* occurs when a director's private interest interferes with the interests of the association. It may also arise when a board member, or a member of his or her immediate family, receives improper personal benefits because of his or her position on the board. Directors should also be mindful of, and seek to avoid, conduct that could reasonably be construed as creating an appearance of a conflict of interest. When a director's actions compromise or undermine his or her fiduciary responsibility to the members of the association, that could also be considered a conflict of interest.

Examples of conflicts of interest follow:

- Making decisions that financially or materially affect the board member or his or her immediate family
- Accepting gifts, bribes, or special favors in order to influence a decision
- Not abiding by the same set of rules as the rest of the members of the association
- Taking advantage of confidential information to gain personally
- Not disclosing a personal interest that the board member may have in a decision

Professional Advisors

Generally speaking, members of the board of directors are not well-versed in all the aspects of overseeing a community. Boards should seek the advice of professionals. Attorneys can help in interpreting and enforcing the governing documents, and they can assist in the creation of new policies. Insurance companies have developed specialized policies for homeowners associations. The board might seek out a broker for such a policy. Contractors are available to handle the buildings, driveways, landscaping, plumbing, electrical issues, and fire protection. The board of directors is not in this alone. Professionals in the industry are ready to help.

Real estate management professionals are available to assist boards in the day-to-day operations of the association. Sometimes this is accomplished by means of a signed contract for a specified period, and other times a board may just want to hire a professional manager on a temporary consulting basis. Like the board of directors, the professional manager has a fiduciary responsibility to act in the best interest of the association at all times. A board looks to its professional manager as someone who knows what he or she is doing. Just as board members want the CPA to help clarify their finances, they want the real estate manager to guide them on the right path when it comes to everyday operations.

The board of directors often looks to the professional association manager as a guide, a coach. Boards look to managers for directions for conducting a meeting, developing a budget, planning maintenance, dealing with difficult homeowners, and staying out of legal trouble. They expect the "pros" to know what they are doing. For that reason, managers must keep themselves informed and educated, staying on top of all of the latest standards and litigation pertinent to the industry.

One way the professional manager can help board members is to provide good directions as to what members of the board are expected to do. The best time for this is when a member is new to the board. The professional manager can produce a board orientation package that includes the following:

- All the association's governing documents along with a brief explanation of their meaning, a list of board members, their phone numbers, and their e-mail addresses
- The code of behavior (includes fiduciary responsibility information)
- The current reserve study
- The current budget
- The current financial statements and audit information
- The past six months' board meeting agendas and minutes as well as the last annual meeting minutes
- The current insurance policy and any pending claims
- A list of all homeowners, including their addresses, phone numbers, and e-mail addresses if available
- Copies of any current contracts (e.g., landscaping, pool, road maintenance)
- Contact phone numbers and e-mail addresses for the professional management team

Ultimately, the professional manager who stays abreast of community developments is situated to serve the association as a competent guide. Effectively communicating this knowledge to the board of directors promotes good community governance, providing information to the board members about priorities the community must face. The professional manager, as a conduit between the association and the board, plays an integral role in a successfully functioning community association by increasing the productivity of board meetings and decision making.

5

Procuring Board and Committee Volunteers

INTRODUCTION

Of the many aspects of community management, obtaining capable, willing volunteers to administer the governance of the community can be the most challenging. This chapter offers assistance to those working in the community management environment—whether directors, committee members, administrators, or managing agents.

Volunteers should bring certain qualities and traits to your community. After all, these individuals will have the responsibility (in most states, even the *fiduciary* responsibility) of maintaining the harmony, asset integrity, stability, and day-to-day governance of your living environment. Volunteering is a demanding (though not as hard as one might think), challenging, and most of all rewarding job because of the successes and accomplishments achieved during one's tenure.

Not everyone possesses the qualities that make a good leader. That is okay because the community needs good followers, too. This chapter presents various leadership roles, the importance of community building, guidance for leadership teams, and ways to acquire leaders from within a community.

VOLUNTEER LEADERSHIP IS PARAMOUNT

Time, talent, and concern are the three main attributes of a good community leader. A volunteer must be readily available, possess the desire and skill, and recognize the need for good community communication. When determining the traits that make a good leader, review your community's needs and expertise shortfalls.

A volunteer who knows an aspect of management that the community needs can be a valuable asset. The occupations community members have chosen provide a potentially endless resource of good, capable volunteers. Mechanics, engineers, architects, accountants, landscapers, and service-oriented professionals in the community have the qualities, experience, and thinking processes needed to be good directors and/or committee members. Some of their capabilities may come not only from their professional backgrounds but also from other interests such as hobbies—for example, landscaping or gardening, journal writing, and architectural or interior design.

One of the most important goals is finding volunteers who simply want to serve, because they will most likely have the time and interest to do so. Such individuals may not have as much special training or talent as some of the others mentioned above, but they could still become real assets to the board or committee.

Good communication is essential. Members may become suspicious of board motives when kept in the dark. A good representative keeps other community members informed about the board's actions.

COMMUNITY LEADER RESPONSIBILITIES AND RIGHTS

All volunteer community leaders—whether board members or committee members—have specific responsibilities to the association they serve. They also have the right to expect certain behaviors from association members in return.

The Board

The ultimate responsibility for all decisions in community management rests with the *board of directors*. Of course, this authority relates only to the common areas, leaving individual unit problems strictly in the hands of the unit owner. This means the board will face problems relating to financial management, legal matters, and inevitable disagreements among neighbors. Board members must help the member owners understand the concept of a common interest community—that its success depends on everyone collectively. The board should remain open to ideas and suggestions from all members of the community.

Board Skills. A successful board is a group of individual unit owners who possess the needed skills and leadership qualities and can work together in the community's best interests. A smoothly run operation is a direct result of a prepared, well-organized board that conducts business in a professional manner. For the board to succeed, board members must demonstrate the ability to do the following:

- Refrain from expressing disruptive political agendas or furthering personal interests
- Remain objective on all issues
- Refrain from voting if the outcome could be of personal benefit
- Use negotiation and communication skills
- Maintain a congenial attitude with others
- Recognize the talents and expertise of other board members, management agents, and other advisors

Board members are often judged on two levels: the time they invest in community activities and the sincerity of their interest in the future of the association.

Board Powers and Duties. Ultimately, the board has responsibility for decisions concerning the operation of the association. Its decisions must correlate with the powers and duties outlined in the governing documents, which may include any or all of the following:

1. Providing for the care, upkeep, operation, maintenance, and surveillance of the community
2. Preparing and adopting an annual budget illustrating the cost to maintain the common areas and other administrative expenses
3. Making assessments against unit owners and determining the method for collecting said amounts and the frequency of payments
4. Opening bank accounts on behalf of the association and designating their signatories
5. Collecting assessments, depositing them in proper bank accounts, and using the funds to carry out the administration of the community
6. Enforcing payment of the assessments from unit owners and adopting methods for handling delinquent payments

7. Designating, hiring, and dismissing the personnel required to maintain, operate, and repair the community
8. Acquiring and maintaining adequate insurance
9. Making additions, repairs, improvements, and alterations to the common areas in the event of damage or destruction by fire or other casualty
10. Enacting rules and regulations governing the use of the property and the conduct of the unit owners
11. Enforcing architectural controls and other compliance issues
12. Levying fines against unit owners for violation of and noncompliance with the rules and regulations
13. Keeping financial books and detailed accounts of the receipts and expenditures related to the property and administration of the community
14. Establishing reasonable reserve funds for future common expenses, including the repair and replacement of common areas and unforeseen contingencies
15. Selecting auditors, attorneys, and any other professionals whose assistance may be required
16. Employing management agents and contractors, outlining their duties, and soliciting RFPs (requests for proposal)
17. Bonding all officers, employees, and agents who have fiscal responsibilities

The above are the basic activities necessary for most associations to operate.

Board Morays. In defining itself as a community leadership group, the board must contemplate certain practices and "morays of business." These *morays* are additional responsibilities each successful board should consider.

A concise list of responsibilities that pertain to the morays mentioned above appears in an article titled "Rights and Responsibilities for Better Communities," from the May/June 2003 *Community Associations Institute (CAI)* publication, sponsored by the CAI President's Club. The list is reproduced below with comments from the author interspersed as notes.

Community leaders have the responsibility to:

1. Fulfill their fiduciary duties to the community and exercise discretion in a manner they reasonably believe to be in the best interests of the community.

Note: The board must exercise governance as provided in the governing documents. Compliance issues will arise, and the board must deal with them on a reasonable, fair basis.

2. Exercise sound business judgment and follow established management practices.

   Note: The board should get at least two to three bids when initiating expensive maintenance projects.

3. Balance the needs and obligations of the community as a whole with those of individual homeowners and residents.

   Note: Consider the best interests of the entire association, not just one homeowner's needs. This means a balanced maintenance program for all the common areas, too.

4. Understand the association's governing documents and become educated with respect to applicable state and local laws, and manage the community association accordingly.

   Note: The board must be diligent in monitoring any new government laws to keep the community in compliance with current statutes.

5. Establish committees or use other methods to obtain input from owners and non–owner residents.

   Note: From the committees come the future leaders. Nurture volunteer involvement.

6. Conduct open, fair, and well-publicized elections.

7. Welcome and educate new members of the community—owners and non–owner residents alike.

   Note: This is your home, and immediate communication with new residents will ensure compliance with the community's specific rules, thus thwarting that old "I didn't know I couldn't do that" response so often heard from new residents.

8. Encourage input from residents on issues affecting them personally and the community as a whole.

   Note: Create a medium for receiving ideas and requests from the residents. Circulate surveys on hot issues, institute a suggestion box, and give directors' e-mail addresses and/or telephone numbers to all residents.

9. Encourage events that foster neighborliness and a sense of community.

10. Conduct business in a transparent manner when feasible and appropriate.

    Note: Be forthright and obvious when discussing the business at hand.

11. Allow homeowners access to appropriate community records, when requested.

    Note: Don't give your constituency a "cloak and dagger" impression. Most legal or assessment delinquency records should have board approval prior to member viewing.

12. Collect all monies due from owners and non–owner residents.

    Note: This means all the community leadership, too. In fact, some associations' governing documents will not allow a director or committee person to function as such if he or she is not current on all assessments.

13. Devise appropriate and reasonable arrangements, when needed and as feasible, to facilitate the ability of individual homeowners to meet their financial obligations to the community.

    Note: The board should do its best to assist residents who experience unexpected financial hardship. Stipulating the arrangements for such a situation via a board resolution before the need actually arises and remaining consistent with the agreed terms will reassure the community and eliminate accusations of favoritism by the board.

14. Provide a process residents can use to appeal decisions affecting their nonroutine financial responsibilities or property rights—as permitted by law and the association's governing documents.

    Note: Most associations' documents provide for a hearing process, whether for contesting a noncompliance issue, for making a special request, or for seeking a variance to other rules and regulations.

15. Initiate foreclosure proceedings only as a measure of last resort.

    Note: This action could have a negative impact on the community—possibly from a public relations (PR) point of view and certainly from an economic one. Definitely consider all other avenues before foreclosing on someone's home.

16. Make covenants, conditions, and restrictions as understandable as possible, adding clarifying "lay" language or supplementary materials when drafting or revising the documents.

    Note: Association leaders all too often disagree on interpretations of the governing documents because the author of the documents left vague or ambiguous statements upon which even the attorneys cannot agree.

17. Provide complete and timely disclosure of personal and financial conflicts of interest related to the actions of community leaders, e.g., officers, the board, and committees. (Community associations may want to develop a code of ethics.)

    Note: Leaders should recuse themselves immediately if conflicts of interest are indicated prior to making a community business decision. Sometimes simply disclosing the potential for a conflict is sufficient. In such cases, the remaining leadership can decide whether the potential conflict would have an impact on business voting. A code of ethics is an excellent tool for the community leadership to adhere to and follow.

Board Rights. Community leadership team members have many responsibilities, as discussed above, but as elected or appointed members of the governance team, they also have certain rights. Their rights dictate the way the association membership should treat them.

Association residents are expected to know and comply with the community's rules and regulations. From time to time, the board may distribute additional policies or governance changes, and residents are expected to read the materials and stay informed.

Board members should expect personal privacy at home. Volunteers, too, are entitled to personal lives outside their leadership roles within the community. It is important for volunteers to set guidelines for the community as to when, how, and where to contact them, if needed. Volunteers must then follow their own guidelines and make no exceptions. In that way, member neighbors will learn to respect the volunteers' time—when representing the association as well as in their personal lives.

Unless an individual manages associations for a living, the leadership is expected to receive education from time to time on the community management operational process. The association should pay for this training. The association expects diligent performance from the board. Take advantage of the many publications and training workshops pertaining to community association management. If a managing agent is part of the team, ask for assistance obtaining this extended knowledge. The manager may have many educational tools, such as videos, tapes, and workbooks he or she would gladly provide. The manager may even put on a mini-seminar with your board and discuss the many pitfalls and tips for good board and committee meetings.

The leadership has the right to conduct positive meetings in a constructive atmosphere. Always have an agenda prior to and during a meeting. Do not allow the meeting to get out of control by letting someone wander from the agenda or by allowing outside membership to interfere with the business meeting at hand. The board controls the atmosphere and should keep the meeting productive or reschedule it to another time and place. The board has a right to expect the residents to be respectful, to give the board fair and honest treatment, and to contribute productively to the community.

Probably the most obvious right of leadership is the expectation that all residents will meet their financial obligations to the community. The association's ability to operate depends on the monthly income from its constituents. Having too many delinquent accounts negatively impacts the community's fiscal performance. Quick resolution of any outstanding assessments is a major priority.

Committees

After the board of directors is in place and officers are chosen, the next step is to appoint committees. Committees play an important role in the governance of the association. Management by committee allows the board to draw upon the expertise of other community members with a broad range of talents. Through committees, the board can delegate specific tasks to other members. Committee members may be willing to serve only for a specific committee; they may possess certain traits and skills that will help the committee successfully achieve its goals.

The size of committees may vary depending on their workload and function. A social committee may require only three members, while a more complex committee, such as maintenance or landscaping, may need six or seven members. A board member or management agent should be an *ex officio member* of each committee. The purpose of the ex officio member is to attend meetings and to offer advice and counsel, but that person does not have a vote in the committee's decision.

Committees can be an area of great strength for any association; they can be invaluable tools when they consist of knowledgeable, willing volunteers.

Committee Types. Many types of committees exist, depending on the size of the association and its needs. *Standing committees* recommend changes in and implementation of policies; they do not establish policy—that is the board's responsibility. The board creates standing committees to take care of the association's recurring needs. The president of the board frequently makes appointments to these committees after seeking the advice of the other board members.

Immediate governance committees include an architectural control committee, the budget and finance committee, the insurance committee, the covenants committee, and the rules and regulations committee. The remaining committees address everyday, recurring community needs; these include the welcoming committee, newsletter committee, social/recreation committee, landscape and grounds committee, and maintenance committee.

The following sections give basic job descriptions for a variety of committees and illustrate the direction and function each committee can provide for your community. Depending on the size of the association, some committee functions can be combined to reduce the number of committees necessary to operate adequately.

Architectural Control Committee. The *architectural control committee (ACC)* is important because its main goal is to preserve the community's architectural integrity. This may be one of the most demanding committees in the community. Members must be available for committee meetings as well as for viewing or inspecting proposed areas of change.

Most governing documents address the guidelines for this process. If they do not, a committee is formed and assigned the task of establishing a system for considering and acting upon proposed architectural changes. Such a system usually involves a four-step process: formal application, review by the committee, recommendation to the board, and approval or rejection by the board. If your association's governing documents call for the committee to approve or reject requests, the third step is eliminated.

Architectural standards may already be in place for your community. Developers frequently address these concerns when establishing the governing documents. These standards consider such areas as fences, patios, exterior paint colors, windows and window coverings, roof types and color, exterior sheds, and porch railings. If such standards are nonexistent, the committee must develop its own specifications consistent with the governing documents and state and local laws.

When managing a community, the manager should be involved in the design-review process. The community manager is an important resource in this process. If he or she is not involved, a manager could find it impossible to manage the covenants administration or the association itself. Associations often accept architectural changes without question and thus fail to consider whether an existing design-review process is obsolete.

Questions to help eliminate out-of-date processes follow:

- Does the design-review process promote the association's general objectives?
- Do the existing rules and regulations allow variations from the permitted architectural style?
- Should the association consider modifying its design principles to meet the standards of the time?

- Is the physical community consistent with its design principles?
- Will acceptance of a proposed change mean changing the scope of present rules, regulations, and restrictions?
- Are the covenants, conditions, and restrictions (CC&Rs) consistent with the applications for change?
- Is an appeal process in place to ensure the fairness and flexibility of the architectural review process?

Budget and Finance Committee. The *budget and finance committee* is an important advisory body of the association that works with the treasurer, management agent, and board on all financial matters. The treasurer is usually a member. The committee assists in preparing the annual budget for submission to and review of the board of directors.

Inviting the chair leaders of the other committees and learning their financial operating needs is an important function of this committee. This understanding allows the budget and finance committee to communicate to the other committees any financial limits or restrictions for the upcoming year. In turn, the finance committee can recommend for the board of directors' review any special assessments that may be needed because projected expenses exceed budgeted costs.

Another function of this committee is to recommend an auditor to perform the annual financial review of the association's books. Many states mandate an annual review or audit of community associations' financials, and it is a good business practice to encourage such an audit if it is not already mandatory. This committee might also prepare the association's income tax return, review its tax status with an attorney, and supervise reserve funds.

Insurance Committee. The *insurance committee* may be a separate committee, or it may be combined with the budget and finance committee. Its function is to evaluate the insurance needs of the association, obtain bids from reputable sources that provide community association insurance, and review such policies each year to ensure the needs of the association are met. Insurance requirements tend to be complex, and the association should consider forming this committee if one does not exist.

If a management agent is employed, that firm may be responsible for certain items mentioned above, and it may assist the committee or board in handling any major claims that might occur.

Rules and Regulations Committee. The *rules and regulations committee*, sometimes called the bylaws committee, provides consistency and continuity for existing rules and regulations and makes recommendations to the board to update regulations as needed. This committee is often an adjunct to, and under the control of, the covenants committee (discussed below).

State regulations usually require a two-thirds or three-fourths vote of all member owners to approve changes in the bylaws. However, most documents are flexible enough to allow the board of directors to adopt house rules and regulations. Provided the rules and regulations adopted in this manner are reasonable, the documents permit the community to function smoothly. The board must remember that every time a change is proposed and ratified, it must be distributed to all member owners.

Covenants Committee. The *covenants committee* may not be included in all communities' committee structures. The board of directors and the management agent at times oversee these needs in the regular course of business. However, this is a viable committee with specific duties. It may assist outside counsel in preliminary work on nonpayment of assessments, violations of association rules and regulations, and foreclosures. More important, however, is the fact that the covenants committee is a judiciary for hearing cases involving violations or infractions of rules and reporting recommendations to the board. Utilizing a covenants committee carries great weight if legal enforcement and judgments of a punitive nature are necessary.

Welcoming Committee. The *welcoming committee* makes the moving transition pleasant and informative for the new resident. This is the opportune time to inform the new resident about the community governance and distribute vital community information. This committee can also function much like a social committee in planning activities to bring neighbors together. A member of the welcoming committee should visit all new residents, possibly providing them with information about shops in the area, a map of neighborhood schools and churches, and a list of other homeowners.

Newsletter/Communications Committee. The *newsletter/communications committee* provides a vital link in the network of communications within an association. The committee should prepare and publish a newsletter on a regular basis. Content for the newsletter may be supplied by the board, committees, a management agent, or other contributors. The advent of e-mail and Web site hosting has opened endless communications possibilities, and many associations use this technology to reach their residents. Many management agents assist in providing a community Web page, thus expediting the dissemination of community information to clients.

The newsletter should be a medium used to bring the association together. It should not be a vehicle for debating issues, creating divisiveness, or promoting negative issues. The newsletter can be a source of valuable information for all homeowners. It should instill goodwill in the community, acknowledge noteworthy occasions, and be a publication community members look forward to reading. Obviously, anyone with experience as a journalist would be ideally suited to serve on this committee.

Social and Recreational Committee. The *social and recreational committee* builds community relations. Planned cookouts, pool parties, tours, card clubs, and so forth generate a friendly atmosphere and camaraderie within the community. Holiday celebrations are great seasonal social events. Many events can be self-supporting if the committee charges fees to help defray the costs.

In large communities with numerous recreational facilities, this committee also evaluates the supervision and operations of existing facilities. Recreational facilities' expenses should be part of the annual budget. Such items include seasonal facilities that may require lifeguards, pool chemicals, or tennis court maintenance. Keep these costs open for competitive bidding. Once a particular season begins, this committee monitors the operation of all recreational facilities, making recommendations for change to the board as necessary. Any amenity rental fee structures, vending machine revenue control, annual swim meets, tennis tournaments, bicycle field trips, and similar functions are concerns of this committee.

Landscape and Grounds Committee. The *landscape and grounds committee* concentrates its efforts on overseeing all common areas and, at times, individual homeowners' grounds. Such areas might be large, open, outdoor areas for playgrounds, parks, parking lots, driveways, and entry areas. A considerable portion of the annual budget is earmarked for landscaping and grounds care. This committee is often referred to as the *outdoor maintenance committee.*

Although few residents wish to do the actual maintenance of the grounds, many take an interest in the outdoor environment. Such individuals are good resources when establishing the committee. The exterior of any community creates the first impression for visitors, so time and effort should be invested in proper care of these common areas.

Working with the management agent to write specifications for landscape and grounds care is an important function of this committee. The preparation of bid packages, evaluation of formal bids, and recommendations to the board of directors are all part of the job description. Once the board has negotiated a contract for outdoor maintenance, the committee should monitor the contractor's performance. The committee works with the management agent to ascertain that contracts are properly prepared and executed. All comments and suggestions should be channeled through the management agent to enhance contractor performance.

The landscape and grounds committee makes expense recommendations for all landscape maintenance and improvements to the board of directors when the annual budget is prepared. Working with the management agent, the committee anticipates long-range, comprehensive improvements. A current reserve study and annual maintenance plan give the committee a good understanding of existing conditions and future capital improvements. Some states mandate that all homeowner communities have a current reserve study plan and a maintenance plan that coincides with the reserve plan.

The architectural control committee or the board frequently asks the landscape and grounds committee to review individual owners' applications to plant shrubs and flowers or to make other changes to the grounds. This committee must keep informed and review all requests to make changes to the grounds because it sets community landscaping and grounds maintenance standards. The committee makes recommendations to the board to approve or reject such applications.

Maintenance Committee. The *maintenance committee* has functions similar to those of the landscape and grounds committee, but it is responsible for the interior and structural portions of the common area. Periodic inspection of the common elements may be necessary in addition to reviewing work specifications and estimates for contractual work. This committee is also expected to work closely with a management agent, if one is employed, in inspecting and checking work projects.

The committee should meet monthly or bimonthly, depending on the size of the community, and do a walk-through of all the common areas, listing any defects. Appropriate recommendations—to replace, repair, or improve—should then be presented to the board of directors and the management agent. In addition, a large part of the maintenance committee's time may be devoted to preparing bid specifications for contracts and presenting recommendations on contractors to the board. Management agents are often experienced in these matters, and they can be especially helpful in assisting with the drafting of specifications.

Again, pool the list of volunteers within your community. Many communities have members experienced in construction or home improvement, such as plumbers or electricians, and those individuals could be excellent maintenance committee members.

The creation of housekeeping subcommittees within this committee allows for daily monitoring of certain maintenance and work schedules. This concept is more prevalent in self-managed communities, and it plays an important role in keeping up with day-to-day maintenance needs. This committee could also review any site employee's salary, benefits, and work schedules with the management agent and recommend any changes to the board.

The above committee structures illustrate the many areas of management concern for any community. Your community may not need all of these committees. You might combine some committees to share the tasks and have fewer committees for which you must find volunteers.

A committee's strengths come from the makeup of its membership and proper guidance from the board of directors. Half of the board's job is the appointment of these leaders. The other half is drafting guidelines that delineate the committee's purpose and its role in the overall administration of the community. To enhance committee effectiveness, the board should establish administrative guidelines and policies for all committees.

Committee Chair Guidelines. Before ending this section on committees, it is important to explain the guidelines for being a committee chair. After all, the chair is the leader of the group, and successful leadership leads to a productive, worthwhile committee.

The committee chair acts as liaison between the board of directors and the committee as a whole. Ideally, the chair has the capacity to work with various other committees. This ability determines the overall effectiveness of a chair; it will help him or her guide the committee toward clearly defined goals. The following ten guidelines are suggestions to assist the committee chair in achieving his or her responsibilities effectively and to enable the chair to play appropriate roles in the overall administrative effort:

1. Begin meetings on time and announce the time of adjournment. Letting members know in advance that the meeting will end at a specific time enhances and expedites the meeting.

2. Use appropriate *parliamentary procedure* to facilitate the flow of the meeting. (Small committees can use less formal, modified procedures.)

3. Have a written agenda and give copies to all committee members.

4. Assign a secretary (note taker) to keep minutes of each meeting and see that all committee members and the board of directors receive copies.

5. Keep control of the meeting so extraneous conversations do not disrupt the business at hand.

6. Summarize briefly what was said after each speaker finishes the discussion of an issue.

7. Encourage reasonable debate and constructive disagreement. Halt rambling discussion that is obviously inconclusive. Appoint subcommittees to research major issues.

8. Avoid hasty actions if time for consideration is inadequate. Table the discussion until the next meeting unless the issue is urgent.

9. Ask committee members at the end of the meeting whether they are satisfied that each subject was given adequate attention.
10. Present complete, brief, formal committee reports to the board of directors. Each report should be in writing. It should present the results of any research and, when applicable, recommend actions to be taken.

Committee Member Guidelines. Guidelines for committee members are equally important. The committee members are instrumental in making decisions on issues together with the committee chair. Each committee member must recognize an obligation to contribute to the effectiveness of the group. The following four rules can help enable committee members to work together toward meeting committee goals:

1. Prepare adequately for each meeting. Complete any required research or reading. Study the agenda prior to the meeting. If reports have been assigned, prepare them in writing and distribute copies to all committee members before the meeting.
2. Ask for the floor when you wish to contribute to the discussion. Speak clearly and loudly enough for everyone to hear.
3. Keep your remarks brief and do not stray from the subject. If a speech must be long, conclude with summary remarks.
4. Avoid issues that are not on the agenda. Refrain from extraneous conversations.

COMMUNITY-BUILDING SKILLS

Common interest development (CID) associations are most successful when homeowner members participate in governance as volunteers and develop a sense of community. To encourage those behaviors, board members and professional managers should learn community-building skills.

The Basics

Community building is the use of strategies intended to create or enhance a sense of community among individuals who live in a particular area or who have a common interest. Community involvement determines the success of community-building efforts, and it is essential when developing a leadership team.

Community leaders need to attract volunteers who can recognize other community members who possess good leadership skills. Such individuals project a positive attitude about living in a community and taking care of their daily responsibilities and duties. The lack of the ability to recognize such potential leaders could diminish prospective volunteerism within the community.

A leader knows that just being a volunteer is not enough; knowing which traits will benefit the community is also essential. Board members and committee members must know the community association's weaknesses and strengths to participate effectively in its day-to-day operational management.

Certain leadership behaviors can enhance the meaning of community. The leadership can distinguish itself by the way it resolves conflict and disputes. When community leaders demonstrate organizational skills by setting goals and attacking problems, the community gains confidence in its leaders. Leadership showing a determination to keep open dialogs with community members, nurturing a sense of shared responsibility for the community's future, and encouraging civic and social gatherings ensures long-term community enthusiasm. Leaders should remember that social elements outside the community are equally important; they should be supportive of nearby businesses, schools, and fire and safety organizations.

An important indication of the community's perception of its leadership is apparent in the residents' (stakeholders') point of view. If that perception is positive, they will show genuine support of the community rules, and many will volunteer to fill the positions and do the work necessary for a prosperous, pleasant community.

It is important to recognize some realities when understanding and implementing community building. Not everything will be successful. No two communities are the same, and just because something works next door does not mean it will work for your community. This process is not static, but dynamic in nature. The association will always need to make adjustments. Not everyone will accept the standards of the community, and that may make some feel very negatively about it. The positives and negatives of many issues can ripple through the community. The benefits may not always be perceptible or quantifiable, and the process and success may involve costs. Most important is that those who benefit within the community must be part of the process in order to benefit. This concept of positive participation among the community members builds the character and strength of the association.

Meaning of Community

Association leaders should ask the question, "What is community?" Knowing what builds positive community bonds helps leadership guide the association.

To determine what *community* means for an association, Brent Herrington, PCAM, in "Learning to Fly: A Time for Change, Growth, and Discovery in America's Community Associations" (an article taken from a reading supplement for CAI's "Advanced ABCs" class), poses the following questions:

> ...is it where you live, is it the environment around you, is it the people you live around, is it the ability to solve problems, is it the civic infrastructure, is it the physical infrastructure, is it based on growth and acceptance, is it isolated to those on the inside track?

Every community has certain benefits and needs. Leadership must recognize the areas of high and low interest among its members. Asking the following questions can lead to a successful analysis of your community:

- Are new homeowners constantly moving in, or is turnover of homes infrequent?
- When homes sell, does the community experience higher resale values?
- Does the board hear very few complaints?
- Is the board known for flexible decision making, creative problem solving, and positive dispute resolution?
- Do member meetings and association activities experience great participation?

The answers to the preceding questions reveal the overall stability and cohesiveness of a community. This provides needed direction to recognize the previously mentioned strengths and weaknesses within the community. Any negative answers to these questions can guide the leadership in a positive direction for change.

Importance of Outside Influences

Leaders and managing agents must acknowledge that the quality of community life can depend on an atmosphere of shared relationships between the community association and many outside influences. These influences include, but are not limited to, local government, entertainment outlets, health centers, day care centers, schools, local businesses, social service agencies, and local area residents.

Keeping a positive relationship with outside influences leaves the impression of a well-organized, cohesive, wonderful community in which to reside. What better testament to the style and type of community leadership management?

Role of Language

Over the years, newer, more positive language has begun to take hold in the community management arena. Expressions that are well received in discussions with owners, directors, or committee members can be useful. For example, instead of "meetings," "gatherings" and "social events" are now prevalent.

The manner in which leadership refers to its constituents and neighborhood is an important element in strengthening the community bond. Using current expressions instead of outdated terminology is another positive approach when discussing your neighborhood. As shown in Exhibit 5.1, newer expressions are softer and add meaning to the communication. "Stakeholder" gives more depth to one's ownership; rules and regulations are much softer when delivered as "neighborhood guidelines."

Communications that in the past involved letters or phone calls are now often achieved through e-mails and Web sites. The days of isolating the community and making it an island have given way to appreciating the importance of being part of the surrounding community and environment.

STRATEGIES AND TACTICS TO HELP LEADERSHIP TEAMS

In addition to community-building skills, leadership teams need approaches to help them plan, reach goals, and find and keep volunteers and leaders.

Strategic Planning Meetings

Frequently throughout a business year, occasions may arise that require special meetings to discuss community business. Aside from the regular annual budget review meeting, periodic board and committee meetings,

Exhibit 5.1

Current versus Outdated Terminology

Current	Outdated
Home	Unit
Stakeholder	Owner
Resident	Renter
Community	Complex
Neighborhood Guidelines	Rules and Regulations

and the annual meeting, another beneficial type of meeting is the leadership strategic planning meeting.

A *strategic planning meeting* is a time for the board president (or chairperson) along with all directors and committee volunteers to meet and discuss the community's governance processes. The time spent strategically planning and accomplishing a list of goals highlights the fact that the association is developing leadership strategies from which the community will benefit.

This is a great opportunity to review the present processes for communicating with one another (interaction procedural guidelines) and to develop the overall camaraderie conducive to successful community management. This is the time to illustrate how unproductive it is to debate countless hours over issues that seldom warrant more than a few minutes of discussion.

Many associations have annual strategic planning meetings and find them to be rewarding and appreciated by the volunteer members elected or appointed to be community leaders.

Volunteer Acknowledgment

Using volunteers' strengths, knowledge, and participation to effectively run the governance of the community is a basic premise for success. However, keeping volunteer leaders active and willing to continue the service is most important.

Community harmony, continuity, and transitional history keep well-run communities going. To accomplish this, the leadership must acknowledge volunteer leaders whenever possible.

People love recognition. Making sure that directors, committee members, and other volunteers receive formal recognition for their efforts is vital to your leadership's health. Use the meetings, minutes, newsletters, and Web page as testaments of appreciation. Use every opportunity in which there is an audience, and be detailed in your accolades.

Presenting certificates of achievement at an annual meeting is a wonderful way of recognizing faithful volunteers. Do not forget the day-to-day volunteers who do the tedious, monotonous tasks like paper pickup and light-bulb checking.

To coin an old phrase, *it is a wise board that makes a point of recognizing mere effort for its own merits.*

Strategies to Find Leaders

From time to time, every community board needs to find new leaders. Two important ways to accomplish that goal are to be sure everyone knows you are looking and to work to ensure future continuation of leaders once you find them.

Communicate the Need. When looking for leadership volunteers, remember to approach anyone who is just moving into the community. Yes, new residents are a great source. Their enthusiasm for the neighborhood is high, thus the rationale for moving in. Capitalize on their positive spirits and invite them into the leadership environment.

Letting a need be known within the community via word of mouth is valuable. Each current leader has friends. What better way to find someone than mentioning the possibility of being part of a team with people who have similar traits and interests? Using these connections is a plus when seeking volunteers.

Posting notices in common areas, using the annual meeting for getting people to sign up, and making announcements at board meetings are all good ways to "get the word out" within your community.

Ensure a Future Continuum of Leadership. As mentioned earlier, publicly acknowledging a volunteer's contributions to the community is vital. The volunteers among the community's committee members will be tomorrow's board members.

The volunteer approach works as long as volunteers continue to enjoy their jobs and do not neglect their responsibilities. A wise board will nurture this need, never forgetting the spirit of volunteerism.

An association must build a great community and assure sound, perpetual future leadership through its daily management processes. Bringing new members into the management arena at staggered intervals is vital to carrying forward a continuum of the community's history, principles, philosophy, and stability.

The perceived attitude of the association's governance team can create harmony or discord among the residents. A happy association will yield many years of productive, willing, volunteer leaders.

PROFESSIONAL MANAGERIAL ROLES

Professional association managers can help their associations develop successful leadership teams. Two important ways managers assist associations are by providing leadership training and by helping them recognize and deal with toxic leadership.

Development of Leadership Training

To ensure success in future leadership governance, the manager should provide tools for volunteer members to succeed. One good way to do this is for the management firm to implement a "board training" function. This could entail inviting board members to joint industry common interest development education sessions with the management firm's staff, and/or distributing periodical management tips to these key community leaders.

Another way to get a new board functioning properly is to hold a governance workshop in the management firm's conference room or on the association's site. The workshop might consist of the following:

- Showing CID industry videos on board management processes
- Explaining the importance of using *Robert's Rules of Order* for controlling meetings
- Covering the legalities and responsibilities of being a director or committee member
- Expressing the importance of community building
- Discussing the board's role in community building within the association

The management firm should use the same training techniques with its CID staff. Constant industry education is a must. Professional firms should know when and where important education sessions are to be held and ensure that the appropriate staff attends regularly. If the firm is large enough to have an HR department, that staff could be in charge of establishing regularly scheduled management/leadership training programs within the company. Industry trade associations are a wonderful resource for training materials and educational sessions.

Dealing with Toxic Leadership

Effective management requires a knowledge and understanding of people's personalities and behavioral traits. A manager does not have to be a sociologist or psychologist, but the ability to recognize and use aspects of everyday life that affect behavior is important.

Associations as well as your management office staff will benefit from a positive leadership style that does not employ *toxic leadership*—a poor leadership style characterized by negative traits. Some traits and tactics of toxic leaders are listed below:

1. *Arrogance.* Such individuals think they are always right. They only accept input from a limited number of yes-men and yes-women. Only their chosen group receives information; they leave others out. Toxic leaders tolerate little discussion about the work being done.
2. *Quick reprisal.* Such leaders are quick to blame those who are not supportive of their decisions if a task is unsuccessful. They are happy

to look good at the expense of others and take credit for others' work. They succeed by tearing others down.

3. *Rigid commitment to an idealized goal.* Toxic leaders do not want any challenges to their goals. Their followers must either be with them 100 percent or be considered a traitor. They are very motivated by their self-interests.

4. *Bullying, threatening, and yelling.* The behavior of these individuals undermines any positive mood among the volunteers. They show lack of concern for the well-being of subordinates.

Many other symptoms of this type of poor leadership exist. Recognizing such traits in your leadership style or that of others is a major step toward successful leadership in the workplace and in the association's governance. Remember these traits, learn to recognize them, and avoid using or being part of this style of management.

Toxic leaders can sap the strength from their associations. Their demands for loyalty can actually cause employees and association volunteers to fear whether they are doing something their leader will think is wrong. Toxic leadership can paralyze an organization.

Leaders are in a position to deal with toxic behavior because they have the authority to counter it. The manager who stays attuned to avoiding the aforementioned traits will benefit from productive associations and a happy staff.

TRANSITION FROM BUILDER/DECLARANT TO SELF-GOVERNED MEMBERSHIP COMMUNITY

Doing business with a builder/declarant is a good way to build a portfolio in CID management. Choosing a builder with a good reputation is important. Knowing that his or her abilities and performance history are positive can eliminate concern about any negative stigma the management firm might acquire from doing business with the builder/declarant.

A builder/declarant may seek your services to manage an association before all the homes have been sold. This beginning management period is very important for the manager—especially if a continuing, long-term contract is expected after the builder/declarant turns the community over to the members.

As mentioned previously, professional managers often fall victim to a scenario in which the members do not recognize that the manager is not part of or affiliated with the builder/declarant. This will definitely affect your management success if your client (the builder/declarant) does not meet the members' needs and expectations. Your good efforts may be perceived negatively. If this happens, your management firm may find redefining a better image to be impossible.

So what can you do to reduce poor relationships with your community when the declarant does not meet member expectations?

Ensure Compliance with Governing Documents

First, make sure the declarant understands that your contract is with and for the association and its members. A manager may feel obligated to the declarant because the declarant was responsible for hiring the professional management firm. However, this does not relieve the manager of his or her fiduciary duties to the association members.

This means the manager must inform the declarant of any issues he or she may be creating by not being in compliance with the governing documents of the homeowners association. If the manager does not perform this compliance function with the declarant, the manager may expose the management firm and the declarant's firm to future legal issues with association members.

Guide the Declarant's Business Practices

The next step is guiding the declarant through good business practices associated with managing any CID. In most states, the declarant is required to diminish board representation as more member homes are sold.

Depending upon the governing documentation, the first election or appointment of one new member director usually occurs after the first 25 percent of the development has been sold. This means the declarant gives up one of his or her appointed director positions to the new member director.

The next increase in member directors can occur at a 50 percent sellout. It should be noted, however, that many times there is not an increase with the 50-percent sold provision, unless the allowed number of directors exceeds three members. This is because the declarant would usually still have the majority-controlling director vote—two members out of the total three—so no vote for another member director could occur because it would shift the control to the members too early.

States frequently dictate that the declarant/builder must make a complete turnover after a 75 percent sellout. Thus, the entire board will then be made up of elected member owners who will control 100 percent of the association, instead of the beginning board being appointed by the declarant/builder and full association control remaining with the declarant.

Encourage Canvassing for Board and Committee Members

As the manager, you should encourage the members of the new community to canvass for potential volunteers for the new board and committee positions. Keep in mind these new volunteers should not have any inherent relationship with the declarant, thus reducing the possibility of any future conflict of interest. The volunteers should have the leadership qualities mentioned earlier in this chapter and those attributes mentioned in Chapter 4, "Board of Directors."

Complete the Turnover Checklist

The professional manager's final task when perfecting the management transition from declarant/builder control to member association control is to assist the declarant in meeting his or her obligations of turning over association control and providing the new governing board all the necessary documentation that was developed and used during the declarant's management, thus keeping consistency and good management history up-to-date. The manager must ensure this process is done in a timely fashion and with precise accounting.

The declarant/builder "Twenty Turnover Checklist" shown in Exhibit 5.2 should be followed as closely as possible to coordinate the timing when full control is turned over to the association members. Many states require such a list with a time stipulation for completion—usually a maximum of 60 days after the transition or turnover date.

Exhibit 5.2

Twenty Turnover Checklist

The declarant should deliver to the association manager all property of the owners and of the association held or controlled by the declarant, including but not limited to the following:

- ❑ 1. An original or photocopy of the recorded declaration and each amendment to the declarations
- ❑ 2. The certificate of incorporation and a copy or duplicate original of the articles as filed with the Secretary of State
- ❑ 3. The bylaws
- ❑ 4. The minute books, including all minutes and other books and records of the association
- ❑ 5. Any rules and regulations that have been adopted
- ❑ 6. Resignations of officers and members of the board who are required to resign because the declarant is required to relinquish control of the association
- ❑ 7. The financial records, including canceled checks, bank statements, and financial statements of the association, and source documents from the time of incorporation of the association through the date of transfer of control to the owners

(continued)

Exhibit 5.2 ***(Continued)***

- ❑ 8. All association funds or the control of the funds of the association
- ❑ 9. All tangible personal property of the association, represented by the declarant to be the property of the association, and inventory of the property
- ❑ 10. Except for alterations to a unit done by a unit owner other than the declarant, the copy of the declarant's plans and specifications utilized in the construction or remodeling of the CID, with a certificate from either the declarant or a licensed architect or engineer stating that the plans and specifications represent, to the best of such person's knowledge and belief, the actual plans and specifications utilized by the declarant in the construction or remodeling of the CID
- ❑ 11. Insurance policies or copies for the CID
- ❑ 12. Copies of any certificates of occupancy that may have been issued for the CID
- ❑ 13. Any other permits issued by governmental bodies applicable to the CID in force or issued up to one year before the transition date
- ❑ 14. All original warranties that are still in effect for the common elements, or any other areas or facilities the association has a responsibility to maintain and repair, from the contractor, subcontractors, suppliers, and manufacturers; and all owners' manuals or instructions furnished to the declarant with respect to installed equipment or building systems
- ❑ 15. A roster of unit owners and eligible mortgagees and their addresses and telephone numbers, if known, as shown on the declarants' records; and the date of closing of the first sale of each unit sold by the declarant
- ❑ 16. Any leases of the common elements or limited common elements and other leases to which the association is a party
- ❑ 17. Any employment contracts or service contracts in which the association is a contracting party or service contracts for which the association or unit owners have an obligation or a responsibility, directly or indirectly, to pay some or all of the fee or charges of the person performing the services
- ❑ 18. All other contracts to which the association is a party
- ❑ 19. Audit of records upon transfer—upon termination of the period during which the declarant had control
- ❑ 20. Termination of contracts and leases made by the declarant, if entered into prior to any board member (unit owner other than declarant) elected taking office

The last item on the checklist in Exhibit 5.2 is crucial to the professional manager. If the declarant hired your services prior to any unit member owners being on the board, your management contract will need to be accepted and ratified by the first new board made up of member-owner representation.

Whether during a management transition or in the process of procuring community volunteers, successful communication is paramount. In the next chapter we turn to a discussion of this skill, which influences many aspects of the professional manager's daily operations.

6

Successful Communication

INTRODUCTION

Communication is the most important element in the success or failure of your day-to-day operations as a professional manager. *Webster's* defines *communication* as "a process by which information is exchanged between individuals through a common system of symbols, signs, or behavior."[1] The key is to recognize that, when communicating about the subjects of management discipline and philosophy, you may need to use a variety of delivery styles to meet the needs of all involved.

This chapter illustrates several methods that professional association managers use to achieve successful communication with the *board of directors* and members of the association. Understanding each entity's needs ensures that your actions as a professional manager will be in accordance with the community's best interests.

Managers and board members do not want your official message to be altered as it is passed around the association. Effective, appropriate, and frequent communication is essential to the success and harmony of your community.

---

[1] Merriam-Webster, Incorporated, *Merriam-Webster's Collegiate Dictionary*, 11th ed. Springfield, MA: Merriam-Webster, Incorporated, 2003.

COMMUNICATING WITH THE ASSOCIATION

The professional association manager must establish efficient, effective lines of communication with the board of directors and the association members. The manager and the board of directors must be consistent in their communications with the membership.

Communication with the Board

As the professional manager, you can use careful, deliberate communications to ensure that you do not experience moments of "the right hand not knowing what the left hand is doing." The dynamic process of communicating with one another allows us to exchange information in many ways—through writing, speaking, and body language. Board members receive these forms of communication in different ways. They must process the spoken word or printed page from the manager and understand it in order to act on it.

The manager communicates with the board of directors in many ways. In the beginning, discussions are detailed and frequent. During this time, the manager becomes familiar with the community, interprets the board of directors' goals, and defines and expresses management's role in relation to the community and the directors. Written policies and compliance-letter formats are developed for the board's review. Many telephone discussions and physical meetings with the directors take place. Later, the writing and talking will decrease, but communication must retain the important ingredients of clarity and effectiveness.

Designated Board Liaison. Management agreements often stipulate that most communications outside of board meetings will be with one designated director—usually the board chair or president of the association. This places immense importance and emphasis on management's communications because they may now reach only one member of the association's governing body. Therefore, it is imperative that there be no misunderstanding or misinterpretation when the liaison goes back to the other directors with information from management.

This single-contact policy can be quite beneficial for the manager, especially if all the directors have been constantly contacting management rather than expressing their need(s) in a collective fashion through the designated management liaison. However, if the liaison begins to have issues with management, opening the doors to the other directors may be best. This process will probably change from board to board, as directors change.

Electronic Communication. The advent of the Internet and e-mail greatly improved communications between management and the board of directors. However, when using e-mail, a manager must establish and maintain certain practices. Be aware that when exchanging information with more than one director in an e-mail, the manager may be placing the directors in the position of conducting an official meeting. One way to avoid this is to e-mail one director directly and blind copy (bcc) the others. This approach maintains the dialog only with the director addressed but keeps the other directors informed about the communication. Be sure to obtain legal advice before implementing e-mail with more than one director at a time.

Establishing a reasonable time for e-mail responses is important. Whatever time frame is used, the directors will learn to expect future responses based on the agreement. When setting a response-time precedent, avoid making it into a daily routine that is unreasonably difficult to maintain. Some directors just will not use e-mail; they prefer the telephone or face-to-face communication.

Telephone and Voicemail. The telephone and voicemail messaging are also useful communications tools. However, as in the e-mail process, be sure to stipulate a reasonable response time for replying to voicemail messages that works for all concerned.

Realizing the importance of customer service, many managers make outgoing voicemail recordings to route certain types of calls to other individuals. This enables the caller or director to reach a live person who can address the issue. Although the person may not be the community manager, he or she should be a capable associate within the management office.

Face-to-Face Communication. The most reliable communication is face-to-face conversation between the director and management. However, since management is probably not hired 24/7 and the director is an unpaid volunteer, constant direct contact is impractical. That very impracticality points out the importance of developing a successful interaction link between the community leaders and management.

Holiday Calendar. Another important management technique is marking a calendar with all the firm's holidays and any other days the management office will not be available to clients and customers. Uninformed directors or residents often become frustrated when the management firm is not open for business—especially if it is because of a floating holiday or an occasional in-office work day for staff only. This is just one of many small but significant procedures that distinguish a successful manager.

Communication with the Members

Yes, the board of directors and the management firm absolutely want to hear from the members. A familiar problem in communication is assuming that it somehow happens all by itself. Do not assume that the members know what the manager and/or directors know or that they share your awareness or opinions. Dispel this illusion by developing and implementing a consistent communication program that educates the members and derives feedback from them. Effective communication promotes informed decision making on the part of members and directors because they are provided with the information they need to make decisions.

Many of the skills used in communicating with the board apply when developing communication channels with association members. The establishment of a reasonable time frame for service delivery is essential. Setting a time to respond to phone calls, e-mails, and maintenance requests from members and to return communications to the board is vital for positive communication between the association members and their leaders. Adhering to time limits demonstrates the efficiency with which a management firm operates.

Management and the board of directors should be consistent in their communications with association members. This will assist members in giving input to the board of directors or management. Most people use basic, good communication skills in daily life, but they generally take those skills for granted. Some everyday communication tips to promote enthusiasm and caring within the association follow.

- *Communicate often.* Using several mediums—newsletters, bulletin boards, front door flyers, Web sites—to repeat important messages is always effective.
- *Communicate in a variety of venues.* The formal annual meeting is a good setting for eliciting input from and encouraging decision making by the majority of the members. If additional explanation is necessary regarding key information about the community, such as budget projections, dues increases, or future policy changes, schedule informal town meetings, coffee gatherings, or other functions that allow members to express their opinions and thoughts.
- *Communicate in a positive, open, and direct manner.* When announcing a board decision to the members, explain and clarify all the factors considered and the reason the decision was made. This is the time to tell all; do not withhold critical information. If bad news must be conveyed, do so as soon as possible, and let the members know what is being done to ameliorate the situation.
- *Let communication be a two-way process.* Listen to members' wishes prior to working toward an end they may not want or appreciate. Getting bids on a common area facility—albeit recreational equipment or playground expansion—before listening to members' needs or desires is a good example of failing to use the two-way process.
- *Communicate to the proper audience.* Do not fall into the practice of chastising the entire community if a few members fail to comply with a rule. Make direct contact with the few; avoid spreading a negative

message to the entire membership. If many residents are violating a rule, use the newsletter or Web site to send a reminder about the noncompliance.

- *Time your communication carefully.* Urgent matters dictate timely notification, whereas future events can be posted or announced in the regular newsletter. A water shutoff tomorrow definitely demands phone calls or front door notification; the summer pool party could be advertised in the newsletter or on a poster.
- *Consider expense and attitude.* Should you use special mailings or the newsletter approach? The form of the communication should express the attitude of the message. Flyers and bulletins regarding special events are much less formal communications than a noncompliance or dues-collection letter. Timely deliverance of critical messages that could affect the health and safety of the members justifies extra expense. The more serious the nature of the news, the greater the importance of using the most effective means of reaching the residents. Registered or certified letters should be used if acknowledgement of the message is important; however, general announcements can go into the newsletter or on the bulletin board.

Welcoming new residents is an important communication link between the association and the member. New owners frequently move into a community completely unnoticed and unexpected; they may feel uninvited. In some communities, a member of the board of directors visits all newcomers and welcomes them to the community. Many associations have a specific *welcoming committee* for this purpose. Among its jobs is providing a hospitality basket of promotional items and the community address directory—a list of important telephone numbers for the board of directors, committee chairs, and management firm. Standard practices in many communities include holding social parties to welcome new residents and placing special articles in the newsletter to inform the entire community of the new neighbor's arrival.

RESOLVING CONFLICTS AMONG MEMBERS

Conflicts among association members can be resolved in many ways. The Association for Conflict Resolution (www.ACRnet.org) states the following:

> Today there has been a movement toward *'Alternative Dispute Resolution'* (ADR), sometimes simply referred to as conflict resolution. The terms ADR and conflict resolution are used somewhat interchangeably and refer to a wide range of processes that encourage nonviolent dispute resolution outside of the traditional court system.

In today's *common interest development (CID)* management, disputes within an association are increasingly resolved through positive conflict resolution processes. Understanding the positive and negative sides of conflict is important in resolving such issues. On the positive side, conflict can encourage change and lead to creative outcomes. On the negative side, unmanaged conflict can lead to frustration, arguments, and the eventual dissipation of the association.

Member Dispute Management

Many associations establish resolutions that give a disciplined structure to the management of member disputes. Exhibit 6.1 is an example of such a resolution.

Exhibit 6.1
Member Dispute Resolution

Community Spirit Resolution

WHEREAS, the Bylaws of the Association charge the Board of Directors with the powers and duties to ensure that Residents who enjoy the privilege of living within the Association also accept the responsibility of not infringing on their neighbors' rights of peaceful enjoyment, safety and sustained property value and;

WHEREAS, it is the intent of the Board of Directors to provide competent leadership and to provide a sense of harmony and community spirit between Residents, Board of Directors and the management company and;

WHEREAS, it is the intent of the Board of Directors to foster a vibrant and responsive community.

THEREFORE, BE IT RESOLVED, the Board requires Residents must first attempt to resolve varying opinions or alleged rule violations among themselves before the Association will assist in any resolution(s).

BE IT FURTHER RESOLVED, in the event of a conflict between Residents that cannot be resolved in good faith by the parties, the Resident alleging a violation has occurred must validate the issue in writing to the Board of Directors, in care of Invest West Management, LLC at 12503 SE Mill Plain, Ste. 260, Vancouver, WA 98684, before the Association will consider any action.

BE IT FURTHER RESOLVED, the report must also include the date and description of the effort the parties involved have made to resolve any issue before the Association can consider any action.

Dated this ______ day of __________________, 20___

______________________________ ______________________

Officer Signature Date

The approach to member dispute management shown in Exhibit 6.1 illustrates one way a board might establish a reasonable procedure for dealing with conflict issues that can be given to all members. It is important to develop strategies that help reach an agreeable resolution for everyone involved.

Conflict Resolution Tactics

Northeastern Illinois University explains some aspects of conflict resolution in a recent white paper. The content is useful and practical for developing association governance and leadership skills. An adapted summary of the report follows:

- *Define the situation.* Let both sides explain the problem and allow each side to acknowledge what it believes the other side is expressing. The problem could be completely misunderstood, thus a possible quick resolution to the issue may be at hand.
- *Get the specifics.* Find out who, what, when, and where—and how the situation could be avoided in the future.
- *Brainstorm options.* Working together reviewing past solutions can help resolve the present issue.
- *What if...?* Predict the likely results of each option, then pick the most viable.
- *Go for it—and don't forget it.* Quick implementation of a plan is essential. Set a future meeting date for parties to discuss the success of the resolution.

Preventative measures

- *Own your feelings.* Use "I feel" statements to reduce defensiveness. For example, "I feel like I never get a chance to speak in our meetings," relays your feelings much more effectively than, "You blab the entire hour and no one else can get a word in edgewise."
- *Dismantle the rumor mill.* Make it happen; rumors stop. Two actions are necessary if you hear gossip: (1) Ask the messenger how he knows the information, how he found out, etc. (2) Go directly to the source to verify or discredit the rumor.
- *Backstabbing—bad; communication—good!* Encourage association members to speak with the person with whom they are experiencing a problem rather than complaining to other members. The key is to open communication. This can prevent most problems before the two members come to blows.

- *Play "win-win."* Create a win-win atmosphere within the association. Work toward solutions that allow everyone involved in the conflict to win. Avoid solutions that have one winner and make the rest of the members losers. Using this technique encourages a supportive, team-based environment.
- *Don't avoid it.* Ignoring a problem will not make it go away. Rather than allowing it to grow to great proportions, confront the conflict and deal with it.
- *Get with the "now."* Many members will not let go of past issues. Stay focused on current issues; the past cannot be changed, and it promotes wasteful, negative energy to keep dwelling on it.

Conflict within an association is a very natural element in CID management, but it can be detrimental if not managed properly. The most important component of conflict management is communication. Most problems can be resolved if the lines of communication are kept open.

Mediation and Arbitration Techniques

Many associations already have a conflict-resolution process in their governing documents. The two distinct processes may be "mediation provisions" and/or "legal arbitration."

Mediation. *Mediation* is an informal process of dispute resolution in which a neutral third party (mediator) helps disputing parties reach an agreement. Each party explains his or her view of the issue to the mediator. The mediator then endeavors to persuade the parties to reach an agreement voluntarily on the disputed issue.

Mediation is helpful because it establishes a nonlegal means of resolving member conflicts. The purpose of mediation is not to establish fault in the past, but rather to look to the future by giving members an opportunity to clear up misunderstandings, define areas of agreement, and design their own solutions. Because decisions are not imposed by an outside authority, mediated agreements have a high rate of voluntary compliance. The mediation process often positively transforms member participants' future relationships with one another.

An association board may create a *mediation committee*—a volunteer member body willing to assist in solving conflicts within the community. This committee sometimes has a board director as a liaison committee member; at other times, the association may choose to have no elected governance on the committee, just member peers helping to resolve conflicts. Any decisions are either final or are brought back to the board for final approval. This is a wonderful process; it lets the members know their voices can be heard by reasonable peers willing to help resolve the conflict.

Do not confuse a conflict issue with improper compliance to a specific declaration or bylaw covenant. Until the association elects to make a specific governance policy change, the board and its members must adhere to all such requirements.

Many states, counties, and cities have mediation bodies established just for the purpose of resolving conflicts between parties. This function is less formal than legal arbitration and is usually free to the taxpayer.

Arbitration. *Arbitration* is a conflict resolution process that is usually sanctioned and implemented by the local courts. Its decisions have a stipulated judgment as the final result. This should be a last resort in resolving issues. It can have a very negative effect on the association—just as any other legal process might.

Many ways to resolve issues are possible within the CID environment. Choosing the proper procedure for the association is vital to maintaining harmony and goodwill among the members.

STRENGTHENING COMMUNICATION TOOLS

Newsletters, surveys, and Web sites are effective communication tools. The professional association manager can assist the board of directors in developing and using these powerful communication aids to great advantage.

Newsletters

What caliber of newsletter is right for your community? This medium for conveying association information should always be a source of pride for the community. Its format, style, and appearance play an important role in communicating the association's message.

Each community has different ideas about its newsletter. Should you produce a 30-page, high-quality, full-color association periodical? Would a less costly, three- or four-page community information brochure with quality content be just as effective? Consider each view's merits when deciding on the type of newsletter. No matter which style your community uses, to make your publication appealing and effective, consider the important tips that follow.

Keep the layout and design simple and orderly. Using too many typefaces, fonts, and colors can detract from the printed message.

Include a letters-to-the-editor or -board feature. This is a great way to find out what the members think and need. Some individuals may disagree with the board, but unless they create massive disruption or division among the members, their letters should not be withheld. A good balance of opinions can help, rather than hinder, the association's governance decisions.

When deciding on newsletter content, cover the association's business meetings, budgets, elections, special projects, and community events. Controversial topics should not be avoided; they should be embraced for the good of the community.

Some communities that use expensive written communications include advertising to offset the high cost of the larger multicolored newsletter. When considering advertising, remember this approach usually involves political as well as fiscal concerns. Many residents may not want to see commercialization of their community, and some may feel the association is giving biased or favored endorsements through its newsletter.

The following are tips for improving association newsletters adapted from a July/August 1995 *Common Ground* article, "12 Tips for Improving Your Newsletter."

1. *Put some zing in your headlines.* Offer specifics; a good headline will pull the reader into the story. For example, a headline that simply says "Annual Meeting Held" will not entice the reader. However, a headline that has a teaser such as "Board Announces Plan to Raise Assessments" indicates an important result of the meeting. Words that trigger the attention of the members will pull them into the story. Being creative will grab people's attention.

2. *Give all of the facts.* Stories and interviews should always include basic "who, what, where, when, and how" information. If a cover story announces a new rule, explain why the rule was enacted. Be sure to illustrate when the board reached the decision, when the rule will take effect, whom it applies to, and how it will be enforced. The members shouldn't read a story or announcement and be left with more questions than answers.

3. *Make the articles easy to scan.* People are flooded with information daily—they often don't have time to read long, detailed pieces. Newsletter articles should be short and easy to scan.

   Many readers will only skim the newsletter. To get their attention, use headings and bullets—"entry points" that grab the readers' eyes as they scan the page. Use boxes to list the most important information. If your newsletter is more than six pages long, put an "Inside This Issue" box on the front cover listing story titles or topics and page numbers.

4. *Don't bury information.* Many times the most interesting and important information will be buried near the end of the article. Downplaying an important fact by placing it too far into the text could cause the reader to loose interest before knowing what the story is really about. For example, your lead may be, "City Councilman I. M. Crooked appeared at an association board meeting on July 1." Then in paragraph three the reader discovers—assuming he or she is still reading—that the councilman announced plans to build an expressway through the community. This should have been your lead: "City Councilman I. M. Crooked announced plans at the July 1 board meeting to build an expressway that could bring 4,000 cars a day through our community."

5. *Proofread every item.* Typographical errors happen, but too many will destroy the credibility of your newsletter. The newsletter will be a reflection of the board. Too many misspelled words get members wondering how the board can manage the affairs of the association. So, at the very least, have someone proofread the article(s)—a second set of eyes is more likely to find mistakes—and always double-check high profile items such as headlines and pulled quotes. Also make sure to double-check the spelling of names. The last thing the board needs is to profile a homeowner and spell his or her name incorrectly.

6. *Be on the lookout for story ideas.* The primary goal of the newsletter is to inform owners of association business. But it can do much more than that.

   Use the newsletter to publicize the efforts of the member volunteers. It can also promote association events. The Kala Point Owners' Association in Port Townsend, Washington profiles new residents in its newsletter, from their careers to their hobbies. The *Kentlands Town Crier*, published by the Kentlands Citizens Assembly in Gaithersburg, includes a section called "Our Town" that shares news regarding residents, from awards to births.

   Including a "Question and Answer" section in the newsletter is another way to get residents to ask questions, and provides a great opportunity for the directors to answer questions on issues from pool rules to pet rules.

7. *Share good news.* When the Quail Creek association in Sparks, Maryland was named Community Association of the Year by CAI's Chesapeake Region Chapter, it was front-page news in the newsletter. The Colonies Condominium in McLean, Virginia includes a regular section titled "Your Condo Fee at Work," which lists all current maintenance repair

and improvement projects. The newsletter is a prime opportunity for the association to publicize its accomplishments. Use it!

8. *Be consistent in your design.* This is important. For example, use no more than three different typefaces. Use the same typeface for body text and the same for headlines. If the design is inconsistent, the newsletter can look cluttered, distracting, and junky.

   One tool for consistency is to develop a blueprint type of vertical grid. It will be a model to be followed every time the newsletter is written. Three column grids are most common. *If you decide to vary the look of the newsletter by using one or two columns in a particular section, it should still follow the grid.*

9. *Don't be afraid of white space.* Your grid should allow margins of at least ¾ inch. This gives it "white space" and makes it look cleaner. It is not necessary to cover every inch of every page with something. Also, use clip art sparingly. Too much will clutter the newsletter and make it look tacky.

10. *Choose a readable typeface.* Too many times an editor will use a hard-to-read artistic typeface style thinking this is part of good journalistic creativity—only to make the newsletter very difficult to read. Use serif typefaces instead of sans serif typefaces in the body text for easier reading. Some examples of serif are Garamond, Times, and New Century. San serif typefaces include Helvetica, Future, and New Gothic. Serif is good for body text; sans serif is good for headlines.

    Also, never set body text in all caps—it's difficult to read. Italics are hard to read as well. Most typefaces are ten points in size. In general, your leading should be two points higher than your font (e.g., a 10-point typeface should have 12-point leading).

11. *Include photographs.* As important visual aids, photographs add variety to the text. This can be particularly helpful in a community association—photos help neighbors see neighbors. And if an association holds an event, what better way to create excitement than to show photos of attendees having fun?

    Black and white photos will generally reproduce better than color photographs. Try to avoid shots of people standing around—instead, print photos that show action and activity. Always include captions.

12. *Have fun.* Producing the newsletter should be a fun and creative experience. Having fun with it will definitely encourage more people to read it.

The preceding information should get your newsletter committee off and running. These same suggestions can be used for other forms of communication, such as an association Web site.

Surveys

In communicating with association members, another valuable process is a periodic survey of the membership to learn what they think about the community. A management firm should have such a format available. Exhibit 6.2 is an example of a survey that was derived from many other surveys presently used in the industry. It is used to encourage feedback from a community's members.

Exhibit 6.2

Example Community Survey

Community Association Survey

Your participation in this annual survey is very important. The board of directors will use the responses to help them make sound decisions and long-range plans for the community. When completed, please return this form to our managing agent either via the community Web site or directly to the management office address below.

1. What physical aspect of this community was the deciding point when you purchased here?

   ○ Location
   ○ House design
   ○ Gated community
   ○ Recreational facilities
   ○ Other ______________________________

2. How would you rate the maintenance of the common areas?

   Repairs…

   ○ Good
   ○ Fair
   ○ Needs improvement

   Physical Appearance…

   ○ Good
   ○ Fair
   ○ Needs improvement

(continued)

Exhibit 6.2 ***(Continued)***

Timeliness...

- ○ Good
- ○ Fair
- ○ Needs improvement

3. What do you like most about living in this community?

   ○ ____

4. Compliance and enforcement of the covenants, conditions, and restrictions (CC&Rs) is a prime responsibility of the association. Would you suggest:

   - ○ More enforcement
   - ○ Less enforcement
   - ○ Changing the CC&Rs for more flexibility
   - ○ Leaving as is

5. How effective is the newsletter—do you feel adequately informed regarding association issues?

   - ○ Yes
   - ○ No
   - ○ No opinion
   - ○ What changes or additions would you recommend? ____________________

6. How effective and timely is the professional management firm when needed?

   - ○ Good
   - ○ Fair
   - ○ Needs improvement
   - ○ Suggestions and comments: ______________________________

7. Is there anything you would change about the community?

   ____

   ____

8. What suggestions, other than noted above, would you have for the association to better serve its members?

   ○ ____

   ____

Please tell us a little more about yourself:

- ○ How long have you owned a home in this community? ________________
- ○ How many occupants are living in the home? _______adults, ______children

Exhibit 6.2 ***(Continued)***

- Do you currently: ___ live in home; ___ rent; ___ use on holidays/vacations
- How many pets are living in the home? ___ dog(s), ___ cat(s)

Thanks for taking the time to complete this survey. Your board of directors will inform all members of the survey results. If you have further questions, please call your community manager; otherwise please fax this to (A Very Professional Management Firm's fax number), send it via e-mail, or return it to the management firm's address noted below.

Source: Invest West Management, LLC, AMO

The board should always review and approve the content of all sanctioned association surveys. This will keep the philosophical goals of the leadership's governance in tune with a realistic outcome. Nothing could be worse than enticing the membership with false hopes about a project that is not feasible. Always communicate the results of surveys back to the members. If possible, include the board's position on the results.

Surveys allow association members to speak their minds; surveys also demonstrate the popularity and importance of member opinions. At the same time, surveys help association leadership take the pulse of the community and determine which direction it wants to go.

Web Sites

Granted, not all communities are populated with members who share an interest in today's high-tech computers or e-mail services. However, with all the new ways of receiving and sending e-mail, it won't be long before virtually all members will possess the machine(s) to connect to this "information superhighway." The information in this section helps acquaint associations with the increasingly popular Web site medium that many communities are already using.

Benefits of a Web Site. The manager and/or board of directors should recognize the benefits of the interactive association Web site. The information superhighway allows easy access to nearly all your members' living rooms. It makes sharing information easy. After all, isn't that what an association needs to do to create a sense of community and unify the residents?

Using the Internet to establish an association Web site provides a powerful tool for the community. It is a great way to keep members up-to-date on the community's events and issues, and it provides easy and increased interaction among the members—on their own time schedules without having to wait for a board meeting.

A Web site allows association committee members to communicate at their leisure rather than taking time out of their day to meet as a group. The flexibility and reduced time constraints can enable the association's governance procedures to be more effective and efficient.

Posting the rules and regulations online can reduce noncompliance by eliminating the excuse that members were not informed. Many member questions can be answered prior to board meetings, which may result in shorter meetings. Additionally, professional management has the option of providing forms and community documents online rather than making members wait for such items to be mailed.

Contents of a Web Site. Creating a public and a private section within the Web site is very important. The public area can be available to everyone on the Internet; it allows access only to certain features the association chooses. The members will one day want to sell their homes, so a "Real Estate Available" section would be valuable. Local realtors might post their listings here, too. Even setting up a classified ads section might be popular. A spot in the Web site that promotes your community to the public by posting neighborhood pictures gives input for undecided buyers who want to know more about the community prior to purchase.

The private section of the Web page is for the homeowner residents, the board of directors, and the management firm. Setting up the site so each homeowner has his or her private ID and password helps to ensure the security of the online material.

Information about the members can appear in this private section. The community address book makes it easy for the members to contact their neighbors, welcome new owners, or communicate for emergency purposes. An online events calendar, a message board section where members can ask questions or make comments to the board of directors, or even a chat room can be developed for live interaction among the residents.

The board of directors and management can use the private section to submit board meeting *minutes* and keep all owners apprised of the community's financial outlook by posting periodic financial statements. The newsletter may still be the main written communication, but the Web site may be the avenue that delivers the newsletter to your residents in a cost-effective manner.

Management can post announcements for residents on the Web site. You can even post survey questions online that residents can answer at their convenience by just pointing and clicking. An example of a survey that could be used online was presented in Exhibit 6.2. Think of it—no more filling out and returning forms. Just push the "send" button, and the board and/or management agent receives the member's answers.

The Web site should have a section on community governance that includes copies of all the covenants, bylaws, and rules and regulations. Any *architectural control committee (ACC)* guidelines and procedures for requesting limited common area or common area changes should be included. Some communities sell ads on their Web site to local service vendors and apply the proceeds toward the site and other communications costs.

Creation of a Web Site. Who creates the Web site? A homeowner volunteer or a communications committee can often fill this need. Many professional community management firms provide Web site design as part of their management services. Of course, many professional firms are available that can build a site for the community. Whoever develops the Web site, be sure to plan ahead so that, when volunteers or management companies change, the site will remain a viable part of the association.

Using an association Web site, whether hosted by the association or by the professional management firm, has become an important trend for CIDs. Many communities see the virtue of the Internet for communicating quick, thorough information to association members.

DELIVERING DIFFICULT COMMUNICATIONS

Professional association managers and association boards must frequently deliver difficult, sensitive, or unpleasant messages. In such situations, success is in the delivery.

Enforcement Communications

Managers are hired for their effective communication skills, advisory abilities, and problem-solving techniques. The manager must gauge the association's sensitivity to certain issues and determine the appropriate time and way to be firm with the noncompliant owner. If management waits too long to contact the violator or gives too much latitude in solving the problem, the board of directors may lose credibility with the association members regarding the effectiveness of using professional management for such issues—or perhaps for any issue.

Softening Strategies. One way of softening the enforcement delivery is to have a friendly telephone conversation or leave a message to say that a letter regarding the noncompliance issue is in the mail. This telephone contact softens the delivery of the mandatory letter of record. When a manager or director can discuss the issue directly instead of in writing, the noncompliant stakeholder will often understand the rationale for the enforcement communication and perceive it as a positive effort to solve the problem. Some management firms may be resistant to calling about all issues; that is understandable, because some violations require a written record that the noncompliant resident was informed. However, when a call is appropriate, it is usually time well spent and very effective for the manager.

Another way to soften enforcement is to address compliance during a routine inspection or walkabout in the community. A board member or management staff may have an opportunity to talk face-to-face with the resident in question. A good manager or director will not approach the subject with malice or contempt, but will display compassion and understanding when explaining the problem. This procedure yields a surprisingly positive response from most offenders. After all, it is their home, too, and they have a vested stakeholder interest that demands respect for and compliance with the associations' *covenants, conditions, and restrictions (CC&Rs).*

Compliance Enforcement Letters. After a phone call or a face-to-face meeting, it is always best to follow up with a letter just in case the resident still doesn't quite agree or understand the violation. It has been said that, for many residents, reading an enforcement letter is like swallowing medicine. A little care and understanding when drafting such communications can ease the defensive response. These letters can be warm, friendly, and to-the-point without provoking angry responses in the recipients. After all, the messenger is only doing his or her job by making sure association compliance is alive, well, and respected.

The management firm is usually the messenger, so the manager would be wise to use a warm, friendly, but firm approach when drafting these communications. Careful thought should go into them. The cold, insensitive, terse, bureaucratic-sounding violation letter may create more problems than the violation. One misguided letter can cause insurmountable problems for management.

Many management firms use form letters when addressing compliance issues. This must be expected if they work with a large portfolio of associations. However, even form letters can have a soft, personalized delivery. Avoid using sentences of all capital letters within the text. This tactic diminishes the softer, more personalized approach and can turn a neighborly resident into a tyrant.

When composing compliance enforcement letters, be sure to cover the essentials of the violation notice. Give a clear description of the alleged violation and point out which provision of the governing documents reflects the infraction. Allow a reasonable time to correct the violation. In most states, the board must inform the resident that a hearing process is available, if he or she disputes the issue.

The board of directors should know the type and style of letters that will be used when dealing with noncompliance issues. One insensitive letter can make the board of directors and/or the management firm the point of attack and turn a peaceful resident into a rebel with a cause. Don't let one normally peaceful—but now irate—resident destroy the stability your hard work has brought to the community.

The Enforcement Process. When owners are given the opportunity to hear why contacting them about the violation is necessary, their resistance is usually diminished and the problem easily corrected. The first letter should be polite, positive, and courteous. Threats and fines usually do not sit well when a member is first notified about noncompliance. If the first letter or telephone discussion does not resolve the issue, a more formal, firmer approach may be necessary.

Most communities' CC&Rs dictate a notice procedure and fine schedule for the repeat offender. A second, third, and final letter are often necessary to correct the problem. Each letter should be firmer than the preceding one. In almost every association, a small percentage of residents will ignore any letter—regardless of style. Do not punish the other 95 percent that does comply once informed.

A good managerial practice is to send a thank-you note to any offender who immediately rectifies the problem after receiving a notice. The offender's actions generally are not out of malice. He or she usually was simply not thinking about the rules or didn't even know about the rule in question. Imagine the positive responses from owners when the association's management sends a thank-you note acknowledging that the owner's respect for the rules has taken care of the problem.

If a community must send many violation notices month after month, management should determine why this is occurring. Have the members lost touch? Do they not know the governance rules? Do they not care about such rules and regulations? The board of directors should be concerned about the community's future if violations are a constant business activity.

Meeting with the members, discussing these matters, and getting their responses and solutions to solving the problems will benefit the community. Perhaps some of the governance guidelines should be modified or dropped. When community rules are largely not observed, trying to enforce them may become a losing proposition.

Records Review

Community associations' governing documents stipulate the members' rights to inspect the association's records. Most requests are legitimate and should be granted; however, some may be inappropriate and should be refused. Some requests for records are simply intended to harass the association or to collect confidential information not intended for individual members. If members have sued or plan to file a lawsuit against the association, sharing certain files could jeopardize the entire community.

The management agent may find himself or herself in conflict with a member if a request is denied. Appropriate responses to requests to review association records are vital to the association's well-being. The wise manager always asks the board of directors for approval prior to opening records to a member. It is equally important that board members know which requests to grant and which to refuse.

General Guidelines. State laws usually specify which records members must be allowed to access. Some states have specific laws forbidding the disclosure of certain information, such as a member's criminal or credit history. If your state does not specifically address this issue, use good common sense when asked to disclose records and have the board get legal advice pertinent to state statutes.

Management practitioners have identified several types of records that nearly all associations may be entitled to keep restricted or confidential. These include personnel job evaluations and disciplinary actions of association employees. The aggregate amount of total salary earnings can be shared, but individual employment records, salaries, benefits, and private files are generally considered private. Such files should only be shared with persons with a need to know, like a supervisor, board member, or management agent. Any records supplied by individual members that contain personal information outside of the association's business affairs are confidential. If a member seeks such information, that member should be asked to present some legal authority or court order allowing such perusal.

Legal Communications. Members often feel that the association attorney represents them, but that is not true. The association attorney is specifically the corporation's attorney—not the attorney of the individual board members or the general membership.

Any correspondence via letter or e-mail between the association's attorney and a member or board member is inappropriate access. Such communications are considered privileged attorney–client communications. Any recorded confidential verbal advice from the association's attorney in meeting minutes is off-limits to members. It becomes privileged anytime legal advice is sought in contemplation of a possible litigation.

Records might exist regarding discussions of a pending lawsuit that the board discussed during and/or recorded in the minutes of an executive session. Members should not be given access to such records. For example, if the board had written discussions about a member who filed a lawsuit against the association, the association would be at a disadvantage if the suing member had access to the discussions.

Contract Bids. Every association spends valuable time and energy procuring service contract bids for the community. These pending contracts are proprietary to the governance bodies involved in managing the association and should not be open for membership review. The reliability of the association's bidding process would be weakened if members were able to access this information prior to vendor selection.

Records Request Form. The association should establish an acceptable written request form that a member can use to request association records. This expedites the member's request by stipulating how much latitude the board gives the managing agent in releasing certain records.

The form should accomplish at least the following:

- Specify which records the member requests for review;
- Explain why the member requests the records;
- Define the process for inspecting such records, any related costs, the time required, and the place of review; and
- Request the member's acknowledgement of this process.

UNDERSTANDING AND BEING UNDERSTOOD

Managers and board members should assess their communication skills. Do you communicate effectively? Do others often misunderstand the ideas you try to convey? Do conversations with others often leave you perplexed—even speechless—because of the response to your communication?

Communication Case Study

Consider a hypothetical discussion with a vendor who did not provide the service you requested and paid for. In fact, his poor work will affect your management firm or board of directors' reputation in the community. This is not the sort of work you like to be associated with. When you call the vendor to find out what happened and try to reach a satisfactory resolution, you get nothing from the vendor, or perhaps the typical, "We got the project done quickly—even if it was wrong—and we didn't make a lot of money on of it anyway." The vendor in this case definitely does not see the situation from your perspective and is unwilling to offer a goodwill gesture like reducing the invoice amount. To add insult to injury, in addition to failing to offer to fix the problem, the vendor tells you that he really doesn't want projects like the one he just did for you. Then he just hangs up, leaving you speechless at the interaction and still stuck with the poor service.

This is not a new story, but it clearly highlights an example of communication not being perceived the way you thought you were delivering it. This might not only be a business scenario; it could also happen in a discussion with a community resident. Some strategies to make the vendor interaction more productive follow.

Make sure you communicate clearly. Stay open to the vendor's perspective and remain curious. Resist giving in to the temptation to assume you are right just because something is important to you. By asking several open-ended questions, you can gather important information: "How do you see this situation?" "What's most important to you in situations like this?" The more you understand about the vendor's point of view, the more realistic—and less frustrating—your conversation will be.

Making sure you and the vendor agree on the core issue (or most important result of the work expected) is paramount. If flawless quality is most important to you and the vendor places major importance on a completion date, you are already on different tracks that may never meet.

To have a less emotional conversation, rely on prior documented conversations kept on a phone log or in a day planner. Back up your opinions with facts. "In reviewing your contract, I listed certain specs and requirements. I do not see those requirements reflected in the completed work."

Do not take responsibility for the vendor's issues. In the example, he set his rates and accepted the job, so his complaints about profit are not (nor should they be) management's concern.

The old saying, "the best defense is a good offense," can be so true. Decide on your alternative course of action before making the first call. Consider the possible responses the vendor may give, and make your decision for each response. Making decisions in the heat of the moment is not good. With prior planning, a response such as, "I hear what you're saying, but that business philosophy does not match the way we like to do business. We'll have to end our relationship," is much easier to say, and you will feel more confident that it was the right decision.

Effective Communication

Many people think communication is easy; actually, talking is easy. Communication, which means an exchange or communion with another, requires much greater skill. In the community management business, managers or directors may be interacting with frustrated, angry, and fearful residents. This can create difficult situations because people are frequently less skillful communicators when caught up in such emotions.

Good communication is an acquired skill. In an *Inc.* article ("A Crash Course in Communication," August 2000), Sarah Fenson gives the following tips for learning to communicate well:

- Don't get personally caught up in another person's reaction or anger, even when being lashed out at. Another person's mood or response is more likely about fear or frustration than it is about you as an individual. This would be a good time to take ten deep breaths and let the other person have this time to vent; then maybe he or she will be able to illustrate what is really on his or her mind.
- Don't forget that most people want to feel heard rather than care about whether you agree with them. This would be a good time to show your listening attentiveness, reinforced with responses such as: *"Tell me more about your concerns." "What is it about (??????) that concerns you?" "I'm very interested in what you've said. Can you give me more detail about what led to that belief?" "What would have to happen for you to be more comfortable with (??????)?"*
- You do not have to provide all the answers. It really is OK to say, *"I don't know."* Possibly the best answer can come from working together to solve the problem.
- Remember to respond with facts and feelings; don't simply react.
- Repeat back what someone says to you. This eliminates any distortion of the message being received.
- Acknowledge inconvenience or frustration and offer a timeline to solve the problem. Be realistic with that timeline.
- Look for some common ground instead of focusing solely on differences.
- Work to keep a positive mental focus.
- Remember to understand that most people, even you, often have a self-serving agenda. This is not necessarily bad, because it does help us protect ourselves. Just don't assume that someone else will share your agenda. Discussing what's most important to each of you will build positively on any conversation.
- Work on and improve your listening skills. Most people think they listen well, but actually most people do not listen at all... they just speak and then think about what they're going to say next. Good listening often means asking good questions and clearing the mind of

> distractions, including what you are going to say next, whom you may be meeting next, or what's going on outside. Remember, when someone makes prickly comments or complaints, there's often a concern or fear lurking nearby.

Be the management detective; ask questions that find the underlying cause of the individual's real concern or agenda. Then and only then can you have a truly genuine, beneficial conversation.

7

Managing the Community Association

INTRODUCTION

So far, we've discussed the many types of community associations, the structural organization of the association, the way a *board of directors* operates, and the "dos" and "don'ts" of association meetings. In subsequent chapters, we will talk about assessment collection, insurance, and property maintenance information. Did you ever ask along the way, "Who will organize and manage all of this?" If you are a board member/director for a small association, does the thought of having to oversee all of this seem overwhelming? Our next discussion centers on the management of the community association. Some communities handle everything themselves (*self-management*), some hire on-site personnel to administer the needs of the association (*on-site management*), and others contract with professional management companies to oversee the management for them (*professional management*).

SELF-MANAGEMENT VERSUS PROFESSIONAL MANAGEMENT

When you sit back and analyze what is required to manage the affairs of the community association, the tasks can seem tremendous. The property must be kept up to maintain property values, a specific quality of life must be maintained for the residents who live in the community, and bills must be paid. The following are just a few of the management tasks an association faces:

- Schedule and conduct routine board meetings, special meetings, and annual meetings
- Enforce governing documents
- Obtain insurance and file claims
- Oversee and pay staff
- Collect *assessments* and pursue delinquent accounts
- Pay the association's bills
- Prepare financial accounting and IRS tax reports
- Maintain the structure and integrity of the physical plant (*common elements*)
- Create an annual budget of operation
- Establish reserves for future capital expenses
- Provide 24/7 emergency contact availability
- Inform the membership of the association's activities
- Maintain the association's records

Sometime in the life of the community association—usually right after the turnover meeting with the *developer*—the membership must decide who will manage the association's operations. Especially in smaller communities, the membership may decide to take care of everything and not pay an outside professional to oversee the affairs of the organization. To keep assessment payments as low as possible, these associations decide to take on the management themselves.

Self-Management

Small communities (and even larger ones) often prefer to save on operating costs by assigning specific duties/tasks to members. Perhaps a member has the skills necessary to run a business—which is exactly what a community association is. The membership might include an attorney or a certified public accountant (CPA) who could provide professional expertise to the group. The association might have a number of retired or "work from home" individuals who could volunteer some of their time to the association's operations. Community associations may also elect to self-manage when not many tasks need to be accomplished. If the homeowners association has little or no *common area* to oversee, the members may elect to attend to rules enforcement and compliance issues themselves. Such associations often collect assessments only once or twice a year, so they decide to collect assessments themselves.

The biggest issue facing community associations that decide to self-manage is the willingness of their members to serve as volunteers. Questions arise: "Who will prepare the budget?" "Who will be available 24/7 when emergencies arise?" "Who will approach the member who is violating the rules?" "Who will shop for insurance?" "Who will keep the members up-to-date on the affairs of the association?" Self-managed associations that rely strictly on volunteers often run into "burn-out" or "move-out" issues. Yes, the volunteer may get tired of doing the work or move out of the community, and the continuity of task responsibilities may suffer. I've seen many associations that have been self-managed for 5, 10, 15, or even more than 25 years. However, the minute they lose their most important volunteer(s), they are in a quandary as to who will take over the all-important task(s) that have been vacated. In addition, an abundance of historical information generally leaves with the outgoing volunteer.

Volunteer Attributes. A self-managed association relies heavily on its volunteers. What makes a good community association volunteer? The following list is adapted from "Highly Effective Volunteers," an article from Health Volunteers Overseas (www.hvousa.org; accessed November 1, 2007):

1. *Common sense.* Volunteers should know right from wrong.
2. *Desire to learn.* Nobody can know everything. Community association volunteers must want to learn the proper policies and procedures for managing the association's affairs.
3. *Good preparation.* Planning ahead of the event (e.g., a board meeting, annual meeting, or budget presentation) will prepare you for questions and concerns that may arise.
4. *Positive attitude.* Sometimes managing the community can have negative aspects. The right attitude will get the volunteer through the rough times.
5. *Patience and open-mindedness.* Not everyone in the community will like the decisions of the directors/volunteers. Manifesting tolerance will help to defuse potentially difficult situations.
6. *Respect for others.* People will treat you the way you treat them.
7. *Personal and professional integrity.* Volunteers should be reliable and accountable; they should maintain the same standard of behavior when representing the community that they do at home.

8. *Ability to communicate.* Good listening skills are invaluable. The ability to speak and write is also important when communicating with the membership.

Volunteer Job Descriptions. One way to assist members who volunteer to participate in the operations of the association is to supply volunteer job descriptions such as the one in Exhibit 7.1.

Exhibit 7.1

Sample Volunteer Job Description

Volunteer Job Description

Volunteer Category:	Community Association Volunteer
Time Commitment:	One to two hours per week; minimum of one year with potential for many more
Involvement Priorities:	Participation in the daily, monthly, and yearly business and social affairs of the association
Qualifications:	1. Sincere concern for the members of the association 2. Desire to maintain the common elements 3. Interest in the welfare of the community 4. Willingness to respond in an emergency 5. Desire to meet new people and make new friends
Knowledge, Skills, & Abilities:	1. Knowledge of the governing documents 2. Ability to make decisions for the betterment of the community 3. Ability to communicate with vendors, members, and staff as necessary—both verbally and in writing 4. Capability to work with people 5. Capacity to solve problems
Education:	Whatever the volunteer can "bring to the table" will be greatly appreciated. If additional education related to association management is necessary, the association will provide it.

On-Site Staff

Community associations must consider many issues when determining their management needs. If volunteers are lacking and if the community's finances allow, the association might consider "in-house," on-site staff or outside professional assistance. Community associations have many reasons for looking to professional assistance in taking care of their needs, including the following:

- Lack of volunteers
- Poor decisions made by volunteers
- Lack of time to oversee the association's affairs
- Lack of skills to perform necessary tasks

Very large and/or well-financed communities may opt to hire on-site personnel to manage the association's everyday affairs. The board is still accountable to the membership to ensure that tasks are accomplished in accordance with the association's governing documents. However, by having someone on-site at all times, board members can be assured that day-to-day responsibilities are addressed.

Professional Management

Another managerial option is a professional management company. Management companies have recently developed *menu-driven services*, meaning that community associations approaching them for services can choose which functions to purchase from a list of services (a *menu of services*). They may want all the services the professional management company provides (sometimes called *full management*), or they may want only one or two of the offered services. Just as an individual would choose from a menu in a restaurant and pay a determined price for that choice, associations have the option to shop for specific services from the menu of services, designing a management assistance package and a fee structure that work best for their organization.

The board may believe volunteer skills are available for most of the tasks required in community operations. However, board members may also sense that skills are lacking in some areas. For example, they might have volunteers who can handle most of the association's management tasks, but they may need to hire an outside source for processing the accounting functions. Hiring a bookkeeper or accounting firm to handle the financial needs could be a consideration. Hiring a community association attorney to assist in amending or reviewing the governing documents is also an option.

Associations decide on full-service professional management when they conclude they don't have the necessary volunteer resources and are not in need of someone on-site. According to attorney Joseph D. Douglass, Esq., of Whiteford, Prestin & Taylor, LLC, "No matter which approach is chosen, successful management depends to a very great degree on the skills, 'smarts,' resources and dedication of the actual people who do the managing." Whether the association chooses self-management, on-site professional management, or full-service professional management, the board of directors is ultimately responsible for association operations. Board members are the ones who decide which management alternative is best for the community.

THE MANAGEMENT OFFICE

Much of the discussion thus far has dealt with community association functions and organization. Just as they have specific policies and procedures for handling the operations for the community and its members, professional management offices must have a well-defined plan of action to meet the needs of the association, be successful, and grow.

The number one difference in managing community associations versus other types of property management is the ownership entity. When managing a high-rise, warehouse, shopping center, or multifamily residential community, the professional property manager generally has minimal interaction with owners and/or the ownership entity, which is usually one individual or a small investor organization. This is not the case with community associations. Even though the management agreement has very specific requirements for management's interaction with the community association, members of the association are often under the impression that the management company and the manager work directly for them personally. The manager may need to educate the members to understand just who (the board of directors) makes operational decisions for the association. Other than that, most of the property management skills necessary for all other property types (e.g., maintenance, financial) come into play when managing community associations.

Office Organization

A significant part of a management company's success depends on its organizational structure and plans of operation. The way the office is set up, files are organized, and forms are created has a great influence on how effective management will be. Structure and organization also affect the ability to attract professional managers to the firm. Managers don't want to work for a company that doesn't provide the support needed to do their jobs productively and effectively. Nothing is worse than the aggravation of disorganization, redundancy, and poor or misplaced documentation. The technology and support equipment a company uses has a dramatic effect on efficient office production.

Before designing an association management office, companies must know what community associations need. Office duties can be broken into three main categories: administrative, financial, and maintenance. Exhibit 7.2 outlines management office duties in these three areas.

To perform all required tasks and support the professional community manager, the management company needs assistant managers, maintenance coordinators, bookkeepers who can perform accounts payable and accounts receivable responsibilities, administrative assistants, and good front desk receptionists/telephone call coordinators. Some firms—especially very large ones—may have CPAs, attorneys, insurance brokers, or general contractors on staff.

Policies and Procedures

Every organization needs guidelines—the "how to," so to speak. Because of the complexities of the tasks assigned to it, the community association

---

Exhibit 7.2

Management Office Duties

Administrative

- ✔ Serve as a professional advisor in the field of association management
- ✔ Maintain records of all legal documents
- ✔ Assist in enforcement of the governing documents
- ✔ Assist with regular, special, and annual meetings
- ✔ Communicate community operations to the members
- ✔ Research appropriate insurance coverage and process claims

Financial

- ✔ Collect assessments
- ✔ Pay bills
- ✔ Provide access to the budgeting processes
- ✔ Produce financial statements
- ✔ Assist with financial auditing
- ✔ Ensure that tax forms are completed and taxes are paid as appropriate

Maintenance

- ✔ Inspect and maintain the common elements
- ✔ Oversee the bidding process for major contracts
- ✔ Negotiate contracts
- ✔ Maintain the maintenance records for common elements and individual units as appropriate

---

management company is no exception. A well-designed manual or computer file of policies and procedures will provide direction for task performance. Some areas of consideration when developing policies and procedures involve the "three *F*s": **f**loor plans, **f**iles, and **f**orms.

Floor Plans. The management company must consider many issues before it can settle on the organizational office *floor plan* that is best suited for its employees and clients. Ask the following:

- Is this a small organization with few employees, or a very large operation?
- Do clients need access to the facility?
- Do the community managers work as individual portfolio managers, doing all the tasks themselves, or are they assigned to a team, with each team member performing specifically assigned tasks?
- What equipment (e.g., phones, computers, printers) is needed to perform the various tasks? Where is the best place to put the equipment so it is easily accessible to those who use it?
- How accessible does everyone need to be? This brings up another important question: Can staff telecommute?
- What kind of budget do you have for setting up the office floor plan?
- What security measures are needed to protect the records of the associations you manage as well as the corporate records of your company?

Whether your company is in a well-established location and you have no plans to move or you are looking to begin anew, how well you design your office floor plans will affect the functionality of your operation.

Some community association management companies use the *team approach* organizational strategy. They have a community association manager, a bookkeeper, an assistant manager, and various support personnel assigned to all the same properties. This group works together as a collective team for the associations under their oversight. If this is the case, the floor plan needs to be designed so all team members have easy access to each other.

Other organizations choose to lay out their floor plans departmentally. In other words, bookkeeping, administrative, support, and property management are grouped as departments throughout the floor plan arrangement. Whatever the organizational structure, the floor plan plays a very important role.

Files. Being unable to locate paperwork and documents for the associations you manage is frustrating. To alleviate this aggravation, many community management companies store most of their important files electronically—either within their own computer systems or with an offsite service. Web services can store and distribute when necessary all of the association's governing documents, board meeting minutes, budgets, resolutions, and other important information.

Electronic or Paper Files. *Historical data* (data over one year old) are generally stored in folders in file cabinets or in electronic files. The following outline suggests one possible way to organize the management company's files—whether electronic or paper:

1. Property Title
2. Declarations
3. Articles of Incorporation
4. Bylaws
5. House Rules & Regulations
6. Resolutions
7. Management Contract
8. Board Meeting Agendas and Minutes
9. Association Manager's Reports
10. Annual Meetings
    a. Notices
    b. Agendas
    c. Sign-in Sheets
    d. Minutes
11. Budgets from Year to Year
12. Delinquency Reports
13. Operating Statements (Financial Statements)
14. Insurance
15. Maintenance/Contracts
16. Board Correspondence
17. Association Correspondence
18. Legal Matters

19. Unit Files
20. E-mails

The Association Manager's Binder. The *binder* generally contains the current year's operations and "immediate access" information. It is designed so the association manager can grab it and take it to a board meeting. This binder can also be developed in an electronic format. Indexes for the binders should be typed as follows:

1. Current Association Correspondence
2. Current Board Correspondence
3. Projects (with dividers for Bid Requests, Proposals Received, and Proposals Accepted)
4. Budget
5. Assessments
6. Board Meeting Agendas and Minutes
7. Property Manager's Reports
8. Annual Meeting Agenda and Minutes
9. On-Site Contracts
10. Insurance
11. Taxes
12. Management Agreement
13. Inspections
14. Homeowner Lists/Maps
15. Declarations/Amendments
16. Articles
17. Bylaws
18. Rules & Regulations
19. Board Resolutions

Record Retention. Another important factor related to files is the length of time the association must retain certain records. The guidelines shown in Exhibit 7.3 are from a January 2003 *Association Times* article titled "Record Retention." It lists the most common business records for a corporation and the length of time recommended for the storage of such records.

Exhibit 7.3
Recommended Record Retention Periods

Accounting Records	Retention Period
Accounts payable	7 years
Accounts receivable	7 years
Audit reports	Permanent
Chart of accounts	Permanent
Depreciation schedules	Permanent
Expense records	7 years
Financial statements (annual)	Permanent
Fixed asset purchases	Permanent
General ledger	Permanent
Inventory records	7 years
Loan payment schedules	7 years
Tax returns	Permanent
Bank Records	**Retention Period**
Bank reconciliations	2 years
Bank statements	7 years
Cancelled checks	7 years
Electronic payment records	7 years
Corporate Records	**Retention Period**
Board minutes	Permanent
Bylaws, articles, covenants, conditions, and restrictions (CC&Rs)	Permanent
Board resolutions	Permanent
Business licenses	Permanent
Contracts—major	Permanent

(continued)

Exhibit 7.3 ***(Continued)***

Contracts—minor	Life + 4 years
Insurance policies	Life + 4 years
Leases/mortgages	Permanent
Patents/trademarks	Permanent
Bids, proposals	Permanent
Homeowner records	Permanent
Employee Records	**Retention Period**
Benefit plans	Permanent
Employee files (ex-employees)	7 years
Employment applications	3 years
Employment taxes	7 years
Payroll records	7 years
Pension/profit sharing plans	Permanent
Real Property Records	**Retention Period**
Construction records	Permanent
Leasehold improvements	Permanent
Lease payment records	Life + 4 years
Real estate purchases	Permanent

A last word of caution regarding files: Whatever you do, be consistent. Such practices as filing new information in the front or back of the folder, filing by address or lot number, or color-coding files will help the people who support you or come after you to find what they need. As trivial as they may seem, write these processes into your organization's policies and procedures.

Forms. Having well-designed forms throughout the company accomplishes two purposes: (1) accuracy of information and (2) timeliness of information. In the course of day-to-day business, we learn what we need to do our jobs effectively. Forms are the result of that learning. Community association management companies have forms for nearly every function:

- *Administrative forms.* Marketing, Association Transition, Property Profile, Insurance, Resale and Transfer, Management Agreements (Exhibit 7.4 is an example of an administrative form.)
- *Accounting forms.* Banking, Charting, New Owner, Collection Policy (Exhibit 7.5 shows a sample accounting form.)
- *Maintenance forms.* Work Orders, Vendor Agreements, Purchase Orders, Inspection Reports, Requests for Proposals, Budgets (Exhibit 7.6 is a sample maintenance form.)
- *Association forms.* Sign-in Sheets, Architectural Control Committee (ACC), Ballots, Compliance, Homeowner Lists, Site Maps (Exhibit 7.7 shows a sample association form.)

Staffing

A community association management company is only as good as its support staff. The staff supports the management company and the professional manager who is responsible to the association. When boards interview new management companies, they look closely at staffing considerations. Board members will ask about the number of properties the company manages, and then they'll ask about the ratio of support staff to properties managed. No formula can determine specifically what that ratio should be. Each community has unique requirements. Every management company designs its particular "organization of efficiency." The task for the management company is to convince the prospective client that the company's organizational structure can fulfill the wants, needs, and desires of the particular association.

When interviewing, community associations want to know the proposed association manager will have the support needed to do a good job for the association. At a very minimum, boards expect the association management company to have staff support for bookkeeping, maintenance and contract negotiation, and membership communications. As mentioned earlier, if the community is large, the board may even expect an attorney, paralegal, CPA, technology expert, or insurance advisor on staff. On-site management situations require a support structure similar to the management company's structure.

The management company should create job descriptions for the duties and tasks of each of its support positions. Develop policies and procedures to detail the way the employee accomplishes assigned duties

Exhibit 7.4

Sample Administrative Form

Association Management Set-Up Information

Account #: __________ Association Name: ______________ Date: ____________________

Type: Condominium/Home/Planned Urban Development (PUD)

Web Site: ____

Manager Assigned: ____

No. of Div.: _____________ # Lots/Units: ________ # of Buildings: ________________

Management Fee per Lot/Unit: $____________ Monthly Rate: $____________________

First Month Prorated? Yes / No If yes, how much: $______________________________

Tax ID #: ____

Bank Account to Open: [ ] Checking [ ] Savings [ ] CD [ ] Other: _________________

Checking #: _________________ Maintenance Reserve: ________________________

Insurance Reserve: _____________________ Other: ______________________________

Board of Directors:

President: ____________________________ HM: ____________ WK: ______________

Mailing Address: ______________________________________ Cell: _______________

E-mail Address: ____________________________________ Term Expires: ___________

Vice President: _________________________ HM: ____________ WK: _____________

Mailing Address: ______________________________________ Cell: _______________

E-mail Address: ____________________________________ Term Expires: ___________

Secretary: ____________________________ HM: ____________ WK: ______________

Mailing Address: ______________________________________ Cell: _______________

E-mail Address: ____________________________________ Term Expires: ___________

Treasurer: ___________________________ HM: ____________ WK: _______________

Mailing Address: ______________________________________ Cell: _______________

E-mail Address: ____________________________________ Term Expires: ___________

MAL (Member at Large): ____________________________ HM: _________WK: ________

Mailing Address: ______________________________________ Cell: _______________

E-mail Address: ____________________________________ Term Expires: ___________

Exhibit 7.5

Sample Accounting Form

Assessments and Fine Charges Policies

Account #: ____________Association: ____________________________________

Dues: ____________________ Annually____ Semi-Annually ____ Monthly ______________

Coupon Ordering Date: ____

Payment Due Dates: ____

Special Assessments

Amount: $ ________ Billing to Begin: ___________ Due Date: ________________________

Billing to End: ____

Cause for Assessment: ____

Deposit/Capital Contribution Amount: $ _________________________________

Late Fee Policy

Flat Fee Amount: $ __________after _________ days

One-Time Interest: ________% after _________ days

Annual Interest Charges: _________% after _________ days

Authority Found: CC&Rs Article: _____________ Section: _____________________

Board Resolution: ____________ Posted: __________________________

General Rules Article: ________ Rule Number: _____________________

Standard Delinquency Notice:

First Notice to Be Sent: ____________________________________

Second Notice to Be Sent: ___________________________________

Sent to Attorney for Lien: ___________________________________

Attorney of Record: ____

Mailing Address: ____

Phone Number: ____

Exhibit 7.6

Sample Maintenance Form

Inspection Report

Property Name: ____________________

Date of Inspection: ____________________ Time: ____________________

Address: ____________ UNIT/LOT ____ Violation _____ Repair____________
List Repair/Violation: ____________________

____

Address: ____________ UNIT/LOT ____ Violation _____ Repair____________
List Repair/Violation: ____________________

____

Address: ____________ UNIT/LOT ____ Violation _____ Repair____________
List Repair/Violation: ____________________

____

Address: ____________ UNIT/LOT ____ Violation _____ Repair____________
List Repair/Violation: ____________________

____

Address: ____________ UNIT/LOT ____ Violation _____ Repair____________
List Repair/Violation: ____________________

____

Address: ____________ UNIT/LOT ____ Violation _____ Repair____________
List Repair/Violation: ____________________

____

Address: ____________ UNIT/LOT ____ Violation _____ Repair____________
List Repair/Violation: ____________________

____

Address: ____________ UNIT/LOT ____ Violation _____ Repair____________
List Repair/Violation: ____________________

____

Address: ____________ UNIT/LOT ____ Violation _____ Repair____________
List Repair/Violation: ____________________

____

Exhibit 7.6 *(Continued)*

Address: ____________________ UNIT/LOT ____ Violation _____ Repair_________________

List Repair/Violation: ____

____

Address: ____________________ UNIT/LOT ____ Violation _____ Repair_________________

List Repair/Violation: ____

____

Address: ____________________ UNIT/LOT ____ Violation _____ Repair_________________

List Repair/Violation: ____

____

Address: ____________________ UNIT/LOT ____ Violation _____ Repair_________________

List Repair/Violation: ____

____

Letters Sent:____________ Bids Requested: ____________ Repairs Ordered: ____________

PM Initials: ____

and tasks. Exhibit 7.8 shows one style of job description for accounts receivable (A/R) that includes job duties and suggested procedures to accomplish them.

Exhibit 7.9 shows another sample job description for accounts payable, with a slightly different format than the A/R example in Exhibit 7.8. This job description defines duties and tasks—and provides the procedures for performing them—in more detail than did the A/R job description. Keep in mind that the company procedural manual should define procedures even more thoroughly.

Management companies should consider developing job descriptions—and the policies and procedures that go with them—for all their staff members. Additional positions not previously discussed that need job descriptions and definitions include the professional association manager, the receptionist, the office manager, the assistant to the manager(s), the maintenance coordinator, and any other support position the company has in place to perform its obligations to the community association.

Staffing Alternatives

As previously discussed, the situation may arise in which a management company chooses to perform all management functions under a single,

Exhibit 7.7

Sample Association Form

Architectural Control Committee Application
Homeowners Association

An approval by the Architectural Control Committee (ACC) of any fence, shed, color change, barn, deck, or other exterior structure or home modification is required before work can begin. This form is the application for approval. Please return this form to the Association Management Office.

Community Name: ______________________________ Lot #: ____________________________

Owner: ____

Address: ____________________________________ Unit #: ___________________________

Mailing Address: ____

____

Telephone: ____

Date: ___/_____/____

(A) Project Description/Lease Rental Information: ____________________________

____

____

____

____

____

____

Present Style: ____

Proposed Style: ____

Present Colors: Main: ____________ Trim: _________________ Accent: _______________

Proposed Colors: Main: ____________ Trim: _________________ Accent: _______________

(B) The exterior finish materials and color (chip for paint to be applied), including roof materials.

Present Material(s): ____

Proposed Material(s): ____

Roofing Material(s): ____

Overall Size: ____

Height: ___________________ Depth: ___________________ Width: ___________________

Exhibit 7.7 ***(Continued)***

(C) Landscape Plan: ______________________________

Other Details of Project: ______________________________

____

Applicant's Signature: ______________________________

Dated this ________ day of ____________, 20___.

ACC RECOMMENDATION: ______________________________

____

____

Also note and include drawings, brochures, and practical samples. All paint requests require paint cards/samples to be included. Moderate hand drawings can be done on back of form and indicated above, but must be legible. A copy will be mailed back to you for your records. If plan specifications are approved, you have 60 days to complete the work. (All fences must be built according to the standard fence detail.)

Signature of Homeowner: ______________________________

Proposed Start/Completion Dates: ____/____/____ TO ____/____/____

Allow 14 days for Committee/Board response, per the CC&Rs

ACC COMMITTEE ONLY

ACC Recommendations: (CIRCLE ONE) APPROVED DENIED

ACC MEMBER'S SIGNATURE: ____________________

ACC MEMBER'S SIGNATURE: ____________________

monthly *full management* fee. Bookkeeping, maintenance, correspondence, and professional manager support are grouped together, and associations pay a standard price. Other management companies take the *menu of services* approach to the services they provide, allowing clients to choose which functions they want to purchase.

A few management companies believe the professional community manager they hire should be capable of performing *all* the functions needed to manage their communities. Needless to say, the manager who keeps the books, writes the letters, attends the meetings, writes the manager's report, inspects the community, and coordinates the maintenance will not be able to handle as many communities as one who has support staff to perform those functions. Management companies may have difficulty finding someone who thoroughly understands the duties and tasks of all those assignments, and such individuals generally demand a much larger salary.

Exhibit 7.8

Accounts Receivable Job Description

Accounts Receivable

Description of Duties:

- Make Bank Deposits
  - Hand Deposits—Dues assessments occasionally come into the office. Process them just as you would other bank deposits.
  - Lock Box Deposits
  - Reserve Deposits
  - File all three
- Handle Returned Mail—Research all returned mail for the associations and file information.
- Submit Short Form Questionnaires for Escrow—Fill out the paperwork, fax back to Escrow Company, and file.
  - Serve as backup on Resale Certificates as well.
  - Move Association Members' escrow papers in and out of unit files, process escrow checks to the Association or Corporate Bookkeeper, make copies, and file.
  - Send out New Owner letters with temporary coupons, make copies, and mail.
  - Charge dues to all Association Members at the beginning of the month.
  - Receive phone calls regarding customer concerns about their account balances, dues, address changes, etc.
- Charge delinquencies and run reports for Property Managers (PMs)—After PM approval, run statements, copy the report for both the PM's file and the Accounts Receivable (A/R) file, and mail.
- After Escrow has closed, initiate refunds to the Association Member, process the report, and provide for Accounts Payable.
- Take voice mail messages from the Delinquency "Hot Line" and return calls within one business day.
- Support the Property Managers when they have questions about Accounts Receivable accounts.
- Process Automated Clearing House (ACH) accounts—Maintain spreadsheets, provide a Corporate Bookkeeper with the report, enter ACH payments in the system, and file.
- Serve as backup on phones—Condo/HOA Support is the main backup, but at times this position must serve as backup as well.
- File all A/R paperwork in the appropriate folders.
- Reconcile bank statements.

Exhibit 7.9

Accounts Payable Job Description

Accounts Payable

Enter Payables into the System. Make notes of anything important, such as account numbers or invoice numbers, as needed. Put invoices into the correct folders with a list of payables for the managers to approve or disapprove. Print checks and return to the managers to review. Print all recurring charges first (e.g., Management Fees, Delinquency Fees).

Check Monthly Financials. Print all reports, put them in order, check for accuracy, and make a copy for the manager to check for accuracy. Research and correct financials as needed by comparing the financial report that was mailed to the board with the computer version and checking for changes. Check for single checks. Check for double deposits. Make necessary corrections and explain to the manager so he or she can explain to the board.

Run Year-End Financials. Year-end financials should be run in January as soon as the December bank reconciliations are complete. The dates for the year-ends are generally from January 1 to December 31 of the closing year. Check against December to be sure ending balances are the same. Copy and store the year-end financials in the current year's financial book for reference and to have on hand for audits. Provide them to the manager to write the account's year-end summary.

Set Up New Associations. Complete the "Association Management Set-Up Information" form when a new association comes on board. All the information needed to set up a new account is on that checklist:

- Tax ID# to open the checking account
- Association number
- Number of units/lots
- Amount of monthly or annual fees
- Amount of management fee

This form also tells you whether the management company must open a reserve account or CDs for the association. Open Lockbox and ACH accounts (if necessary). Add units for the new associations. Add owners into the system.

Prepare Budget Spreadsheets. Using August's year-to-date actuals, create an Excel spreadsheet for the managers to take to their boards. The spreadsheet should include the present year's budget, previous year's budget, and the previous year's actual year-to-date figures. These spreadsheets serve as worksheets for the board and the association manager. Maintain these worksheets from year to year.

Enter Budgets. Budgets generally are created once a year. Occasionally, associations make changes midyear due to shortages in their budgets. Update them when necessary.

Track Miscellaneous Information on Spreadsheets

1. Ledgers
2. Insurance expenses
3. Reserve accounts
4. Multiple bills from utility companies

(continued)

Exhibit 7.9 ***(Continued)***

Meet with Boards on Financials. Assist the boards in understanding their financial reports. Explain accrual- versus cash-basis accounting.

Prepare Payroll. Enter payroll into the system, prepare the quarterly payroll taxes, and make quarterly deposits for the taxes.

Organize Income Tax Information. Match 1099s as received to bank statements for interest earned. Print out the balance sheet for the year end, make copies of all 1099s and yearend bank statements if needed. Staple them all together for the auditor who will do the actual tax paperwork.

Add Vendors. Enter new vendors into the system. Contact the vendors as needed for information, such as tax ID numbers or Social Security numbers, so they can be paid. Verify that each vendor has provided all appropriate paperwork, including the vendor agreement with signatures, insurance information, and a license copy.

Add and Close Bank Accounts. Set up new bank accounts in the system. Close old bank accounts as needed.

Take Phone Calls from Vendors and Homeowners. Research vendors' and members' accounts so you can explain any concerns they may have.

Research and Return Members' Credit Balances. Conduct a thorough investigation for all apparent credit balances. Contact homeowners to determine if they want a refund or to leave the credit balance.

Another staffing alternative that community association management companies use is the outsourcing of some of the services provided to their associations. They may choose to subcontract the accounting, payroll, staffing, and maintenance services. More often than not, smaller management companies use this arrangement. These companies can provide very qualified professional management services. They just spend their time in the professional manager's role and leave the other management functions to the subcontractors they hire. Generally, associations still pay a flat monthly fee to the management company for this arrangement.

Turnovers and Transitions

Community associations choose to hire and fire management companies all the time. Management companies sometimes decide to dismiss associations for which they work. It works both ways. What constitutes a good or bad community association client? Exhibit 7.10 compares traits that make good and bad clients for an association management company.

Exhibit 7.10

Comparison of Association Traits

GOOD

- The board understands that its position is to represent the best interests of the association at all times and make appropriate business decisions.
- The board is prepared for meetings and all interactions with the association's membership.
- The board makes financial decisions that are in the best interests of its members.
- The board recognizes the professional experience of its manager and consults with the manager on matters pertaining to the association.

BAD

- The board/association fails to listen to or accept the recommendations and advice of the management company and its professional manager.
- The board makes decisions contradictory to the association's governing documents.
- The board wants to micromanage the manager and other support staff.
- The board makes financial choices that could harm the association.
- The board and its members perform actions or behaviors that are contradictory to federal, state, or local laws.
- The board fails to stop harassment of the professional manager by its association members or board members.

Community associations may also look for a change of professional management services for many reasons. Contrary to what many may believe, contract pricing is not the main reason community associations look for new management—even though it is often mentioned when an association leaves a firm. There is no easy answer. Frequently, association members may feel they have not gotten the service for which they originally contracted. Perhaps the professional manager no longer returns phone calls in a timely manner or does not respond to maintenance requests as needed. The board may have been receiving inaccurate accounts of the association's financial matters. When a board of directors and its membership start feeling they are doing the work of the professional manager, they start looking for someone else to help with the association's affairs. Sometimes, the association may want to align itself with a company it believes to be more in tune with the most up-to-date services (e.g., accounting software, Web sites, other technology). Therefore, association members may feel they need to look for a management firm that offers such services.

Management companies should establish policies and procedures regarding the turnover/transition of associations. The management agreement should outline the processes necessary to cancel a contract. The procedure should provide a timeline for closing the account and turning over all of the association's records to the association itself or to the new management firm. Whenever an association is transitioning into the firm or leaving the firm, a formal checklist helps ensure that nothing is overlooked in the process, as displayed in Exhibit 7.11.

The checklist in Exhibit 7.11 serves two purposes: (1) to verify that that you requested all the pertinent information for managing the association, and (2) to organize the receipt of the materials. This transition checklist can be modified when the management company turns over an association's records. An important issue with the turnover checklist is to be sure the former management company receives a signed receipt from the person who picks up the check and records. This serves as evidence that the turnover has been handled appropriately.

PROFESSIONAL COMMUNITY MANAGERS

According to Bulletin 2600 of the U.S. Department of Labor's Bureau of Labor Statistics (last modified December 20, 2005):

> Developments of new homes increasingly are being organized with community or homeowners associations that provide community services and oversee jointly owned common areas requiring professional management.... To help properties become more profitable or to enhance the resale values of homes... property owners are expected to place their investment in the hands of professional managers.

The bulletin goes on to state, "Opportunities should be best for those with a college degree in business administration, real estate, or a related field or for those who attain a professional designation." In a 2005 survey conducted by Zogby International for The Foundation for Community Association Research, more than half (52 percent) of the associations interviewed said they had a professional manager for their community association, and 80 percent of respondents said the manager provided value and support. Also according to the survey, those who had interacted with their managers felt that 90 percent of the interactions were positive.

According to an *Association Times* article ("Wanted, Community Association Managers") published in January 2006, the National Association of Home Builders (NAHB; www.nahb.org) projected that 25,000 new community associations would be formed in 2006 and 2007. This would in turn generate

Exhibit 7.11

Sample Transition Checklist

ASSOCIATION TRANSITION

The following documents and information are requested for transition to ABC Management. Please indicate each item furnished.

Please issue an initial check in the amount of $500.00 made payable to: **Your Association. This will be used to open a new operating checking account.**

ASSOCIATION DOCUMENTS

- ❑ Declaration and Bylaws
- ❑ Plat, Site Map(s) (Common/Limited Common Areas, Parking Assignments, etc.)
- ❑ Building Plans, As-Built Plans, Occupancy Permit, etc.
- ❑ Articles of Incorporation
- ❑ House Rules and Regulations and Board Resolutions
- ❑ Late Charge Policy
- ❑ Move In/Out or Change of Occupancy Fee Policy
- ❑ Date of Transition from Declarant/Developer: ______________________________
- ❑ Fine/Fee Schedule & Policy (Move-In Fee, Late Charge, etc.)
- ❑ Minutes of Meetings (Homeowners' and Board Meetings)
- ❑ Resale Certificate Files
- ❑ Eligible Mortgagee Folder/List
- ❑ Current Contracts (Landscaping, Janitorial, Fire/Life Safety, Pest Control, etc.)
- ❑ Employee Records
- ❑ Equipment Inventory List Owned by Association
- ❑ Insurance Information (Company, Agent, Copy of Declaration Page, Including Endorsements)
- ❑ Site Plan of Master Shut-off(s) (Water, Sprinkler, Gas, etc.)
- ❑ Any and All Other Association Records and Files in Your Custody

UNIT INFORMATION

- ❑ Ownership Roster Including Unit Number, Owner and Occupant/Tenant Information, Mailing Addresses, Phone Numbers, etc.
- ❑ List of Assigned Parking and Applicable Use Fees
- ❑ List of Assigned Storage Lockers and Applicable Use Fees

(continued)

Exhibit 7.11 ***(Continued)***

- ❑ Report of Monthly Unit Assessments—Regular and Special
- ❑ Percentage of Ownership for Each Unit
- ❑ Unit Account Ledgers—Balance, Including History of Credits and Charges
- ❑ Unit Files—Rule Violations, Communications, etc.

ACCOUNTING AND FINANCIAL INFORMATION

- ❑ Federal Tax ID Number: ______________________________
- ❑ Corporate Name: ___________________________________
- ❑ Financial Statements/Reports for Previous Year(s)
- ❑ Copy of Most Recent Audit and Annual Financial Report of Prior Fiscal/Calendar Year
- ❑ Tax Return(s)
- ❑ Federal Tax Deposit Payment Coupons
- ❑ Current Budget
- ❑ Balance(s) and Information Concerning Any Special Assessments—Current or within Previous Year
- ❑ Replacement Reserve Analysis Report
- ❑ Replacement Fund Bank Statements, Signature Card Information, Certificate of Deposit Information
- ❑ Operating Account Statement(s), Checkbooks, Signature Card Information
- ❑ Assessor's Personal and Real Property Tax Affidavits
- ❑ Payroll Information and Records, Including Name, Address, Phone Numbers, Social Security No., W-4, I-9, Rate of Pay Information, Job Description
- ❑ Final Income and Expense Reports for Prior Fiscal/Calendar Year

GENERAL RECORDS AND VENDOR ACCOUNT INFORMATION

- ❑ Originals or Copies of All Association Records and Files, Including All Current Contracts, Current Correspondence, and Other Current Activity
- ❑ Legal File, Including Any Current or Recent Past Litigation Issue(s)
- ❑ Complete Information for All Utilities, Maintenance Vendors, and Contract Vendors, Including Contact Name(s), Phone Number(s), Addresses, etc.
- ❑ File of All Insurance Claims in the Past Three Years, Including Disposition (Pending, Type, and Amount of Claim(s)
- ❑ Keys to Buildings, Common Areas, and Facilities

Exhibit 7.11 ***(Continued)***

Include any additional and pertinent information that will help in this transition and specify any ***matters needing immediate attention.***

Please facilitate the closing of the Operating Checking Account(s). Please forward a check made payable to the Association c/o this office to close the Operating Checking Account.

Please contact this office when these items are ready for pickup.

THANK YOU FOR YOUR HELP IN THIS TRANSITION.

Sincerely,

ABC Management

a need for approximately 2,500 new community managers. As of 2006, many regions of the United States were already experiencing severe shortages of professional association managers. Contributing to the need for professional managers is the changing demographic population. The aging population will want the convenience afforded by living in a community association.

The Role of the Professional Community Manager

Every community association has specific wants, needs, and desires. Just as associations hire attorneys to interpret and/or modify their governing documents and CPAs to handle their financial matters, they look to professional community managers as consultants to help with their everyday operations.

What do associations look for in professional managers? Good managers have excellent people skills. They know how to motivate and invigorate. Their ability to listen highlights their communication skills. A positive attitude in an oftentimes negative environment will get them through the day, and an ability to stay organized will keep them from drowning.

Duties of the Professional Community Manager Community association management must often be customized to the particular community. Even so, the duties and job functions of the professional community manager are nearly universal—no matter what the assignment. Community association managers frequently perform the following duties:

- Maintain communication with the board, association members, and vendors

- Welcome new members
- Verify and code payables
- Ensure bills are paid
- Disburse payments and attachments to vendors
- Check monthly financial statements for accuracy
- Respond to letters from association members
- Maintain a log of all calls from association members
- Maintain files for each member in the association
- Advise the board of directors of anything that may be an issue in the future
- Advise the board as to the governing documents
- Refer the board to other professional advisors (e.g., attorneys, CPAs, engineers)
- Send notices of annual meetings
- Establish a rough draft budget for the board to use in finalizing the annual budget
- Implement budget policy
- Interview, hire, supervise, and terminate association employees, when pertinent
- Send out compliance letters for violations of the CC&Rs
- Ensure proper notice of dues and statements
- Maintain records for the association
- Process initial ACC applications
- Notify homeowners of ACC application approvals and denials
- Assist the association in collection of delinquencies, liens, and foreclosures
- Assist in association mailings
- Negotiate contracts—with board approval
- Monitor contract vendors, such as landscapers and custodial services
- Contract and monitor needed common area repairs

- Handle emergency situations
- Research governing documents, state laws, federal laws, count records, and FCC guidelines for the board of directors

In a nutshell, community association managers don't have to know everything, but they certainly must know a little about a whole lot! Boards hire professional managers to act as a third party in many of the association's functions. Board members often have difficulty confronting noncompliant neighbors in the community—especially because they may live right next door. To a certain extent, professional community managers can insulate the board. However, all final decisions and directions must come from the association's board of directors.

Misconceptions about the Community Manager's Duties. Misconceptions abound as to what the professional community manager does and does not do. These misunderstandings come from both association members and the board of directors. Let's look at what the professional manager does *not* do:

- *Act as a peacemaker.* The manager is often asked to step in and oversee or negotiate membership disputes. Certainly if whatever caused the dispute is a violation of the governing documents, the manager, under the direction of the board, can write letters or assess fines. However, there is no reason for the manager to step in and negotiate a solution just because two members can't get along.
- *Advise on legal matters.* Issues that require legal advice frequently come before the association. The manager advises the board when he or she feels an attorney must be consulted on an issue. Boards should never ask the professional community manager for legal advice, and the manager should never feel free to give it (unless that manager is an attorney, of course).
- *Be available 24/7.* Many community members and board members feel they should be able to pick up the phone, walk into the management office, or talk to the manager anytime they please. *Note:* Professional community managers have lives outside their secular jobs. A well-organized management company has a system in place to address the association's emergency needs. Otherwise, a good rule of thumb is for the manager to return all phone calls within 24 hours or at a specific time each day. This is true even for on-site managers; they like scheduled appointments—just like everyone else.

- *Be on-site whenever contractors are at the property.* Unless they are on-site managers, community association managers usually have oversight of more than one community. They become very skilled at assigning their available time. Most management contracts do not require the manager to be at the site every time a contractor is working there. A good policy would be to meet initially with the contractor and a board representative, go over the "rules of engagement," check periodically, and perform a final inspection—again with a board representative. Some management contracts allow for a project management fee for extensive involvement on the part of the community manager.

- *Report to individual association members.* Many members feel they can tell their association's manager what to do, how to do it, and when to do it. They have the mistaken impression that "the manager works for me, and I have every right to tell him or her what to do." The management contract is with the board of directors, not with the individual members. Members should address their concerns to the board of directors. The same is true of the individual board members. The management contract usually specifies the establishment of a board liaison who will take the matters of the board to the manager.

Certifications and Designations

Most professions have certification and/or designation programs that identify individuals who excel at what they do for a living. Association management is no different. Upon receipt of the following credentials, professional association managers have demonstrated that they meet specific educational, experiential, and ethical standards for the industry:

- *Certified Manager of Community Associations (CMCA).* This professional has demonstrated a fundamental knowledge in the management of community associations.

- *Association Management Specialist (AMS).* This manager has demonstrated professional competence by having two years' experience managing the finances, administration, and facilities of at least one association.

- *Professional Community Association Manager (PCAM).* This designation requires much more educational and management experience as well as the completion of a case study.

- *Certified Property Manager (CPM).* This designation identifies the recipient as a real estate management professional.

SUPPORT EQUIPMENT

Thus far, we have discussed the human factors needed to manage the business affairs of a community association. As we know today, nothing is accomplished in business without the proper equipment. Just as no two communities or no two management companies are alike, so will their support equipment needs not be the same. However, the basics are standard: everyone needs phones, copy and fax machines, mail-processing machines, computers, monitors, and printers.

Phone Systems

If you've ever been to an association management company in the middle of the day, you know the phones never stop ringing. Calls pour in from vendors, association boards and members, legal advisors, financial consultants, and an occasional friend or relative. A phone system must be in place to handle the load of phone calls the firm receives and initiates daily. The phone system should be designed to improve communication over the telephone and through the Internet. Conveniences such as three-way calling, call forwarding, "Do Not Disturb," voice mail, call waiting, caller ID, and transfer capabilities are necessities for any business phone system. Another important consideration is the speed with which the company can access the Internet, which precipitates the choice among T-1, broadband, DSL, and dial-up connections.

Many small companies increasingly choose *voice over Internet protocol (VoIP)* packages instead of conventional telephone systems. The greater versatility and cost savings of VoIP allow businesses to tailor packages specifically to meet their needs without spending heavily on communications equipment or maintaining an information technology (IT) staff. All that's needed is a broadband connection and VoIP to create a low-cost, professional telephone system—even for companies with as few as three employees. Another important advantage of VoIP is that it dispenses with the need for a phone call router, possibly saving the cost of a full-time employee. Systems can route incoming calls to the appropriate department or person.

Copiers and Fax Machines

A firm's need for copying and faxing depends on the volume of paperwork it processes. Smaller companies can get by with stand-alone desktop machines at staff members' workstations. Larger companies handling large communities need machines able to generate thousands of copies a month. These large units are multifunctional. They not only copy but also print, duplex (print on both sides of the paper), scan, fax, and even e-mail. The more advanced models can sort, staple, punch holes, and saddle stitch the large reports they produce. These machines are generally placed in a central location and can be configured to work from multiple workstations throughout the building. Providing black and white or color copies for clients is a decision the management company must make.

For a price, association management companies can have just about any type of copier or fax machine they want. Highly advanced models are very expensive. However, most office machine companies will set up loans or leasing arrangements for the equipment they sell. If your firm needs to finance the equipment, thoroughly analyzing the contract is imperative. Know what your company is getting into! Copiers have the ability to track the number of copies produced for different associations—a feature that can help recover some of the loan/lease expenses. Leases have cancellation and automatic renewal clauses as well as maintenance agreements. Both leases and loans come with financing expenses, as with buying or leasing a car.

Postage Meters

Management companies send out copious amounts of mail. This calls for a postage meter. Selecting the best meter for your company's needs can take a lot of time. According to the buyer's guide on the BuyerZone Web site (www.buyerzone.com; accessed December 19, 2006), one should ask these basic questions before purchasing a postage meter:

- How much does my office spend on postage each month?
- How many pieces of mail does my office send on both an average and a busy day?
- Does my office send mostly standard letters or a variety of packages of different weights?

The answers to these questions will help in the selection of the piece of equipment with the appropriate features for your company's needs.

Postage meters themselves cannot be bought. Under federal statute, they can only be leased. The bases they sit on can be purchased, but generally they are leased along with the meters. The postage meter will feed, sort, seal, and stack the mail. Additional options that may be available are password-protected access and accounting codes. These options are essential to track the postage for different associations and charge that cost back to the appropriate association (just like copying charges). Scales can be attached to the meter to weigh heavier pieces. Service contracts are a part of the meter leasing agreement.

Information Technology

There is no such thing as operating without information technology in today's business world. This was not true 20 years ago. But today, "you can't live with it and you can't live without it." The management company must consider the size and quantity of its associations as well as the quality of its services when contemplating its technology needs. An outside resource is often needed to assist in this process. Large management companies have IT personnel on staff. Community associations and their boards shop for firms that make conducting business as convenient as possible. They also often like the "bells and whistles."

The association management company must ask itself the following questions:

- Can my client send and receive e-mail on a consistent basis?
- Does the staff have the ability to communicate effectively with each other and with clients?
- How easily can my existing and potential customers find and use our company's services?
- What storage capacity is needed for the association's information and the company's data?
- To what extent is outside access required?
- What format should the management company's operating system take to service the client?
- Are staff members provided the proper tools to do their jobs?

Once the company answers these basic questions, it can generate an information technology plan for its operations. The plan must be flexible because, as we know, technology changes at a faster pace than most people manage. Association management companies must invest in good IT systems and programs. The client/customer expects them to keep up with the latest in equipment and applications. At a CEO retreat for community association management companies, it was stated that approximately 5 to 10 percent of a firm's total income is spent on technology and related services. To be competitive, it is vital that association management companies budget for continual changes and upgrades to their information technology plans.

8

Keeping the Books

INTRODUCTION

Keeping track of the money is the number one task members of a community association (*common interest development*) ask the board of directors and the professional manager to perform. Members pay their assessments in good faith, and they expect those in charge to keep an account of what has been collected and what has been paid. They want to know that the market values of their real estate investments are being protected.

The association treasurer has primary oversight for the community's accounting functions and financial records. However, all board members should have a rudimentary understanding of the way the money flows into and out of the community. The board is responsible for protecting the association's money, thus board members must control the community's banking, auditing, and investment strategies. The professional manager of the community association is also entrusted with safeguarding the community's financial interests. Managers can make or break their professional reputations based on the effectiveness of their financial reports to the board.

In the life of the community association, operations may call for funding the association does not have. Due to such shortfalls in finances, the association may need to shop for money. This chapter addresses the process of saving money (reserve funding) so shortfalls are unlikely to occur; however, just in case they do, the chapter also discusses how to shop for money (secure a loan).

ACCOUNTING TERMS

Financial accounting has a terminology all its own. To perform every phase of financial tracking and reporting, the board, the treasurer, and the professional manager should first become familiar with accounting terminology. Some basic accounting terms are explained below. Rather than appearing in alphabetical order, they are presented in logical groupings.

- *Accounting*. The process of recording, classifying, reporting, and analyzing financial data. While the accounting requirements of businesses vary, all organizations need a way to keep track of their money. Businesses use three accounting methods:

  1. *Cash basis*. Income (*revenue*) is recognized when cash is received and deposited. Expenses are recorded in the accounting period in which bills are paid. This type of accounting works very much like a checkbook. You deposit money and you write checks, all the time keeping a running balance of your funds.
  2. *Accrual basis*. Income is declared within the accounting period in which it is earned, regardless of when it is received. Expenses are declared in the accounting period in which they are incurred, but not necessarily when they are paid. This is the preferred method of accounting for community associations because it gives the most accurate picture of a community's financial position.
  3. *Modified accrual/cash basis*. A mixture of cash-basis and accrual-basis accounting. Some items are charted on a cash basis (e.g., utilities) and some on an accrual basis (e.g., insurance and real estate taxes).

- *Chart of accounts*. A numbering system used for classifying financial transactions. The chart of accounts is central to accurate information and can be customized to each association's needs.
- *Revenues*. The flow of funds into a community (e.g., cash, receipts, rent).
- *Expenses*. The flow of funds out of a community (e.g., payments, disbursements).
- *Accounts receivable (A/R)*. Revenues to be collected and money owed to the community association.
- *Accounts payable (A/P)*. Revenues to be paid out and/or money, such as debts or loans, owed to someone or something else. (In the accounting world, A/R and A/P are considered "short-term" issues. In

other words, they are settled during the current accounting period and generally within one year.)

- *Financial statements.* Formal records of an association's financial activities that give an overview of the organization's short- and long-term profitability and financial condition. A community produces four kinds of financial statements on a monthly, quarterly, or yearly basis:

  1. *Balance sheet.* A quick snapshot of a community's financial stability. Just as the name implies, everything must balance: assets equal liabilities and members' equity (net worth). (*Assets*, *liabilities*, and *equity* are balance sheet terms.)

     a. *Asset.* An item that is owned by or owed to the community. This may be in the form of cash, accounts receivable, property, or loans made to others. Assets are a community's economic resource should it need funds in the future.

     b. *Liability.* An item owed to others. This is usually in the form of debts or obligations, accounts payable, and loans. Businesses generally have two kinds of liabilities:

        i. *Current liabilities* are obligations that fall due within a comparably short time (usually within one year).

        ii. *Long-term liabilities* are obligations that are due over a longer period. An example is a long-term loan.

           a. *Equity.* The community's investments and/or net worth. This is the amount that remains after the organization's liabilities are subtracted from its assets.

  2. *Profit and loss statement (revenues & expense, income & expense).* A summary of financial activity for a given period. Shows how successful a community is after all bills are paid.

  3. *Cash flow statement.* A report of the actual inflow and outflow of cash and its related sources and uses in a given accounting period; typically a 12-month spreadsheet showing a month-to-month picture of the flow of money through a property.

  4. *Budget variance statement.* A financial statement that compares what the association expected to receive/spend with the amount actually received/spent.

- *General ledger.* A record of all the financial transactions that have taken place on a property. It uses the chart of accounts to identify the classification of each transaction. It employs double-entry accounting in which debits must equal credits: debits increase assets and decrease liabilities and equity; credits increase liability and equity and decrease assets.

- *Generally accepted accounting principles (GAAP).* The principles used to establish the accounting procedures. GAAP help to establish uniformity in the financial statements that community associations receive.

INFLOWS AND OUTFLOWS OF MONEY

Tracking the way money comes in and goes out is a major function of the community association, the treasurer, and the professional manager. An organized process is necessary to accomplish this task. A well-designed chart of accounts, together with the short- and long-term budgets, provides the information the association needs to produce detailed, accurate financial statements for the community.

Chart of Accounts

A lot happens to the money that flows into and out of a community association. A well-planned listing of financial transactions can assist in tracking just how the money flows. That list is the *chart of accounts.* It is a list of accounts that are given a specific definition as to the part they play in the movement of money. This list is the foundation of financial reporting. When designing a chart of accounts, make sure it accurately reflects the operations of the community association. Only chart financial functions that are pertinent to the community.

The chart of accounts is divided into five sections or categories: assets, liabilities, equity, income (revenue), and expenses. Each category is assigned a list of numbers. Generally, assets are 100 accounts, liabilities are 200 accounts, equity is 300 accounts, income (revenue) is 400 accounts, and expenses are 500 to 900 accounts. Exhibit 8.1 shows a sample chart of accounts that follows this numbering system.

Some accounting processes use four digits to categorize charts of accounts. Each money transaction is assigned an identifying number within one of the five categories. A good guide in the design of your association's chart of accounts is to keep it as simple as possible. Chances of misinterpreting where to account for a transaction increase when the design is too complex.

The chart of accounts often assigns one number to define the category and another number to define further the financial transactions within that category. In the chart of accounts in Exhibit 8.1, 500 = Utilities, 510 = Electricity, 515 = Water, 520 = Sewer, and so forth. In another example, 700 = Administrative, 710 = Insurance, 720 = Management Fees, and 730 = Professional Services.

Every community's chart of accounts must be designed exclusively for the particular association. The directors, and especially the association treasurer, must keep in mind exactly what they want to track. They will be reading and assimilating the financial reports, so they must be sure the financial transactions for their community are charted appropriately. For example, some communities only want one account for office expenses (720 in Exhibit 8.1). Others want to see specifically how much they spend on postage, copies, envelopes, coupons, and file storage, so they create individual account numbers for those functions. Professional managers must have the capability to customize their accounting software programs to meet the chart of accounts needs of the properties they manage. Most accounting software programs for community associations today have the ability to do that.

Budgets

No analysis of the flow of money in and out of a community association is complete without a budget, or, as some would like to call it, the *financial plan*. The *budget* is the guide to the association's current and future financial operations. Some like to call it the "educated guess" as to what is expected to happen with the money coming and going through the community. It is "educated" because, through gathered factual financial information, one can develop a good idea of what will happen with the association's money. It is a "guess" because the budget speculates what one anticipates the income and expenditures to be for the association. The budget guides the board in determining how much the association's assessments must be to meet its financial obligations. Budgets are used for short-term financial planning (e.g., a one-year program), long-term financial planning (e.g., a three-year or five-year program), and reserve replacement funding.

The board of directors, the treasurer, and the professional manager (if the association has one) must start working early on the upcoming year's budget. Sometimes budget responsibilities are mandated to a finance committee. August or September is not too early to start if your association operates on a January to December fiscal year. In any case, start your budget planning a minimum of four to five months before it is to go into operation. The professional manager often works closely with the association treasurer/finance committee before presenting a draft to the board, and sometimes even prepares the initial worksheet for the treasurer/finance committee to review.

Preparing an Initial Budget Worksheet/Spreadsheet. When preparing a budget, first consider actual historical data gathered from previous years. This information is extremely pertinent to determining whether the association collects enough money to pay operating expenses and provide funding for future reserve replacements. One of the biggest mistakes in preparing an

Exhibit 8.1
Chart of Accounts

Chart of Accounts
ABC Community Association

Current Assets		**Expenses**	
110	Cash	500	Utilities
115	Money Market	510	Electricity
124	Owner Deposits	515	Water
126	Replacement Reserves	520	Sewer
127	Insurance Reserves	530	Garbage
128	CD #1 (5/26/07)	540	Telephone
129	CD #2 (11/1/07)	550	Gas
150	Accounts Receivable	560	Cable TV
Current Liabilities		600	Maintenance & Repairs
210	Accounts Payable	601	General Maintenance
220	Loan Payable	602	Maintenance Supplies
230	Sec. Deposit Liability	605	Landscape Contract
		608	Landscape Improvements
Equity		620	Pool/Spa Maintenance
310	Transfer Funds	622	Back Flow Testing
390	Association Equity	623	Gate Repairs
399	Retained Earnings	625	Pest Control
		628	Fire/Safety Tests
Income		635	Security
420	Dues	645	Elevator Maintenance
425	Key/Gate Deposits	670	Window Washing
430	Late Charges	686	Custodial
432	NSF Fees		
445	Interest	700	Administrative
455	Fines	701	Insurance

(continued)

Exhibit 8.1 ***(Continued)***

460	Move Ins/Move Outs	702	Insurance Claims
475	Special Assessments	710	Management Fees
480	Insurance Claims	720	Office Expenses
487	Escrow Transfer Fees	725	Legal Services
490	Other Income	730	Accounting Services
		735	Professional Services
		740	Payroll Expenses
		745	Bank Charges
		755	Social
		800	Taxes and Permits
		855	Quarterly Taxes
		860	Income Tax
		865	Property Tax
		870	License and Permits
		899	Misc. Expenses
		900	Capital Expenses
		910	Painting
		911	Skylight Repairs
		915	Asphalt

(***Note:*** This chart of accounts is a sample. It is not meant to represent any specific community association. As mentioned earlier, each association must have a customized chart of accounts designed to meet its exclusive needs.)

annual budget is attempting to make the expenses meet a predetermined assessment payment. That is not possible, and is a major reason community associations get into trouble with financial planning.

In preparing your annual budget, develop a spreadsheet showing the previous two to three years of historical data, like the sample shown in Exhibit 8.2. Plug in the actual figures for each respective year. Next, include the current year-to-date information on the spreadsheet. If you were preparing your worksheet in August as shown in the example, you would have a column with all the totals of your income and expenses for the first eight months of the year. The next column would be for the "predicted" actuals

Exhibit 8.2

Budget Worksheet/Spreadsheet

	2003 Actual Figures	2004 Actual Figures	2005 Budget Figures	Aug. 2005 Actual Figures	2005 Predicted to 12/31/05
Income					
Assessments	200,000	210,000	220,000	150,000	225,000
Expenses					
Utilities	58,000	60,900	63,800	43,500	65,250
Maintenance	62,000	65,100	68,200	46,500	69,750
Administrative	22,000	23,100	24,200	16,500	24,750
Taxes & Permits	4,000	4,200	4,400	3,000	4,500
Reserves	54,000	56,700	59,400	39,600	59,400
Net Income (Loss)	0	0	0	900	1,350

(*Note:* This sample is not meant to represent any community association. The figures are given only to demonstrate a budget worksheet/spreadsheet.)

to the end of the year (the additional four months). Using the eight months of actual income and expenses, you would predict the actual figures for the end of the year. Unless you know about some outstanding windfall of income or outlay of expense that will take place before year-end, a simple means of obtaining the estimated year-end figures is to divide the actual figure by eight (because you are using eight months of actual figures) and multiply the result by 12. (Example: Utilities = $43,500 for August 2005; 43,500 ÷ 8 × 12 = 65,250). This is the "actual prediction" in the simplest of processes. There are other ways to do this, and the authors highly recommend that you get professional advice as needed.

Making Budget Predictions. Once you have prepared the worksheet to this point, plug in educated-guess figures for the upcoming year. Begin by analyzing the actual year and the predicted year-end figures. What do they tell you? Are they increasing at a predicted rate (i.e., by a certain percentage or specific dollar amount each year)? Sometimes you will see a pattern. Other times you won't see any increase at all.

Next, start calling your vendors and suppliers. Ask if they anticipate increases in the upcoming year and, if so, the amount. Utility companies will frequently tell you if a 5 percent or 15 percent rate increase is on the horizon. Likewise, the insurance company, the pool maintenance personnel, and the landscaper may also be able to inform you whether increases are likely. You should know exactly what increases or decreases to predict from vendors or suppliers with whom you have a current contract. Don't miss anyone to whom you pay bills on a continual basis.

If your community association has employees, don't forget anticipated pay increases and increased benefit expenses for your upcoming annual budget. Health insurance premiums have escalated at phenomenal rates recently. If your association offers mileage reimbursement, be sure to take into consideration the anticipated price of fuel and service on automobiles.

Once all of the research and analysis is complete for anticipated income and expenditures, start plugging your figures into the budget worksheet/spreadsheet as shown in Exhibit 8.3. Some of the figures in Exhibit 8.3 are averages of the previous years' actuals along with the predicted year-end; others were obtained by talking to vendor/suppliers about anticipated increases.

This draft budget worksheet is given to the board of directors for review. During the entire budget development phase, the board should keep its

Exhibit 8.3

Worksheet/Spreadsheet with Proposed Budget

	2003 Actual Figures	2004 Actual Figures	2005 Budget Figures	Aug. 2005 Actual Figures	2005 Predicted to 12/31/05	2006 Proposed Budget
Income						
Assessments	200,000	210,000	220,000	150,000	225,000	228,000
Expenses						
Utilities	58,000	60,900	63,800	43,500	65,250	69,800
Maintenance	62,000	65,100	68,200	46,500	69,750	66,600
Administrative	22,000	23,100	24,200	16,500	24,750	24,000
Taxes & Permits	4,000	4,200	4,400	3,000	4,500	4,600
Reserves	54,000	56,700	59,400	39,600	59,400	62,300
Net Income (Loss)	0	0	0	900	1,350	700

Worksheet explanation:

- **Utilities:** Represents 7% increase. (Year 2003 to 2004 was a 5% increase; year 2004 to the 2005 prediction was 7%.)
- **Maintenance:** Represents a 3% increase. (Most major maintenance items were addressed in 2005. Only a slight increase was anticipated in this category.)
- **Reserves:** Represents a 5% increase. (In order to maintain appropriate reserve funding, the board's policy is a steady 5% increase every year.)

members informed and use any constructive suggestions from membership. The board will decide if any final changes are made.

Once board members agree on the budget, they present it to the entire membership. They can do this by simply mailing the budget to the members for review. The association's *governing documents* or state statutes define the way this is to be accomplished. Sometimes an open meeting before the membership is required before the board can actually adopt the budget. At other times, the board has to have a budget ratification meeting that allows the membership to overturn the budget with a majority vote. Whatever the process, the board must ensure it is done correctly.

Financial Statements

Financial statements provide a plethora of information for the community association. These financial reports let the members and the board know just how financially healthy the association is. When Jerry McGuire said, "Show me the money," he could have been asking to look at financial statements. Probably not, but it makes a good analogy because it is in financial statements that one "sees" the money. Financial statements show how money is collected (flows in), how it is disbursed (flows out), and what effect those actions have on the overall financial health of the association. Financial statements should provide the following:

- Information the board can use to make monetary decisions for the association
- Information regarding the inflow and outflow of money during a particular financial accounting period
- Information about the association's financial health
- Reports regarding the collection of assessments
- Budget analyses comparing actual monetary events as they relate to budgeted monetary events
- Information regarding any outstanding financial obligations the association has

The American Institute of Certified Public Accountants (AICPA) has established guidelines for community association accounting. The guidelines state that financial reports for community associations should be prepared on the accrual basis. As discussed earlier in the chapter, this method provides a much more accurate picture of an association's financial health than does cash-basis accounting. Accrual-basis accounting introduces accounts receivable and accounts payable into the financial report. These accounts help the association determine how much it still owes and is owed by others. Cash-basis accounting does not give that depth to the financial picture.

At a minimum, a community association should compile the following financial statements:

- Balance Sheet
- Income and Expense Report (also called Revenue & Expense or Profit & Loss)
- Member Balance Report
- Check Register
- Budget Variance Report
- Bank Reconciliation
- General Ledger Report

The AICPA guidelines also recommend *fund accounting*. This means a financial report should be made for the reserve replacement funds. This can be done as an addition to the balance sheet and the income and expense report. Fund accounting segregates the association's financial activities into two funds: the operating fund and the replacement fund.

A written narrative should accompany the financial statements. The narrative clarifies any irregularities, any special actions taken, and any budget variance details that may need explanation. When reviewing the financial statements, the board should pay close attention to the following:

- Past due assessments
- Severe differences between budgeted figures and actual figures
- Unusually large expenses
- Any unexplained situations

Probably more than any other responsibility, the association members expect the board to maintain control of the inflow and outflow of money; the financial statements assist the board in accomplishing that.

In his "Understanding Financial Statements" article in the July 2003 *Association Times* (www.AssociationTimes.com/articles2003), Mark Southall, CPM, PCAM, addresses the board's need for internal controls to ensure the community's finances are in order. Exhibit 8.4 shows some of the questions he suggests a board should consider.

Exhibit 8.4
Financial Questions to Consider

Cash and Bank Accounts

Are bank reconciliations reviewed by the board?

Are outstanding checks dated over 90 days reviewed and is action taken?

Are cash deposits in FDIC-insured accounts?

Is the total cash balance in any one financial institution over $100,000?

Are bank accounts (operating and reserve) in the name of the association?

Is the management company responsible for handling the cash bonded?

Cash Disbursements

Are vendor invoices paid in a timely manner to avoid late fees/penalties?

Do reserve transfers between accounts require two signatures?

Are checks prenumbered and accounted for in sequence?

Are vendor invoices reviewed and approved for payment?

Are vendor payments posted to the proper general ledger account?

Accounts Receivable

Is there a written, approved collection/delinquency policy in place? If so, is the policy followed?

Are late charges being levied on past due balances?

Is the accounts receivable aging reviewed each month?

Are past due balances vigorously pursued by a collection agency, an attorney, or other legal action?

Are liens and lien releases filed on a timely basis?

Are assessments properly charged in compliance with the governing documents and the budget?

Financial Statement

Do the board members and/or treasurer review the financial statements each month?

Exhibit 8.4 ***(Continued)***

Is there an income statement to budget comparison reports?

Are variances noted on the financial reports?

Are the financial statements prepared promptly?

Is the general ledger chart of accounts adequate for tracking association transactions?

Accounting Administration

Are there accurate minutes of board meetings in which financial decisions are approved?

Is the budget prepared and approved by the board each year?

Is the budget approval process in compliance with the governing documents?

ASSESSMENTS

Residents of a community association like to have running water, green grass, a roof that doesn't leak, and an overall well-maintained home. They also desire to preserve the real estate market value of their property. All of this has a price. To establish operating funds that take care of these items and more, the association must collect money from its members. As previously mentioned, these funds are often called *assessments*, but depending on the type of community association, they may also be called *dues* or *maintenance fees*.

The governing documents give the community association the authority to impose assessments to cover operating costs and build funds for major *capital expenditures*. The money collected is used to pay utilities, maintain the property, pay administrative costs including insurance expenses, and establish reserve funds for future major expenses such as siding replacement, roof replacement, and painting if the association is a condominium, a cooperative, or any other entity with *common elements* that must be maintained.

Assessment Types

There are three types of assessments:

1. *Regular assessments*. These are the monthly, quarterly, semiannual, or annual payments the members are charged based on the financial needs addressed in the association's annual operating budget and the authority of the governing documents. Each owner's share of the

annual budget is specified in the governing documents. The amount the homeowner pays is sometimes based on a percentage of the property's overall square footage; at other times, it is based on the number of units. These assessments are mandatory, and they can be pursued through legal means if not paid in a timely manner.

2. *Special assessments.* These are special-purpose assessments meant to meet a specific need. The governing documents include a provision for imposing special assessments—generally one-time or short-term payments. The association may be unable to meet its routine financial obligations (be underbudgeted), or it may recognize a need to build up the reserve funds for future capital expenditures. Special assessments sometimes result from poor financial planning, such as when the membership consistently refuses to authorize increases in assessments, causing shortfalls when major repairs, emergencies, or replacements arise.
3. *Individual or personal assessments.* These are assessments imposed on a single owner, usually as the result of something the owner did or did not do. The most common individual assessment is probably the one imposed on the individual member owner for not paying regular assessments in a timely manner. This assessment may be in the form of a fine, a late charge, or another monetary penalty. An individual assessment might also be imposed to reimburse the association for any maintenance repairs that are the sole responsibility of one owner.

Assessments are the lifeblood of a community association. The association must be able to meet its financial obligations and put money in savings for future major expenditures. This will result in a better community and protect property values.

Collections

It is no surprise to those living in or managing a community association that some owners/members do not pay their assessments in the manner established by the association and its governing documents. Fortunately for everyone, most community members are very responsive to timely payment of assessments. For those who are not, the association must establish well-written policies for collection that are frequently published and distributed to the membership. Exhibit 8.5 is an example of a collection policy.

Some vital elements must be included in any document adopted regarding the association's collection policy. The association attorney can assist in formalizing this resolution.

Exhibit 8.5

Collection Policy/Resolution

_______________ CONDOMINIUM ASSOCIATION

Collection Policy for Delinquent Assessments
(Effective January 1, 20__)

WHEREAS the board of directors for ________________ is charged with the responsibility of collecting Assessments for common expenses from homeowners pursuant to the Association's Governing Documents;

WHEREAS from time to time homeowners become delinquent in payment of those Assessments and fail to bring their accounts current;

WHEREAS the board deems it to be in the best interests of the Association to adopt a uniform and systematic procedure for dealing with delinquent accounts in a timely manner and further believes it to be in the best interests of the Association to refer these accounts promptly to an attorney for collection so as to minimize the Association's loss of assessment revenue;

NOW, THEREFORE, IT IS RESOLVED that:

1. Pursuant to the Governing Documents and RCW (state law) __________, there is hereby levied against any assessment account that is not paid in full as of the tenth (10th) day of the month a late fee in the amount of $25.00 which the Treasurer or Association Manager is authorized and directed to charge to and collect from any delinquent unit owner;
2. The Board shall retain an Association Collection Attorney experienced in representing condominium and homeowners associations in collections and related matters;
3. The Board shall direct such Association Collection Attorney to represent the Association on the terms outlined in this resolution;
4. The Association Collection Attorney is hereby directed to pursue all collection and other related matters that the Board, acting through the Treasurer or Association Manager, may from time to time refer to the attorney and to provide any advice and counsel which the Board may require;
5. The Treasurer or Association Manager, acting on behalf of the Association, is directed to pay the Association Collection Attorney the attorney's usual and customary charges for time incurred in connection with the attorney's representation of the Association, together with all costs incurred by the attorney, including but not limited to fees and charges for filing, service of process, messenger service, court reporters, electronic or computer-assisted legal research, photocopies, postage, long distance calls, investigator's services, credit reports, and title reports, promptly upon receipt of the attorney's monthly invoice;
6. The Board may direct the Treasurer or Association Manager to refer any unit owner who is more than ________days delinquent in the payment of any regular or special Assessment amount, or other charges authorized by the Association's Governing Documents (hereinafter referred to as "Assessments"), to the Association

Exhibit 8.5 ***(Continued)***

Collection Attorney for collection action (which includes, without limitation, the recording of a lien against the property owned by the delinquent unit owner) and is authorized and directed to consult with the Association Collection Attorney on all accounts referred for collection;

7. The owner whose account has been referred for collection will be liable for payment of the minimum charge imposed by the Association Collection Attorney to cover fees and costs charged to the Association;
8. The Treasurer or Association Manager is authorized and directed to consult with the Association Collection Attorney and to immediately refer for collection any account for which the homeowner files or is the subject of a petition for relief in bankruptcy or a lender has commenced any action for foreclosure of its lien against the property;
9. The following policies shall apply to all delinquent accounts turned over to the Association Collection Attorney for collection:
   a. All contacts with a delinquent owner shall be handled through the Association Collection Attorney. Neither the Treasurer, the Association Manager, nor any Association officer or director shall have authority to settle the collection of the account directly with a homeowner after it has been turned over to the Association Collection Attorney without prior consultation with the Association Collection Attorney.
   b. All sums collected on a delinquent account shall be remitted to the Association in care of the Association's Collection Attorney until the account has been brought current.
   c. In accordance with Section ____ of the Amended and Restated Declaration, any owner who has been delinquent in paying monthly Assessments for three of the five preceding months shall be required to make and maintain a security deposit in the amount of three months' estimated monthly Assessments. However, the Treasurer or Association Manager and Association Collection Attorney are hereby granted discretionary authority to waive this acceleration in whole or in part under circumstances that they deem to be appropriate.
   d. In accordance with Section ______ of the Amended and Restated Declaration, any owner who is more than 90 days delinquent in payment of Assessments shall be required to make and maintain a security deposit in the amount of 12 months' estimated monthly Assessments. However, the Treasurer or Association Manager and Association Collection Attorney are hereby granted discretionary authority to waive this acceleration in whole or in part under circumstances that they deem to be appropriate.
   e. In accordance with Section_______, the Association Collection Attorney is authorized and directed to demand and collect the rent from an owner/landlord's tenant if the account of the owner/landlord is 30 or more days delinquent.
   f. Interest at the rate provided by the Governing Documents or otherwise at the legal rate shall be collected on all delinquent Assessment amounts, including

(continued)

Exhibit 8.5 ***(Continued)***

but not limited to late charges and legal fees and costs. The Association's Treasurer or Association Manager and Association Collection Attorney are, however, granted the discretionary authority to waive this requirement in whole or in part under circumstances that they deem to be appropriate.

g. The Association Collection Attorney's minimum legal fee shall be assessed against each delinquent property and its owner (including repeat collections) when the account is turned over to counsel for collection. All legal fees and costs incurred in the collection of a delinquent account shall be assessed against the delinquent unit and owner and shall be collectible as an Assessment as provided in the Declaration and RCW ____________.

ATTESTED that this collection policy resolution was duly adopted at a meeting of the Board of Directors held ________________, 20__, and shall take effect January 1, 20__.

_____________ Condominium Association, a
nonprofit corporation,

By: ______________________________
Secretary

Minimum elements of a good collection policy:

- Establish the reasons for timely collection of the association assessments.
- Establish the authority the board has to pursue delinquent assessments. Generally, the authority comes from state statutes and the governing documents.
- Levy fines, late charges, interest charges, and any costs associated with the collection of the delinquent assessment (i.e., attorney fees, mailings, copy charges, etc.).
- Define how the collection process will progress, including payment acceleration and/or utility termination if allowable in the governing documents or state statutes.
- Explain how late assessment payments will be credited.
- Provide contact information and addresses where appropriate.

An association's collection policy is of no use unless it is enforced immediately and aggressively. The association should be consistent with its enforcement in order to be seen as treating all members fairly and equally. With timely collection, the association may be able to stay ahead of a mortgage foreclosure that could prevent the association from collecting any unpaid assessments.

Liens, Foreclosures, and Bankruptcy

The board has taken all the appropriate steps, followed all procedural policies, and still some members will not pay their delinquent assessments. Associations often see individual owners file for bankruptcy, thus attempting to tie the "collection hands" of the association. Attorney Kris Sundberg (KSundberg@sundberglaw.com) said, "Don't lose hope and give up on collecting unpaid assessments simply because delinquent owners file for bankruptcy or their property is in foreclosure with the lender… by using all of the tricks in the legal bag, substantial recoveries can be made."

Kris stated, "Keep in mind that there are two separate and distinct sources for payment of delinquent assessments. The first source is the owner's personal liability. This means that the association can look to the owner's personal assets (e.g., bank accounts, wages, etc.) for payment. The second source of payment is the association's lien against the owner's property. This means that the association can look to the property as an independent and separate source of payment. To realize on the property it will have to be sold at a public sale (or at least have the process started), either by the sheriff or a private trustee. Except for the case of the private trustee's sale, both sources of payment (i.e., owner's personal liability and the lien against the property) are affected by way of a lawsuit. The owner is sued for both a personal judgment and also to foreclose the association's lien on the property."

Attorney Sundberg further advised, "Many delinquent owners (and even their attorneys) have the mistaken notion that if they just file for bankruptcy then all of their problems with the association will be over. This will be true if and only if the owner forever abandons the property in connection with the bankruptcy filing. The bankruptcy will only eliminate the owner's personal liability. It will not eliminate the association's separate lien against the property. Therefore the association can lose the owner's personal liability through bankruptcy but still collect under the lien. Conversely, the lien can be lost in a lender's foreclosure but the association can still collect under the owner's personal liability. And until the association loses both the personal liability of the owners and the lien against the property, there's always a possibility to collect."

BANKING

Any way you look at it, the community association has to develop a system for managing the money that flows into and out of the organization. The board and/or its professional management company must build a healthy working relationship with experts who understand money and how it works for them. So they turn to the banks. Many banks have created specific departments that specialize in working with community associations. They understand assessment collection and reserve funding. If the community needs to borrow money, these same banks offer programs for that. (We will discuss reserves and loans later in this chapter.)

If a bank wants your association's business—which could amount to thousands or even millions of dollars—it must find ways to work with the association, even if that means ocassionally going against routine banking procedures. Boards and professional managers must ask questions such as:

- How flexible is the bank in meeting the association's money needs?
- What does the bank know about community associations and assessment collection?
- Can the bank provide a primary contact person?
- What are the bank's "checks and balances" to protect the association's finances?
- What are the bank's fees, charges, and hidden costs?

Working with its bank, an association can make assessment payment convenient for homeowners in a number of ways:

- *Coupons.* Just as many of us get coupons to make mortgage and car payments, the association can print coupons to be mailed to the homeowners for assessment payments. The association or management company can print them in-house, or the association can use a professional printing company to create the coupons. These printing companies are equipped to handle large quantities. They can print, insert, and mail the coupons in accordance with each association's needs. Of course, using this outside source involves a cost. However, the association must take into consideration the cost of staff time and the equipment and supplies needed to produce the coupons. That analysis often turns in favor of using an outside source for coupon production.
- *Lock box.* The lock box receives and processes the assessment payments. This feature can be offered by the association's bank or by a private lock box company. Banks generally do not charge for lock boxes; a private lock box company does. Then why consider paying this additional fee? If the bank does not provide competitive returns on the association's money, the association might be wise to consider the cost-effectiveness of using a private company. Costs

aren't everything, even though they are extremely important. The association must also take into consideration reliability, accuracy, technology requirements, and timeliness of assessment deposits.

This is how it works: Coupons and payments are sent to the lock box. The lock box processes them by depositing the payment and applying it to the specific homeowner's account. Then the deposit information is downloaded on a disk (and sent to the association or management company) or sent via e-mail to be downloaded into the association's or management company's computer program. With today's banking and accounting software programs, the time saved in this process is invaluable.

- *Automatic bank debit.* To eliminate check writing and processing procedures, associations can take advantage of automatic withdrawals from members' bank accounts. The association must get each member's permission to do this. The member signs an Automated Clearing House (ACH) agreement that authorizes his or her bank to make automated, electronic deposits into the association's bank account. Once the authorization is signed, the association and the bank use the Federal Reserve System's Automated Clearing House to make electronic transfers. In this manner, assessments are collected immediately when due. No more do the association's members have to worry about making their payments in a timely manner. If they become ill or go on vacation, they will know that their assessment payments will still be made on time and will not jeopardize their financial standing with the association.

- *Internet-based collections.* Web sites, such as www.NoteMinder.net, provide coupon books, collection, posting, ACH management, reports, late notices, and monthly bank reconciliation. Such services are especially helpful for self-managed associations. Accounting software available to community associations allows boards to review their association's financial situation and allows individual members to investigate their accounts online. Such tools can greatly enhance the efficiency of the community association's operations. In addition, everything is password protected for added security.

- *Check scanning.* If the association is self-managed or the professional manager chooses to process the assessment payments, a check scanning system might be considered. When checks are run through a piece of scanning equipment, the information is converted to an ACH transaction. Special software is also required. This process is highly regulated by the Automated Clearing House using National Automated Clearing House Association (NACHA) rules for all transactions. For more information on the rules and regulations governing the process, go to www.nacha.org. Many have found this procedure very cost-effective in handling assessment collection for community associations.

Banks are an integral part of financial operations for community associations. Building a trusting, reliable relationship with a bank can enhance an association's overall success.

AUDITS AND TAXES

Accurate financial records support the community association's day-to-day operations. They also assist the board and professional manager in meeting their fiduciary responsibilities to the membership. Association members expect their monies to be put to good use and not to be misappropriated or embezzled. Financial reviews or audits are performed to verify that the association's financial operations are handled appropriately. In conjunction with the reviews and audits, the board can determine whether the association owes taxes.

Audits

Wikipedia, the free encyclopedia, defines *financial audit* as "the examination by an independent third party of the financial statements" of an organization, "resulting in the publication of an independent opinion on whether or not those financial statements are relevant, accurate, complete, and fairly presented" (www.wikipedia.org; accessed November 7, 2007). Financial audits exist to ensure that financial statements correctly represent the association's financial position for a given period. Audits are designed to reduce the possibility of false, misleading, or inaccurate information. Many states and governing documents require community associations to conduct an annual financial examination. However, even when not required, it is good business practice for the association to have its financial records examined on a routine basis.

The annual financial examination can take the form of a review or a full-fledged audit. The *review* is a check of the association's financial statements. The auditor is not required to corroborate the information provided for the review. Through interviews with board members, the professional manager, and others involved with operations, the auditor assesses the association's financial procedures, compares the current financial statements with the previous year's statements, and provides a report or opinion of the association's financial health. Reviews are less expensive to conduct than audits.

An *audit* is a much more thorough examination of the association's financial records and procedures. The auditor, usually a Certified Public

Accountant (CPA), typically performs audits in conformity with GAAP. The auditor also obtains independent evidence to corroborate the information supplied. This is done by means of a physical inspection of all association records, including but not limited to minutes, legal documents, contracts, and financial statements. The auditor then prepares a written opinion report either assuring that everything is in order or noting areas of concern. An audit costs more than a review, but if properly anticipated and budgeted, it can protect the association in matters of litigation.

Barry Wuntch, a CPA from Houston, Texas, suggests in his *FACETS* newsletter article, "How to Make Preparing for Your Year-End Audit as Easy as One, Two, Three" (published October 11, 2004 by the Houston Chapter of CAI), the following list of records to have available for an audit:

- Year-end and year-to-date general ledger
- Aged accounts receivable and accounts payable reports
- Bank statements and reconciliations (including reserve account statements)
- Paid and unpaid vendor invoices
- Insurance policies
- Approved annual budget
- Bad debt write-off information
- Minutes for the year being audited
- Governing documents
- Open vendor contracts and vendor proposals
- Prior year's audit reports and income tax returns

Taxes

Every community association must file a federal income tax return every year. Although the association may not have created any taxable income for the year, that does not negate the requirement to file. Filing must be done no later then the 15th day of the third month following the close of the tax year. This means that, if the association's fiscal year closes on December 31, taxes must be filed by March 15 of the next year.

Associations have the option to file as a corporation using form 1120 or as a homeowners association using form 1120-H. When using form 1120-H, the association must meet very specific requirements related to its revenues and expenses. This method has no tax consequences related to replacement reserves and/or excess membership income. As the association's financial position changes from year to year, board members may want to change the form they use. According to Howard Goldklang, CPA, MBA, in "Six Questions (And Answers) To Survive Tax Time" (*Community Management*, March/April 2001), some associations have tax-exempt status under Section 501c of the Internal Revenue Code, although this is rare and relatively hard to obtain. Cooperatives file form 1120, subchapter T. Community associations should consult their accountants or tax advisors as to which form to use when it is time to file a return. For a good explanation of forms 1120 and 1120-H, go to www.1120accountant.com/homeowners-associations.htm.

RESERVE PLANNING

As monies come in and out of the community association's coffers to pay for the day-to-day operations of the organization, the necessity to set aside funds for future maintenance and replacements is often forgotten. Members of a community association want their assessments to remain at a tolerable level. They don't want to pay any more than necessary. Robert Norlund, P.E., of Association Reserves, Inc., wrote, "The Governing Documents of most associations require the Board to collect an 'appropriate' amount of money on a regular basis to offset the ongoing deterioration of the common areas."

The board of directors can have a hard time convincing members that they must pay a large amount of money (a *special assessment*) to address the need for a roof replacement, pool resurfacing, or siding paint. However, the board would be irresponsible to neglect its fiduciary responsibility to ensure that a plan is in place to care for common elements with a limited life expectancy. With good, long-term financial planning, an association can avoid members' hatred and discontentment that result from having no financial plan at all. This means developing a reserve plan. *Reserves* (also called *capital replacement reserves*) are monies the association sets aside on a continuing basis for future expenditures. The reserves are a savings account into which the association deposits money to pay for major replacements that could become necessary. Many states (e.g., California, Florida, Hawaii) and community association governing documents require reserve planning.

A *reserve plan* identifies all common area maintenance components and establishes a funding plan to address them as necessary. The association first conducts an analysis of the common area components that are expected to wear out in 3 to 30 years. Most associations choose not to do this analysis themselves. Professional companies exist whose sole purpose is to conduct this analysis and provide a written report, called a *reserve study*, to the association. The Association of Professional Reserve Analysts (APRA) is the national trade organization for reserve study professionals. Information about the organization is available at www.apra-usa.com.

Again according to Robert Norlund of Association Reserves, Inc., "The primary responsibility of the Board of Directors is to maintain, protect, and enhance the assets of the association. The reserve study (or reserve plan) is the document that helps keep the physical and financial assets of the association in balance." This study determines each component's remaining useful life and the cost to repair or replace it at predicted inflationary prices. When completed, the study also provides a detailed report on the means the association should use to collect reserve funds from association members to meet these projected future expenses. Once an association has completed an initial reserve study, it should plan for periodic updates (e.g., at one year, two years, five years), because things change over time. An association might not be able to follow its reserve plan if an emergency or other expense causes a slight detour from the plan.

The key element for the board of directors and the professional association manager in understanding a community's written reserve study (plan) is the *executive summary*. This is a brief summation analysis giving an encapsulated view of the physical assets of the property and the financial status of the community. By reading the executive summary, the board can see the estimated initial useful life of all common area components (e.g., roof, siding, pools), the remaining useful life, the average cost to replace, the future dollar value of the cost to replace, and a thorough analysis of the funds presently set aside and those needed for future replacements. That sounds like a lot, but the summary is generally only a few pages, and it provides a snapshot view of the community's reserve funding situation. In most reserve study reports, the executive summary is followed by supporting documents, including inventory pictures and an analysis of all the community's common elements.

Reserve Funds and Investing

The reserve study identifies the funds that have to be set aside on a regular basis to meet the replacement costs of the community association's major capital expenses. The association's annual and long-term budgets should have line items for reserve funds. As the association collects the funds, it must develop prudent investment strategies to protect the members' monies. The governing documents often set parameters restricting reserve investments. Boards should never risk the association's money simply because they believe they can get a higher rate of return on the money in a shorter time. For that reason, reserve funds should generally not be invested in the stock market. Stocks have an extremely high degree of risk and potentially jeopardize reserve funds.

Unless the board has received a written mandate from their members to the contrary, it is recommended that the association invest reserve funds in FDIC-insured accounts. Money market checking or passbook savings accounts, even though immediately accessible, do not have the rate of return that do treasury bills or certificates of deposits (CDs). Because the FDIC only insures deposits up to $100,000, the association may need to invest its money in different banks. However, a few banks today do offer insurance protection for funds over $100,000. One advantage of CDs is that the association can stagger the maturity dates (e.g., a 6-month CD, 1-year CD, and 3-year CD) so funds are available at different times. Generally, the longer the maturity date, the higher the rate of return (interest) on the CD.

Reserve planning and funding are imperative for every community association that has common elements. Each association should create a written policy, possibly by way of an amendment to the bylaws, that specifies the following:

- How often reserve analysis should be done
- For what reserve funds are to be used
- What types of investment vehicles are to be used
- Who controls access to the reserve funds

Reserve planning can help protect the financial future of the association and its members year after year.

Loans

From time to time, the association may need additional funds for any number of reasons—such as the underfunding of reserves, the aging of the property, emergency damages, and even poor leadership/management. Special assessments, for which members are assessed payments equal to their portion of the entire price of a project, have historically addressed these needs. Members have the choice of paying cash, applying for financing (which creates a lien on the member's individual unit), or obtaining a credit card advance. Such assessments are often substantial because of the costs involved. Assessments of $10,000, $20,000, or $50,000 can create considerable ill will within the community association, especially when members are given a short time to come up with the money.

An alternative to the special assessment is the bank loan. If the association's governing documents allow and the membership passes a vote of approval, the board of directors may be able to seek a bank loan. The difficulty for the bank is that, other than the common elements/areas, the association has no collateral to secure the loan. Except for cooperatives, which hold title to the entire structure containing the cooperative units, most community associations do not own real property they can offer as collateral. In most cases, the bank obtains its security by taking *assignment* of the association's assets. This means that, should the association default on the loan, the lender has the ability to take over the management of the association, including but not limited to taking over the responsibilities of the board of directors.

When applying for a bank loan, the association may be asked to produce the following:

- Evidence of owner/occupancy (Banks prefer to see that at least 70 to 75 percent of the unit owners also occupy them.)
- Two to three years of historical operating records
- The current year's budget with year-to-date information
- Aged receivables reports
- The most current audit
- The reserve study with reserve plan and funding information
- Tax returns
- Current financial statements
- Board meeting minutes
- Plans, bids, and proposals for anticipated work that needs the financing

The lender will visit the property and meet with its directors before making the final decision. Most loans have a "construction phase" at the completion of which a term loan with a fixed interest rate is instituted. Loans can be from three to ten years. The association incorporates the loan payoff into the annual budget and member assessments. Banks are expressing an increasing interest in community associations and their borrowing needs. Should the need to fund a major capital expense arise, the association should investigate the possibility of securing a loan from a financial institution.

It is important to members and the wellbeing of the community that associations make the most of paid assessments and any additional secured financing. Effective community maintenance is essential to making the most of these funds and ensuring competitive real estate market values. In the next chapter, we turn to a discussion of the maintenance procedures that are so closely linked with the financial decisions and welfare of any community association.

9

Maintenance Processes

INTRODUCTION

The initial impression of a community is based on its appearance, which is evidence of the way it is maintained. Understanding maintenance functions is only half the maintenance job. The other half is establishing a program to perform those functions. The *board of directors* and the manager of the community association must review and understand many factors to accomplish effective day-to-day operational maintenance.

MAINTENANCE COORDINATION AND TRACKING

Common interest communities are different from apartment environments, yet they have some similar maintenance needs. When given the task of community management, the manager must understand the differences.

Establish the Rules

Before a community association can initiate a working maintenance plan, it must address certain "rules of engagement." The main rule illustrates the difference between apartment community maintenance and association maintenance: Know which maintenance is the association's responsibility and which is the resident's responsibility. The *covenants, conditions, and restrictions (CC&Rs)* of most governing documents dictate which elements of the association are common to all and which elements are limited common elements, and they stipulate whose dollars pay for the repairs—the association's or the property owners'. Knowing the difference between common and limited common elements assists the board and the manager in determining who must pay for repairs.

Common Elements versus Limited Common Elements. As discussed in Chapter 3, *common elements* are generally defined as portions of the association other than residences, including all portions of the roofs, walls, floors, or ceilings that are not a part of or within residence boundaries. Common elements also comprise other elements such as chutes, flues, ducts, wires, conduits, bearing walls, bearing columns, and any other fixtures that lie partially within and partially outside the designated boundaries of a residence and serve more than one residence or any portion of a common element.

Limited common elements are best defined as parts of the common elements that have limited use exclusively for the owner or resident of a particular unit, such as private patios or lanais, entryways, garages, and exterior doors and windows. The association must generally ensure that all repairs are done, but the individual resident owner may have to pay for needed repairs that are within the association's control.

Processes for Monitoring Maintenance. The managing agent must fully understand the community's processes for monitoring maintenance. Associations often establish *maintenance committees*; their role is to inform management of association needs and to make budget and special project recommendations to the board for approval. After approving projects, the board commissions management to implement them. The board and the managing agent schedule the maintenance and agree upon the order in which necessary maintenance will be performed. Then the work order is completed by an outside vendor, an on-site employee, or the management agent's staff.

Responsibility for Maintenance Requests. Many management firms have specialized staff, usually called *maintenance administrators*, supervisors, or coordinators, who receive requests, create work orders, and determine the best response to maintenance issues. According to Maria Garcia, Maintenance Coordinator for Bell-Anderson & Associates, LLC, AMO, a person in this position calls, e-mails, or faxes maintenance requests to vendors for repairs. For a minor maintenance call (e.g., a water stain from a previous leak, an overflowing gutter, a screen door off the track), someone should call back within 24 to 48 hours to schedule the repair. Emergencies (e.g., water going everywhere, an electrical wiring smell, underground leaks) should be handled immediately. The coordinator follows up on emergency and routine maintenance calls to make sure all work has been completed, so a maintenance coordinator must have a reliable tracking system.

Other management firms assign the community manager as the first contact with the association members. In that case, the manager addresses any maintenance problems from the community.

Tracking of Maintenance Requests. To provide the best service response, the manager must use a good system for tracking the community's maintenance requests. Maintenance software is available to help gather and track reports for the community's maintenance. Many firms set up a tracking matrix using a spreadsheet program like Microsoft Excel, and/or they have in-house management accounting software with a maintenance/vendor module for monitoring needed maintenance as well as its progress and completion.

A manager must use an effective system to keep a community's maintenance efficient. The association board looks to the professional management firm to maintain the community and to inform the board of deferred, preventive, custodial, and emergency maintenance needs.

Know the Property's Needs

Preserving and protecting common areas requires an association to prepare for both expected and emergency repairs and replacements. Every association should have a maintenance program, and a reserve study should be an integral part of the program.

Prepare a Reserve Study. As mentioned in Chapter 8, a *reserve study* is an analysis of common area components that may wear out in 3 to 30 years. Every community eventually needs major repairs and replacements. Establishing adequate reserves helps assure resident owners that they are unlikely to encounter large special assessments they may be unable to pay. Boards of directors increasingly establish appropriate reserves for working capital, operations, contingencies, and replacements. Annually or semiannually, boards determine the reserves needed by reassessing the useful lives of their building components and the costs to replace them. Many states require that a formal reserve study be done for every community association; Oregon requires that a "maintenance plan" be part of the reserve study.

It is important to recognize the benefit of a reserve study for the community. Many associations work with their managers to develop their own reserve plans, or they hire other professionals who specialize in developing formal reserve studies. The plan then becomes part of the long-range budget planning. It dovetails into the projected *annual budget* as the reserve fund allocation.

Exhibit 9.1 is a worksheet illustrating a thorough reserve analysis for a community. The format is a compilation of formats used by professionals who develop such studies, most notably Dave Schwindt, CPA, of Portland's Schwindt & Co.

Exhibit 9.1
Reserve Study Worksheet

Association Common Area Component Checklist

Association Information:

Community Name:
Property Address:

Checklist Completed by: ____________________ **Phone:** ________________

Component Details:

1. **Shingle Roofing—Renewal** Not Applicable ☐
   - Material type: ______________________________
   - Will roof be layered? ____________ Removed/replaced? ____________
   - Total shingle roof area: ______________________________
   - Useful life of component: ______________________________
   - Estimated cost: $______________________________

2. **Gutters & Downspouts—Replace** Not Applicable ☐
   - Gutter type: ______________________________
   - Total gutter length: __________ Total downspout length: ______________
   - Useful life of component: ______________________________
   - Estimated cost: $ ______________________________

3. **Membrane Roofing—Renewal** Not Applicable ☐
   - Material type: ______________________________
   - Will roof be layered? ____________ Removed/replaced? ____________
   - Total membrane roof area: ______________________________
   - Useful life of component: ______________________________
   - Estimated cost: $______________________________

4. **Exterior Siding (1)—Renewal** Not Applicable ☐
   - Material type: ______________________________
   - Estimated total area: ______________________________
   - Percent to be replaced: ________% Percent to be repaired: __________%
   - Useful life of component: ______________________________
   - Estimated cost: $______________________________

(continued)

Exhibit 9.1 ***(Continued)***

5. Exterior Siding (2)—Renewal Not Applicable ☐
(complete for each type of exterior siding)

- Material type: ______________________________
- Estimated total area: ______________________________
- Percent to be replaced: __________% Percent to be repaired: __________%
- Useful life of component: ______________________________
- Estimated cost: ______________________________

6. Exterior Siding (3)—Renewal Not Applicable ☐
(complete for each type of exterior siding)

- Material type: ______________________________
- Estimated total area: ______________________________
- Percent to be replaced: __________% Percent to be repaired: __________%
- Useful life of component: ______________________________
- Estimated cost: ______________________________

7. Exterior Trim—Renewal Not Applicable ☐

- Material type: ______________________________
- Estimated total area: ______________________________
- Percent to be replaced: __________% Percent to be repaired: __________%
- Useful life of component: ______________________________
- Estimated cost: ______________________________

8. Exterior Siding—Paint/Stain/Seal Not Applicable ☐

- Material type: ______________________________
- Estimated total area: ______________________________
- Percent to be painted: __________% Percent to be stained: __________%
  Percent to be sealed: __________%
- Useful life of component: ______________________________
- Estimated cost: ______________________________

9. Exterior Masonry & Brickwork—Renewal Not Applicable ☐

- Material type: ______________________________
- Estimated total area: ______________________________
- Percent to be replaced: __________% Percent to be repaired: __________%
- Useful life of component: ______________________________
- Estimated cost: ______________________________

Exhibit 9.1 *(Continued)*

10. Exterior Masonry & Brickwork—Grout & Seal Not Applicable ☐

- Material type: ______
- Estimated total area: ______
- Sealant type: ______
- Useful life of component: ______
- Estimated cost: ______

11. Common Area Balconies & Decks—Renewal Not Applicable ☐

- Material type: Concrete: _____ Wood: _____ Other: _____ (Type?) ______
- Total area concrete: _____ Total area wood: _____ Total area other: ______
- Are any of these surfaces waterproofed? ______
- Percent repaired: Concrete: ______% Wood: ______% Other: ______%
- Percent replaced: Concrete: ______% Wood: ______% Other: ______%
- Useful life of component: ______
- Estimated cost: ______

12. Common Area Balconies & Decks—Maintenance Not Applicable ☐

- Material type: Concrete: _____ Wood: _____ Other: _____ (Type?) ______
- Total area concrete: _____ Total area wood: _____ Total area other: ______
- Are any of these surfaces waterproofed? ______
- Percent replaced: Concrete: ______% Wood: ______% Other: ______%
- Percent repaired: Concrete: ______% Wood: ______% Other: ______%
- Useful life of component: ______
- Estimated cost: ______

13. Common Area Stairs—Renewal Not Applicable ☐

- Material type: ______
- Number of staircases: One story: ______ Two stories: ______
  Three stories: ______
- Repair or replacement anticipated? ______
- Useful life of component: ______
- Estimated cost: ______

(continued)

Exhibit 9.1 ***(Continued)***

14. Common Area Stairs—Maintenance Not Applicable ☐

- Material type: ______
- Number of staircases: One story: ______ Two stories: ______ Three stories: ______
- Describe anticipated maintenance: ______
- Useful life of component: ______
- Estimated cost: ______

15. Handrails & Guardrails—Renewal Not Applicable ☐

- Material type: Wood: ______ Metal: ______ Other: (Type?) ______
- Total length: Wood: ______ Metal: ______ Other: ______
- Percent to be replaced: ______% Percent to be repaired: ______%
- Useful life of component: ______
- Estimated cost: ______

16. Handrails & Guardrails—Painting & Sealing Not Applicable ☐

- Material type: Wood: ______ Metal: ______ Other: (Type?) ______
- Total length: Wood: ______ Metal: ______ Other: ______
- Percent to be replaced: ______% Percent to be repaired: ______%
- Useful life of component: ______
- Estimated cost: ______

17. Asphalt Paving—Driveways & Parking—Renewal Not Applicable ☐

- Total area subject to vehicular traffic: ______
- Total parking area: ______
- Total non-parking areas: ______
- Useful life of component: ______
- Estimated cost: ______

18. Asphalt Paving—Driveways & Parking—Maintenance Not Applicable ☐

- Total area subject to vehicular traffic: ______
- Year it was last seal-coated: ______
- Year it was last skim-coated: ______
- Useful life of component: ______
- Estimated cost: Seal-coat: ______ Skim-coat: ______

Exhibit 9.1 ***(Continued)***

19. Asphalt Paving—Renewal (surfaces not subject to vehicular traffic) Not Applicable ☐

- Total area: ____________________
- Are these areas accessible by maintenance equipment? Yes ______ No ______
- Year it was last seal-coated: ____________________
- Useful life of component: ____________________
- Estimated cost: ____________________

20. Concrete Paving—Renewal Not Applicable ☐

- Total area: ____________________
- Total driving areas: ____________________
- Non-driving areas: ____________________
- Useful life of component: ____________________
- Estimated cost: ____________________

21. Concrete Curbing & Wheel-Stops—Renewal Not Applicable ☐

- Total length of continuous curb: ____________________
- Total number of wheel-stops: ____________________
- Useful life of component: ____________________
- Estimated cost: ____________________

22. Common Area Walkways—Renewal Not Applicable ☐

- Material type: Concrete: ______ Wood: ______ Other: (Type?) ______
- Total area concrete: _____ Total area wood: _____ Total area other: ______
- Are any of these surfaces waterproofed? ____________________
- Percent replaced: Concrete: ________% Wood: ________% Other: ________%
- Percent repaired: Concrete: ________% Wood: ________% Other: ________%
- Useful life of component: ____________________
- Estimated cost: ____________________

23. Common Area Lighting—Renewal Not Applicable ☐

- Total number of exterior fixtures: ____________________
- Number attached to building: ____________ (Do not include unit entry lights)
- Number of unattached or freestanding fixtures: ____________________
- Fixture type(s): Attached: ____________________

  Unattached: ____________________
- Number of unit entry lights: ____________________ (If HOA maintained)
- Useful life of component: ____________________
- Estimated cost: ____________________

(continued)

Exhibit 9.1 ***(Continued)***

24. Lawn Irrigation System—Renewal Not Applicable ☐

- Installed cost of new system: ____________________
- Estimated replacement cost: ____________________
- Useful life of component: ____________________
- Estimated cost: ____________________

25. Elevators—Renewal/Upgrade Not Applicable ☐

- Number of elevators: ____________________
- Number of floors served by each elevator: ____________________
- Elevator maintenance company: ____________________
- Useful life of component: ____________________
- Estimated cost: ____________________

26. Pool & Spa—Renewal Not Applicable ☐

- Material type: Pool: ____________________ Spa: ____________________
- Pool dimensions: ____________________
- Concrete deck area: ____________________ Wood deck area: ____________________
- Useful life of component: ____________________
- Estimated cost: ____________________

27. Pool & Spa Equipment—Renewal Not Applicable ☐

- Pool equipment cost & useful life:

  Heater cost: ____________________ Lifespan: ____________________

  Pump cost: ____________________ Lifespan: ____________________

  Filter cost: ____________________ Lifespan: ____________________

  Spa pump cost: ____________________ Lifespan: ____________________
- Other components: ____________________
- Useful life of component(s): ____________________
- Estimated cost: ____________________

28. Clubhouse/Recreation Facilities—Renewal Not Applicable ☐

(Does not include building components such as siding, roofing, windows, doors)

- Type of facilities: ____________________
- Floor area: ____________________ Flooring type: ____________________
- Amenities description: ____________________

  ____
- Furniture description: ____________________

  ____
- Useful life of component(s): ____________________
- Estimated cost to replace amenities and building contents: ____________________

  ____

Exhibit 9.1 ***(Continued)***

29. Clubhouse/Recreation Facilities—Renewal Not Applicable ☐
(Interior and exterior building components only)

- Building description: ____________
- Exterior siding area: ____________ Material type: ____________
- Roofing area: ____________ Material type: ____________
- Interior wall area: ____________ Material type: ____________
- Ceiling area: ____________ Material type: ____________
- Useful life of component(s): ____________
  ____
- Cost/useful life of components:
  Roofing: ____________ Lifespan: ____________
  Exterior siding: ____________ Lifespan: ____________
  Paint & decoration: ____________ Lifespan: ____________
- Other components: ____________

30. Other Common Area Components—Renewal Not Applicable ☐
(Describe any other common area components that are not listed on this checklist, please provide as much detail as possible)

- ____________
- ____________
- ____________

The format of the reserve study worksheet in Exhibit 9.1 may seem involved and time-consuming; however, all of its components need to be considered to perform an effective and valid reserve analysis. Taking the time to properly perform this analysis will ensure the accuracy of the reserve projections.

Review All Maintenance. The physical maintenance of any community can be extensive. For the maintenance of many elements, the board of directors can contract outside professional vendors and have the managing agent monitor these vendors: landscapers for mowing; arborists for pruning and trimming; trash removal, elevator, and garage door experts; and even weed and pest control contractors.

Other areas requiring constant attention are paved areas, sidewalks, stairs, and curbs. These elements may need only minor patching and cleaning, or they may require major replacement.

In addition to the grounds and paved areas of the association, the exteriors of the buildings must be carefully maintained. Areas not commonly noticed by owners, such as roofs, gutters, and downspouts, can become major sources of complaint if they do not function properly. Other exterior elements that must be inspected and maintained include eaves, soffits, shutters, and miscellaneous outside items such as:

- Fencing, including the underground portion of posts that must be treated with a safe preservative to avoid rotting;
- Light poles and underground wiring;
- Electrical timers;
- Public doorways, including the closers, hinges, locks, and other hardware;
- Patios—owners should be notified of needed corrections;
- Balconies, particularly those with wooden cantilevers and decks, since these are subject to deterioration and rot;
- Trash enclosures;
- Public area lighting fixtures; and
- All cracked or chipped glass in common areas.

Each association has different maintenance needs. When developing a maintenance program, the board and management should always consider the four areas of maintenance previously mentioned: deferred, preventive, custodial, and emergency.

Deferred Maintenance. Some maintenance can be *deferred* and scheduled for completion at a future date. If the problem can wait until a more opportune time, the association can defer it—as long as the delay does not permit a minor problem to become a major disaster. This type of maintenance is a likely candidate for a reserve study or future capital repair/replacement plan.

Preventive Maintenance. On the other hand, *preventive maintenance* is crucial. By providing regular care and making regular inspections of mechanical equipment and structural elements, those responsible for maintenance can detect potential problems early or prevent them altogether. This type of maintenance should be scheduled on a regular basis. Associations with strong preventive maintenance programs typically have lower operating costs than those that make repairs only when major work is needed.

Exhibit 9.2 is an inspection report that can be used for the initial maintenance evaluation for any community. The elements on this report may not all be present for every property analyzed. The report is one of many good tools managers can use to help track and plan for future needs.

Exhibit 9.2

Initial Inspection Report

ASSOCIATION PROPERTY INSPECTION REPORT

Property ________________________________

Inspected by ____________________ Date ______________

Item	Condition	Repairs Needed	Estimated Cost	Next Inspection
Grounds				
Foundation				
Exterior Walls				
Roof				
Gutters & Downspouts				
Windows & Casings				
Lobby				
Common Areas				
Elevators				
Stairways				
Boiler/Furnace Room				
Air-Conditioning Plant				
Electrical System				
Plumbing				
Gas Lines				
Fire Safety Equipment				
Garbage Disposal Area				

This particular format was retrieved from the IREM Web site, www.irem.org.[1] As a member of IREM, the management agent would have free access to many downloadable management forms. Use this one to establish a more specific form for the type of community studied.

Custodial Maintenance. *Custodial maintenance* refers to all policing and housekeeping functions as they relate to the common areas. Preparing a maintenance schedule for routine custodial duties is less difficult but no less important than drafting a preventive maintenance schedule. Residents are more aware of the effectiveness of custodial maintenance than they are of preventive maintenance that is performed.

Recreational amenity maintenance helps assure association members of the safety and cleanliness of association facilities. The areas in and around clubhouses, swimming pools, tennis courts, Jacuzzis, and other outdoor or indoor amenities should be routinely policed for litter. These facilities are showcase amenities for the community. Keeping them in pristine, sparkling condition should be one of management's goals.

An inspection of the physical areas, including lobbies, hallways, elevator cars, recreational areas, and other public places, should be done at the same time as the major common elements inspection. The custodial maintenance schedule acts as a reminder of the work that must be performed daily and provides a guideline to determine if adequate staff is available to perform routine housekeeping tasks. Use a daily checklist to monitor what is done.

Emergency Maintenance. Unexpected repairs are certain to be needed. Creating an *emergency maintenance plan* will help expedite the unexpected. To be prepared for emergencies, each board member and the management firm should keep a list of critical telephone numbers and other contact information easily accessible at all times. The list should include utility companies, a plumber, an electrician, all other maintenance-related contractors, and police and fire departments.

In larger associations, a manager may need to be aware of more extensive mechanical and building systems maintenance. The manager, board of

---

[1] *Disclaimer*: These sample forms and agreements are not endorsed by the Institute of Real Estate Management. They are presented for informational purposes only and should not be relied upon for accuracy, completeness, or consistency with applicable law. The user is advised to check all applicable state and federal laws before using these forms, agreements, or parts thereof. Because certain forms have legal implications (e.g., management agreements, rental applications), it is recommended that downloaded versions of such forms be reviewed with legal counsel prior to their use and that any modifications made by the user also be reviewed by legal counsel.

directors, and maintenance committee must know the location and repair requirements of all mechanical and building systems. Equipment manufacturers usually provide instruction manuals that should be kept on-site. The manuals offer guidelines to repairing and maintaining most equipment. The association should receive such manuals, together with plumbing and wiring schematics, from the *developer* at the time of turnover.

Associations may have a variety of mechanical equipment, including *heating, ventilation, and air conditioning (HVAC) systems*, boilers and closed loop heat systems, electric motors, cooling towers, pumps, elevators, fans, tanks, and other equipment needing regularly scheduled maintenance. The board, management agent, and maintenance committee should become familiar with the basic operations and maintenance requirements of each piece of equipment. Although contracts for professional maintenance service are common, knowing something about the mechanical equipment allows the board to work more effectively with the management agent and contractors.

Other important areas of knowledge are the primary building systems—plumbing and waterline maintenance. A schematic illustrating the location of all main shut-off valves and service areas is extremely important. Should water begin leaking uncontrollably throughout the building, time is of the essence in getting it under control. Protecting exterior pipes from freezing weather and knowing the location of air conditioning condensation lines in case of blockage are critical strategies to avoid potential damage.

Knowledge of the electrical wiring of a building, including the locations of all panel boxes and meters, is essential. Keeping replacement circuit breakers on hand is also beneficial. Periodic electrical and fire inspections help ensure that everything complies with building and fire codes.

Implement Seasonal Planning. Every association must be aware of and prepare for *seasonal maintenance*. This maintenance should be scheduled for certain elements that need the same maintenance year after year, at or near the same time each year. Cost estimates can be procured well in advance of the work—possibly with great savings due to early planning. Seasonal maintenance can include but is not limited to the following: pruning and trimming of trees and shrubs, weeding, fertilizing, mulching, and watering. Monitoring a sensible irrigation water use plan can save an association hundreds if not thousands of dollars in its annual *operating budget*.

Another important seasonal maintenance concern is preparing for ice and snow removal. This is a major consideration in many parts of the country. If the association has large open areas, such as parking lots and sidewalks, the board should consider hiring a snow removal service. Contracted landscaping firms often provide these cold weather services. A good manager plans ahead and has a sufficient stock of snow-melting chemicals or sand, which is so crucial to the community's health and safety during cold weather.

Resurfacing of paved areas must be seasonally planned, as well. Asphalt lasts for many years with proper resealing and care; however, paved surfaces cannot be patched repeatedly, and eventually they must be replaced. Extensive asphalt work should always be done when the weather is dry and warm. This work usually begins in late spring and ends in the fall when temperatures fall below 50 to 55 degrees.

Gutter, downspout, and storm drain cleaning can be seasonally planned. In most parts of the country, trees shed their leaves from late fall to early winter. After that is the best time to clean gutters and drains and unblock any downspouts. A late spring cleaning is frequently needed to keep summer rainwater flowing easily through these areas. The location of association buildings in relation to surrounding tall trees dictates the timing and frequency of cleanings. The community may not need all the gutters or drains cleaned at once. Performing a preliminary inspection and deciding which gutters and storm drains need cleaning can save many dollars in the maintenance expense budget.

NEGOTIATING CONTRACTS

Preventive and custodial maintenance schedules are meaningless unless the assigned tasks are completed. No matter what maintenance arrangements the association makes, certain services must be contracted and contracts must be negotiated in order for the maintenance responsibilities to be accomplished.

Decision Process

If the association is self-managed and utilizes a self-help maintenance program, many of the maintenance functions may be assigned to volunteer members or a staff hired by the board. If a management firm is employed, the firm should establish the maintenance schedules and provide the necessary personnel to perform required tasks. If an on-site manager is hired to run the community, he or she may be responsible for doing much of the work alone or for hiring personnel to complete the work.

As a rule, outside service is needed whenever complex machinery is involved or special equipment or skills are required. In addition to technical and special skill functions, other services may be performed more efficiently or more effectively by contractors. For example, an association may find it appropriate to contract for janitorial or grounds care services. Local and state regulations may stipulate that only licensed individuals may perform certain services such as extermination, trash removal, and sprinkler and fire extinguisher services. See Exhibit 9.3 for a sample service contract record.

Exhibit 9.3

Service Contract Record

Company	Type Of Service	Frequency Of Service	Termination Date	Amount (Monthly)	Cancellation Provision
	Pool				
	Gardening				
	Janitorial				
	Elevator Maintenance				
	Security Services				
	Trash Removal				

Bid Proposals

If the association recognizes a need for service contractors, it must be prepared to become involved in the contract negotiation process. The first step is getting a bid proposal accompanied by a statement of specifications detailing all the elements of work in writing. Most associations should procure at least three bid proposals from reputable contractors and set a deadline for all submissions. The management firm or the maintenance committee may assist in collecting the bids and then present all written bids to the board for review and acceptance.

In some cases, soliciting three bids may not be practical. Associations frequently develop close relationships with certain service companies, and mutual respect and trust evolve. When the association has a comfort level that a particular contractor remains competitive and performs to standard, the board or managing agent may not wish to rebid to the outside at renewal time. Insurance policies and competitive costs may be such an area of tenured trust.

Management and the board should share a common goal when soliciting a contractor: to find the best service for the most reasonable cost (not necessarily the cheapest) while using contractors with the best industry and client reputations.

Contract Elements

In order to formalize a working agreement between the contractor and the association, a contract must be prepared. At a minimum, the contract should include:

- A detailed statement as to when and how the services are to be performed. (Lacking such specific instructions, the board has no way to evaluate the performance of the contracted services.)
- The amount and terms of compensation to the contractor.
- The circumstances under which either party may be released from the agreement by exercising a cancellation clause.
- A statement on the lines of authority; that is, who will be the liaison on the project. (The designated liaison may be a committee chair, a board member, the management agent, or another person.)

The association board should designate who has the authority to sign on behalf of the association for entering into any contracts. The management agent often accepts this authority. In that case, to avoid future misunderstandings, the board should confirm the procedure in the management contract or by a resolution approved by the board and placed in the business minutes.

Insurance Considerations

To help ensure that the association is protected under workers' compensation, liability insurance, bonding, and any other potential areas of exposure when dealing with contracts, the association's attorney or management agent should review all contracts before they are signed. At the time each contract is awarded, the board should require the contractor to present certificates of four types of insurance:

1. *Vehicle-related injury and property damage insurance.* Protects the association against claims if a vehicle is to be used on the association premises.
2. *Comprehensive general liability (CGL) insurance.* Covers the contractor's employees against bodily injury or property damage while on the premises.
3. *Blanket fidelity bond.* Protects the association if the contractor's employees divert funds illegally or if there is theft of materials designed for use on association premises.
4. *Workers' compensation insurance.* Provides for the payment of benefits determined according to the law for covered occupational injuries or disease incurred regardless of employer fault. (It is important to remember that, in the event that employees are not covered, the association may be required to pay for injuries or damages.)

The board may also require contractors to show proof of *completed operations and products liability coverage.* This type of insurance is intended to cover accidents that occur while the contracted services are being performed—for example, if a hot water heater bursts while being installed by a plumber. The secondary damage from such a water leak could be a costly problem.

Contract Follow-Up

Once the work has been awarded, the management agent or the appropriate liaison is responsible for holding periodic follow-up meetings with the contractor to determine that the work is being completed satisfactorily and invoices are being paid in a timely fashion. Many contractors become upset with associations that delay paying bills even though the work performed has been acceptable. The association should not hold back payment unless work is unsatisfactory. Even when withholding payment is justified, the reason should be adequately communicated to the contractor.

Reviewing annual contracts should be a regular board procedure. If a particular contractor renders proper services, strong consideration should be given to continuing the contract for another year—even when prices escalate. Associations too often mistakenly change contractors annually and damage their reputation in the industry. That could artificially drive their costs up when bids are submitted, or contractors may even decline to submit a bid. The annual review would be the time to discuss contract changes or modifications relating to performance issues or requirements.

Resident Involvement

Finally, the board should establish a firm policy regarding resident involvement with contractors. The board must inform the members that one liaison is responsible for coordinating the work with any contractor or its staff. Any unauthorized interruption in the contractor's work could be at the expense of the association and/or the unauthorized person. Such interference may aggravate contractors and may cause them to quit before completing the job or to refuse to bid on future work. A professional working relationship must be maintained at all times.

EMERGENCY AND DISASTER PLANNING

The advent of large, multifamily community associations has increased the demand to prepare and maintain sophisticated security and life-safety systems. Townhouse and garden projects are lower in density and height than mid- or high-rise developments and do not usually maintain high levels of security or surveillance programs. They may have drive-through car security or entrance gate cameras. Higher-density communities, however, demand more security performance—especially in mid- and high-rise buildings. Life-safety measures, although more complex in a high-density building, are essential for all communities. The following information focuses mainly on the needs of mid- to high-rise communities.

Security Systems

The best time to install an electronic security system is while the building is under construction. Most buildings erected since 1965 contain elaborate limited access systems and alert devices. The cost of installation of such a network in a completed building should be weighed against other security means available and the benefits derived. All residents and the board of directors must be informed of the proper use of their security technology through an ongoing education process. These safety systems have often been upgraded to provide the community with the latest state-of-the-art developments. The management agent must become an expert on the use and care of these resources.

To increase an association's security, the manager should consider many avenues:

- *Lighting.* Adding lighting is one of the least expensive methods of improving security.
- *Intercom systems.* An intercom can be installed between the entrance and the resident's home, allowing electronic, keyless entry by activating an electronic door strike.

- *Computer security systems.* The management agent usually has a master control operated by a computer software program. The system allows management constant monitoring and easy changing of the card key code for new residents, lost cards, or restriction of use on certain entryways, i.e., pools, restrooms, garages, clubhouses, and even residents' main entry doors.
- *Elevator lockouts.* A security system using key or card switches to operate the elevators restricts their use to key- or card-holding members. The same cards can be tracked electronically so the community has a log of which card was used and the time at which entry was granted.
- *Alarms.* Fire suppression–sprinkler systems and strategically placed police monitor alarms can be secured and monitored as additional security measures.
- *Closed-circuit televisions.* Many high-rise communities have closed-circuit television installations. When combined with the installation of camera monitors at various locations, they can provide residents with visual control of all visitor accesses. A resident who wishes to deny access to someone viewed in the monitor can refuse to depress the electronic door release located in his or her home.
- *Guards.* A contract guard service may be used as an auxiliary to the electronic surveillance systems. This could be very expensive and must be carefully evaluated against the total cost of all security measures considered.

Life-Safety Systems

Each community is unique, so one emergency and disaster plan will not necessarily work for all communities managed. Each plan has particulars that are germane to the community it serves; it is a compilation of the efforts of the members, board of directors, and managing agent.

The association's emergency plan should be publicized and posted in appropriate places within the community, and should be given to all members individually. If an urgent circumstance arises, a prepared community will react in a more sensible and predictable manner than a population caught off guard. Knowledge of fire alarm systems, the ability to operate emergency generators, and access to lifesaving equipment, storm warnings, and *emergency procedures* with detailed plans for evacuation facilitate the ability to handle a serious situation properly.

Fire Alarms. Most state and local building codes now stipulate a monitored fire alarm system within a multifamily residential dwelling. Building fire codes and *Building Officials and Code Administrators (BOCA) International* codes require that elevators automatically return to the first-floor level where they are isolated in the event of a fire alarm. This prevents their use by anyone other than the fire department in an emergency. If full-time staff members are available, they should be instructed to immediately contact the fire department to confirm the emergency in the building.

Emergency Lights and Generators. At a minimum, building codes now require battery-operated lighting packs in main corridors and stairways to allow ample time and lighting for vacating the premises in the event of a major system failure or a general power outage. The emergency lighting system should be tested weekly.

Some codes require emergency generator systems. Generators can be vital to preserving life and safety, and should be under a regular maintenance program.

Lifesaving Techniques and Equipment. The knowledge and use of *cardiopulmonary resuscitation (CPR)* techniques has dramatically improved lifesaving ability for many. Everyone in the community should be prepared to save another person's life, and consequently many associations sponsor CPR classes. Some communities supply portable oxygen systems and heart defibrillator kits as life-sustaining measures that association members can use while awaiting the arrival of paramedics.

Evacuation Plans. Most municipalities require buildings of four stories or more to have a detailed, written, and posted plan of evacuation. The local fire marshal or fire prevention bureau reviews these preparations on a regular basis. The plan should include the following:

- Emergency exit locations
- Fire department telephone numbers
- Methods of evacuation
- Procedures for assisting the handicapped

Some communities appoint "floor captains" or "floor fire wardens" to ensure that all residents have evacuated the building in an emergency. Most fire departments will gladly assist in the preparation of an evacuation strategy.

Preparing to take the proper steps in case of a bomb threat is vital for management and building staff. If the association receives such a threat, the local police and fire departments should be notified immediately. They will advise what steps to take. Just as for a fire emergency, a bomb threat evacuation plan should be devised in advance. The management agent and board members must have full knowledge of all areas of their buildings—such as crawlspaces, storage areas, boiler rooms, stairwells, and parking garages—in which an explosive device could be hidden.

In areas subject to tornadoes, hurricanes, or similar natural disasters, communities must have plans in place to respond to storm warnings and handle such emergencies. They must be prepared to assist with resident evacuation if necessary. Prior arrangements should be made for boarding windows or securing areas where flooding or wind damage may occur.

Construction Defects and Toxic Mold

A potential problem for all associations and their managers is the discovery of construction defects within the community. This phenomenon has been around for a number of years and is becoming more prevalent with every passing day. Today's building codes, which make the exterior building envelope watertight and airtight, have brought about many construction defects in this country's newer residences. The problem is exacerbated when moisture gets behind an exterior siding that is so watertight/airtight that it cannot breathe. The moisture trapped inside the wall membrane creates the ideal condition for rot and mold to form. The manager and board of directors must be cognizant of this potentially major issue and take immediate action to remediate the problem.

The manager should contact professional contractors experienced in construction defects, including an attorney and a construction expert. Many attorneys have the needed expertise, and many legal firms will evaluate the association's situation free of charge. The construction expert will determine the extent of and remedy for the problem, and the attorney will give advice on the association's legal rights and any deadlines before implied warranties from the developer expire. Each state has its own statute of limitations, and management needs to know that period before it can perfect any construction defect litigation.

Construction defect and community association attorneys at the law firm of Goff & DeWalt, LLP, in Washington state, provide valuable information concerning mold in their legal resource publication, *In Brief*. Their article titled "Construction Defects & Toxic Mold" states, "The harmful effects of toxic mold have been over-exposed by experts and novices alike in recent years." They point out that extensive research has been done on the "complex chemical reactive and emissions from mold growth." Naturally, some parts of the country are more susceptible to mold than others, and areas with abundant rainfall and moisture will likely have higher mold concentrations than dryer climate areas.

Mold is a common and essential part of our ecosystem, aiding in the role of organic decomposition (the breakdown of dead organic matter such as leaves, dead grass, and tree limbs); but experts say that its presence in our homes can be dangerous and often misunderstood. Most types of mold appear to have no harmful effects. Medical research has identified a link, however, between certain types of mold growth and negative effects on human health. The greenish-black fungus *Stachybotrys chartarum* is the mold that has received the most attention in toxic mold claims.

To combat *any* type of mold growth, it is imperative that expert investigation is initiated to determine the type of mold present at a given location. Homeowners must be aware of the seriousness of problematic molds in their homes and their possible relation to construction deficiencies. The most common ailments to look for associated with mold contamination among homeowners are headaches, coughing, breathlessness, bronchial asthma, skin rashes, eye irritation, drowsiness, and dizziness. More serious conditions include lung disease, brain damage, and cancer.

Mold (or fungus) can live on nearly anything. Common surfaces on which mold growth occurs in buildings are wood, carpet, paper, and so forth. The two main elements that promote the development of fungus on any organic substance are oxygen and moisture. Building materials like wood and paper backing on drywall provide a wonderful growth medium for mold.

The aforementioned *In Brief* article says that, "Whenever there is water intrusion into a building, there is a possibility for mold growth to occur." There can be many areas where water penetration will contribute to mold contamination in a community. Some of the possibilities that promote this growth and should be recognized are:

- Damp storage or crawl spaces;
- Building materials installed while still wet with moisture;
- Reoccurring water penetration into the building due to defective construction;
- Improper design, construction, or maintenance of the building envelope (including siding, roofing, windows, doors, etc.);
- Improper design, installation or maintenance of the HVAC system;
- Leaking water from a burst pipe;
- Building humidifiers not working properly; and
- Encapsulated moisture due to paints or lacquers applied to wet building materials.

When investigating a mold claim, services of an experienced, qualified industrial hygienist should be retained. The association should also acquire legal counsel qualified in handling this type of complex litigation. An expert's opinion can guide the association through the investigation, claim, and (if necessary) litigation.

An association manager must not only be aware of mold and construction defects but also must realize the importance of the immediate remediation of these problems when they are discovered. The difficulty with this maintenance requirement arises from the fact that mold and deterioration are not readily seen without invasive building inspections.

Legal deadlines that apply to associations with construction defects vary from state to state. However, it is important for the managing agent to immediately make the association board aware should any mold be found. An implied warranty from the developer may still be in effect, and in order to prevent a breach of warranty claim, certain legal deadlines must be met. Know the deadline timeframes and work within the guidelines, and the developer may have to pay the cost to remedy the defects.

Appropriate legal action can save considerable resources and promote the wellbeing of the entire association. In the next chapter we will turn to additional insurance and legal matters that concern the professional manager.

10

Legal and Insurance Issues

Specific aspects of community association management often require knowledge from other professionals. For example, insurance professionals can provide legal management ramifications and risk management expertise. Two such experts who contributed their time and energy to this chapter are Kevin Harker, an attorney from Vial Fotheringham, LLP, Portland, Oregon, and Vern Nuecomb, Insurance Broker with American Benefits, also from Portland, Oregon. We have incorporated their expert opinions into our discussion of today's common interest development (CID) management techniques.

INTRODUCTION

Legal and insurance issues are extremely important considerations in the management of community associations. Association managers, board members, and homeowners must have some awareness and understanding of the ways these issues affect them and their property.

LEGAL ISSUES

As planned communities and condominiums become larger and more popular forms of home ownership, homeowners associations increasingly hire professional managers to ensure efficient and proper operation of their communities. While the board typically makes the decisions in both large and small communities, it often opts to have a property management company handle the day-to-day issues that arise. For property managers to have the authority to perform their services, a legal relationship must exist between the homeowners association (or community association) and the property manager. Reviewing Chapter 2 and implementing a management contract similar to the one shown there will help better define the legal relationship for both manager and association.

The board vests the property manager with powers that allow the manager to make necessary decisions over certain aspects of the community association. Because of these powers, the manager becomes potentially liable to anyone injured as a result of any of the manager's decisions or actions.

Legally, the relationship between the community association and the manager is characterized as a principal–agent relationship in which the community association is the principal and the property manager is the agent. Under common-law agency doctrines, the agent acts on behalf of the principal in matters for which the agent is authorized to act. If the agent (property manager) takes unauthorized action, the property manager may become liable to the community association for any damages, and in some cases, may be liable to third parties for his or her unauthorized actions.

For any management decision that could be construed to be solely a professional management decision and not one sanctioned by the board, having the association board ratify or grant the power to the managing agent by resolution is important. If the management contract does not specify your authority to process an association request or demand, have the board memorialize its request and approval in writing.

Role of the Attorney

Not only should the community association consider the services of a professional property manager and a certified public accountant (CPA) as mentioned in previous chapters, but it should also, upon occasion, consider the services of an attorney—preferably one whose expertise is in real estate law and/or community association law. Boards of directors often shy away from hiring legal representatives because of the cost involved. Few associations have attorneys among their members, and even when they do, the attorney members either do not have proficiency in the field or are not able to give their services pro bono (for free).

Even so, as mentioned in Chapter 4, the board is responsible for making good business decisions. Association members will hold the board accountable if they fail to work with a legal specialist when their decisions may jeopardize the community. Associations have been sued, and *liens* have been placed on their members' homes to pay the awards from those suits.

The following are a few services that may require an attorney's assistance:

- Original drafting of the *covenants, conditions, and restrictions (CC&Rs)*, *bylaws*, and *articles of incorporation* (the *governing documents*)
- Interpretation and enforcement of the governing documents
- Assistance with the collection of past-due assessments, including placing liens and following up on foreclosure actions
- Representation of the community association in litigation brought by members of the association or third parties
- Guidance in proper operations and assistance to board members in understanding their roles and responsibilities
- Assistance in rewriting and/or amending the governing documents
- Occasional attendance at meetings that have the potential of "spinning out of control" (often because of a heated issue on the meeting agenda)

Before the community looks for an attorney, the board members must first identify what they need an attorney to do. What issues may require legal assistance? Once they have determined what they need, they can look for a legal specialist in a number of places.

- Local and state bar associations list their members online and in the yellow pages.
- A great place to find attorneys in your community's geographical area is www.lawyers.com.
- Trade associations that represent community associations (e.g., see www.irem.org and www.CAIonline.org) have many members who are attorneys specializing in the field. Generally, attorneys in trade associations are active in their respective organizations and often share invaluable information, at no cost, with their fellow members.

Boards should do their homework carefully when selecting a legal representative. As mentioned, be sure to look for attorneys who specialize in community associations.

Areas of Liability

Lawsuits are usually brought by aggrieved members of community associations. Managers are often named in lawsuits regarding personal injuries or property damage that may have happened on the managed property. This occurs more often today than in years past. Your management agreement should ensure that your firm is held harmless and represented by the association's insurance carrier should such a lawsuit occur. (For further discussion, see the section entitled "Management Contract Indemnification Provisions" below.)

Premises Liability. Property managers are often named as defendants in *premises liability* cases. Premises liability cases stem from personal injuries sustained on the property of others. They include slip and fall incidents and other injuries that result from hazards, defects, or poor maintenance.

Depending on the nature of the relationship between the property manager and the owner, the property manager may have limited duties or may be deemed to have "entire charge" of the premises. In either case, property managers or other independent contractors may be liable for negligence in discharging duties they have assumed. In the instance of a property manager who has taken entire charge of the property, the scope of duty and liability is the same as if he or she were the owner of the property. However, since an owner's duties may be deemed nondelegable in some jurisdictions, the existence of a property manager relationship may not relieve landowners of liability.[1]

Property Damage Liability. Property managers are also named in property damage liability cases that involve allowing certain covenants, conditions, and restrictions (CC&Rs) to be breached. For example, the managed association might be involved in construction defect litigation—especially if the managing agent performed any of the needed repairs or was hired as an expert project manager with the duty to oversee the completion of approved contract work on behalf of the association.

Property damage liability insurance affords protection against liability for damage to the property of another, including loss of the use of property, as distinguished from liability for bodily injury or personal injury to another. In the majority of cases, it is written along with bodily liability protection.

Breach of Contract Community associations also bring suits against property managers. These suits are typically *breach of contract* suits, which are brought for failure to perform a duty in a contract. A property manager may be liable to the community association under his or her employment contract.

---

[1] Karl Baker & Dwight H. Merriam, Homeland Security and Premises Liability, SK002 A.L.I.-A.B.A. 1267, 1271 (Aug. 26–28, 2004).

Debt Collections. Many associations face the problem of trying to collect delinquent assessments. The *Fair Debt Collection Practices Act (FDCPA)* outlawed abusive debt collection practices. While many associations do not fall under the federal law, most states have similar laws. Many managers are responsible for the initial attempts to collect debts. Managers should make sure any attempts to collect debts conform to the FDCPA and/or state laws.

Libel and Slander. Associations have been sued over statements made against certain members. An example of this is a case in which allegedly defamatory statements were made in a letter that management sent out to homeowners, responding to allegations against the management company.[2] Ultimately, the letter was held not to be defamatory.

Fair Housing Act Violations. The *Fair Housing Act* mandates that discrimination based on race, color, religion, sex, or national origin is unlawful. If the association discriminates, it opens itself up to lawsuits. This particularly exposes associations to liability when combined with the *Americans with Disabilities Act.* For instance, handicapped individuals may request closer parking spots if their parking spots are far away from their units. This is a reasonable request in most cases, and the association must make every effort to accommodate such a request. Failure to do so could end in the association defending against a lawsuit. A manager must take care to alert the association and take the correct action to make sure all reasonable accommodations are granted.

Real-World Cases. Property management companies have been sued for negligence in a number of cases. In one case, a homeowner sued the management company for injuries sustained because of negligence in maintaining common property.[3] The court found that the management company did not have a duty to warn of a dangerous condition on the roof. In another instance, a community association and its management company were sued by a mail carrier for injuries sustained.[4] The case was dismissed due to evidence showing that the defendants had no notice of the defects that caused the injury.

Another community association and its management company were sued for defects to the property.[5] The court granted summary judgment (making a judgment without a full trial) and granted in favor of the community association and management company.

---

[2] *Ampleman v. Scheweppe,* 972 S.W.2d 329 (Mo. Ct. App 1998).

[3] *Crown Management, Inc. v. Superior Ct.* 2002 WL 798267 (Cal. Ct. App. 2002).

[4] *Wellington Green Homeowners' Assoc. v. Parsons* 768 NE 2d 923 (Ind. 2002).

[5] *Meute v. City of El Paso* 2000 WL 1204836 (Tex. App. 2000).

In yet another case, a condominium owner sued the Veterans Administration (from which the owner bought the unit), five members of the board, and the property manager, alleging the unit to be structurally unsound.[6] The court dismissed the complaint against the members of the board and the property manager. Keep in mind that, while this was the desired result for the board and property manager, they still both had to pay legal fees to defend against the lawsuit.

In all the cases mentioned above, the property management company was not found liable. However, that did not mean they were not sued. While avoiding being named in a suit may be impossible, this chapter outlines certain steps property managers can take to protect themselves.

No matter how they defend themselves, property managers are sometimes dismissed. In one case, the court remanded to a lower court after going up to an appellate court for further proceedings on a homeowner's complaint including breach of contract, fraud, and breach of *fiduciary* duty.[7]

Lawsuits against property management companies can involve issues other than property liability. For instance, one homeowner sued a community and its management company for *libel*.[8] The management company was consequently dismissed. Issues concerning the Fair Housing Act also arise. One court found that whether the association or property managers could take retaliatory actions against residents of a condominium was an issue for a jury to decide.[9]

Minimizing Liability

In the face of so many potential liabilities, property managers and their companies are wise to implement every available strategy to minimize their liability. Several useful suggestions follow.

Management Contract Indemnification Provisions. One way to minimize potential liability is to have the community association *indemnify* the property manager against third parties. This protects the property manager against claims by members of the community association or the public regarding the manager's work. However, the property manager typically is given the right to contract with third parties regarding maintenance and emergency issues related to the community association. Property managers

---

[6] *Whyte v. United States* 59 Fed. CL. 493 (2004).

[7] *LaGoye v. Civtoria Wood Condominium Association*, 112 S.W.3d 777 (Tex. App. 2003).

[8] *Ampleman v. Scheweppe* 2005 CL 1324782 (Cal. Ct. App. 2005).

[9] *Hamad v. Woodcrest Condominium Association* 328 F.3d 224 (6th Cir. 2003).

must also protect themselves in their own third-party contracts—for example, with landscapers—with a similar *indemnification* provision.

Most indemnification provisions require the community association to indemnify the property manager in all situations unless the property manager acts with gross negligence. The following is typical language found in contracts between community associations and property managers:

> Association shall indemnify, defend, and hold harmless Agent and its employees, agents, officers and directors from and against any and all claims, demands, losses, costs, expenses, obligations, liabilities, judgments, orders and damages, including interest, penalties and attorney's fees, that Agent shall incur or suffer, which arise, result from or relate to the performance by Agent of its duties under this Agreement in good faith and in the ordinary course of business, except for the willful misconduct or gross negligence of Agent. This includes, without limitation and, for example, a situation in which Agent is made a party to litigation, arbitration or other proceeding brought by a Member, a contract vendor of the Association, or an outside party by reason of Agent's position as Agent or its activities hereunder. This provision shall survive any termination of this agreement.

Stipulating in your management agreement that the association will defend you is a very important contract term.

Insurance. Unfortunately, in today's litigious society, it is difficult to avoid lawsuits. The best protection against future lawsuits is proper insurance coverage. *Coverage* is the scope of the protection provided under an insurance contract. A wise manager carries additional insurance coverages like *errors and omissions (E&O) insurance* along with the other protective policies discussed in detail later in this chapter. E&O policies are imperative for working professionals. Managers often require community associations to obtain coverage for them.

Standard Policies and Procedures. To help minimize liability, a manager may adopt standard policies and procedures when conducting association business. While the adoption of such policies and procedures may be time-consuming because the manager must make sure all policies and procedures conform to the law, in the end it will help reduce the possibility of errors that could cause potential liability.

Regular Accounting Audits. To reduce fiscal accounting liability, each association should have regular accounting audits. Audits ensure both manager and association that the money is where it should be; audits also point out errors so they can be corrected. They are a good business practice for managers, and they are invaluable to associations.

Many states and/or association governing documents require an annual *audit* of an association's accounting records. Even if an audit is not required, associations should consider having one performed annually, or at least every two to three years.

Liability-Minimizing Checklist. Exhibit 10.1 can be used as a constructive list of areas that may cause potential claims against professional managers. The information in the checklist gives a good perspective on what the professional manager should know and do to keep unfavorable legal issues from arising. As in any business, time will be spent assisting an association with its legal problems and/or defending the manager's own firm's past management positions.

Another crucial aspect of association management is the implementation of risk management through insurance practices. The rest of this chapter discusses these specific areas of great importance to association communities.

INSURANCE PRACTICES

All businesses face a certain amount of risk in their operations. *Risk management* means dealing with the pure risk to which an organization might be subject. It involves analyzing all exposures to the possibility of loss and determining how to handle these exposures through such practices as avoiding, reducing, retaining, or transferring the risk—usually by means of insurance.

This section presents an introduction to insurance contracts, and to many types of insurance necessary for community associations. The community manager should refer to the CC&Rs, applicable state statutes, and lending institution requirements to determine the types of coverage the association requires. This should be one of the manager's first tasks with the commencement of a new managing contract. Understanding the insurance required by the association's CC&Rs keeps the governing body on track and gives association members a clearer picture of the insurance coverage they should carry. To determine the necessary amounts of coverage, the community manager should always enlist the expertise of a licensed insurance agent who is well-versed in common interest developments.

The Insurance Contract

An *insurance contract* is a legal agreement between two parties: the *insured* and the *insurer*. It promises a certain performance, such as payment for an insured's covered loss, in exchange for certain considerations, such a

Exhibit 10.1

Potential Claims Checklist

- **Main Areas to Avoid Liability**
  - ***Condition of Property.*** Make sure the board does its part by not having deferred maintenance issues.
  - ***Incidents.*** Have there been or are there any ongoing incidents to which the manager should be privy? Even if these were ongoing at the commencement of your management, you could become legally involved before attaining resolution.
  - ***Operations.*** Has the board been operating in a prudent manner? While you are managing, be sure to emphasize the importance of governance according to the association's recorded documents.
  - ***Bookkeeping.*** Does the association have a good fiscal history? Follow ***generally** accepted accounting principles (GAAP)* when implementing the fiscal accounting process.

- **Property and Incidents**
  - ***Pre-Incident***
    - *Preventive maintenance inspections.* Be proactive rather than reactive with any needed maintenance. Develop effective maintenance inspections for present needs and plan for future maintenance needs. Document these needs and submit your findings to the association board. Immediately make the board aware of any health or safety issues.
    - *Routine schedules.* Establish a routine schedule for each property managed, and be faithful in keeping to those schedules.
    - *Internal policy.* Be able to show that your firm has written routine procedures, if requested.
    - *Follow-up repairs.* Follow up on any maintenance process or owner need within a reasonable time. This is one of the most important considerations in preventing legal issues.
    - *Recordkeeping.* Keep association records easily available to the owners. The management firm provides consistency and serves as the historian of past events for each new director elected to the board. Failure to keep such records could be interpreted as not fulfilling a manager's fiduciary role. The absence of a documented history of events can open the door for misinterpretation and deception.
    - *Emergency plans.* Implement sound emergency procedures as needed within the association. Planning ahead in this area could save thousands of dollars in legal expenses if the association is responsible for providing safe emergency procedures.
  - ***Post-Incident***
    - *Follow emergency plans/procedures.* Follow the specifics of the plan that is in place—unless a procedure is officially changed. Going outside the scope of the procedure could create liability for the manager and the association.
    - *Take care of the injured party first.* Providing immediate care is mandatory. Then consider the economic consequences.
    - *Take photos of the area involved after any injured party has left.* Document the incident to the best of your ability and as soon as possible. Photos can be worth a thousand words.

Exhibit 10.1 *(Continued)*

- *Keep records of witnesses.* Get the names and telephone numbers of all witnesses to the incident. Should litigation arise, you may need these contacts.

- *Advise with an insurance broker and/or attorney.* Notify the insurance broker and/or the attorney immediately. Too often, insurance may not be available due to lack of timely notification of the carrier. Most insurance carriers want notification any time potential claims may exist against their policies. Get an attorney involved early in the process.

❖ **Association Operations and Record Keeping**

○ ***Avoidance of Liability***

- *Review the community association's declaration, bylaws, rules and regulations, and policies and procedures.* The management agent must be knowledgeable about an association's governing documents and should adhere to such documents when implementing any of these provisions. All directors on the board must also adhere to such policies. Do not let a board member begin any self-serving action that could be construed as deviating from association governance. Some associations require a separate statement of governance acknowledgment from all newly elected directors before they begin the board position.

- *Observe ongoing practices not otherwise documented.* Precedence can play a role in any future legal outcome, so the manager and the board should be consistent when implementing any compliance issues within the association.

- *Review the community association's current insurance coverage.* Managing agents and directors could be liable if they know the association is underinsured. Requesting a risk appraisal from time to time is prudent.

- *Consult with the association's attorney and insurance broker.* These experts work for the association and want to make sure proper procedures are effected when needed. The managing agent is covered as an additional insured under most association policies, so everyone is on the same team. The manager should get the association's approval prior to consulting with legal counsel due to the potential costs involved.

- *Recommend necessary changes to the board.* The manager's job is also advisory, so recommending changes to the board is appropriate. If the board does not accept your recommendations and liability could be incurred, have your suggestion documented in the board meeting minutes. The association board hires the manager, and the final operating disposition comes from the board, so the manager can either respect the board's policy-making decisions or be prepared to cancel the management agreement if the board appears to be heading into a litigious situation.

○ ***Documentation of Every Position's Authority and Purpose***

- *Volunteers (board and committees).* Brief descriptions of each committee's goals and objectives and officer job descriptions greatly assist in defining responsibilities and provide a snapshot of what is expected.

- *Managers.* The management contract should emphasize management's authority and responsibilities as well as its working relationship with the board and association members.

- *Membership.* Members often do not understand their influential role as owners within an association. Information from the board and managing agent introduces owners to the policies and dealings of an association. This

(continued)

Exhibit 10.1 *(Continued)*

information explains the members' responsibilities and the board's compliance expectations.

- ***Member Communication***
  - *Ongoing*
    - *Welcome letter.* This letter can explain the association's governance and rules and regulations to the new owner. Owners often complain they do not know the procedures for contacting the board or management agent if they need assistance.
    - *Newsletters.* Being informed about important happenings in the community gives owners a sense of involvement in community affairs. That is preferable to owners thinking something might be happening, but not officially being told about issues that may directly affect them.
    - *Web site.* The Internet has given new meaning to associations keeping their public informed. Publishing architectural guidelines with application forms and posting all governance documents on the Web site can increase the effectiveness of the association's policies and procedures.
  - *New rules and regulations from the board or policies and procedures from the management company*
    - *Governance changes.* The board should give all changes in the rules and regulations to all owners in a timely manner before they go into effect. Too often associations make changes and do not follow the proper notice requirements to inform their members.
    - *Policy and procedure changes.* The management company should likewise give timely notice of changes well before they go into effect.

❖ **Proactive Approach**

- ***Standard Contract Forms.*** Maintaining consistent language in all management contracts is important. Allowing wide variances of management operations by having different contracts could cause the agent to be negligent in fulfilling his or her duties due to forgetting the exceptions rather than remembering a constant rule.
- ***Policies and Practices Audits.*** Good managers periodically review the everyday policies and practices to be sure they are followed and to make positive adjustments as needed. Becoming complacent about management review could spell operational inconsistencies that might later become legal issues.
- ***Manager Education.*** A manager who has a good understanding of acceptable business practices and standards is an asset to any business. An avocation of further business relations education should be part of the manager's job description.
- ***Training for Board Members and Other Key Volunteers.*** Regular training programs for the manager and the association's volunteers should be utilized. Many other professionals (e.g., attorneys, insurance agents, and CPAs) offer informative events that expand the association's operational and management knowledge.
- ***Training for On-Site Personnel (Maintenance, Landscapers, Pool Contractors).*** Keeping the association vendors and working staff up-to-date on current trends and procedures instills confidence in the management firm. It also helps the manager be consistent with association members regarding management policies and procedures.

premiums paid. A *covered loss* is any illness, injury, death, property loss, legal liability, or any other situation or loss for which an insurance company will pay benefits under a policy when such an event occurs. A *premium* is the price of insurance protection for a specified risk for a particular period.

Principle of Indemnity. An insurance contract shares characteristics with other contracts. It also has a unique identity in that it follows the principle of indemnity. The *principle of indemnity* states that when a loss occurs, an individual should be restored to the approximate financial condition he or she was in before the loss—no more and no less.

The principle of indemnity closely relates to the requirement of an insurable interest and the exclusion of speculative risks. An insured may only be indemnified to the extent of his or her *insurable interest*—the financial loss the person would experience if the property were damaged or destroyed. *Speculative risks* (those risks for which the final outcome is uncertain) create the possibility of gain or loss—such as in a poker game—and are therefore excluded. Keep in mind that having insurance is not comparable to gambling. The policyholder does not "win" or "lose." The insured may only be returned to the approximate financial condition that existed before the loss occurred.

Parts of a Contract. Because an insurance policy is a legal contract, it must be very specific about the agreements between the insured and the insurer. Most policies contain four parts: declarations, insuring agreements, conditions, and exclusions. The acronym *DICE* can help you remember the four parts:

1. ***D**eclarations.* This part of the contract contains basic information, such as the name of the insured, address, amount of coverage provided, description of the property, and cost of the policy. It is usually on the first page.
2. ***I**nsuring agreements.* The "heart" of the policy, this part states in general what is to be covered: the losses for which the insured will be indemnified. It describes the type of property covered and the perils against which it is insured.
3. ***C**onditions.* This part states the "ground rules" of the policy. It describes the responsibilities and the obligations of both the insurance company and the insured and defines the terms used in the policy. Policy terms are sometimes defined in a separate "definitions" section.
4. ***E**xclusions.* This section describes the losses against which the insured is *not* protected. If an excluded loss occurs, the insured will not be indemnified.

If a change is made to any part of an insurance contract, it is enacted through an endorsement. An *endorsement* is a document that is attached to the policy and modifies or changes the original policy in some way. One might never need to modify the policy using an endorsement change; however, the insurance contract will always contain the four basic parts: declarations, insuring agreements, conditions, and exclusions (DICE).

Deductible. The "self-insured retention," most commonly known as the policy *deductible*, is a very important aspect of any insurance policy. It specifies the amount the insured party must pay before the insurer pays on a claim. The amount of this deductible may determine the annual premium cost to the association; if it is too low, the long-term relationship with the insurance carrier may be jeopardized. Community managers are finding that insurance carriers may decide not to renew policies if there have been many claims against them.

Thus, a good reason to increase the limit of the deductible to a higher rate is to ensure that many potential small claims do not become a burden on the association's master policy. Individual member owners should be sure their insurance policies dovetail with the master association policy—especially if any deductible would be their responsibility when making a claim.

Insurance carriers often cover claims even if, under the association's CC&Rs, a claim is not specified and stipulated as covered by the master policy. Many such claims are specified as the responsibility of the individual homeowner member, not of the association. For example, some of the *limited common elements* maintenance and replacements may be a member's sole responsibility. In high-rises, if serious leaks from equipment that must be maintained by the unit owner go beyond the owner's perimeter, that owner could be liable for all the collateral damage to any common element, limited common element, or other owner's property.

If the present CC&Rs do not address a higher deductible with the burden of the deductible to be that of the entity covered—that is, by the association versus individual member—the association might consider making a resolution or amendment to the CC&Rs similar to the one provided in Exhibit 10.2. Before implementing such a resolution or amendment, be sure to obtain legal advice as to whether such an amendment is legal in your state. Some associations have agreed to pay a member's lower deductible rather than institute a claim against the association's insurance—especially if doubt may exist as to which policy should cover the loss.

Insurance Responsibility Checklist

A checklist of areas of responsibility for insurance, such as the one shown in Exhibit 10.3, is an excellent tool for managed communities. Each

Exhibit 10.2

Insurance Deductible Resolution

THE GOOD CONDOMINIUM ASSOCIATION
BOARD OF DIRECTORS
RESOLUTION DATE: APRIL 30, 2007
RE: INSURANCE

A. The Declaration of Condominium Ownership for THE GOOD CONDOMINIUM Association, a nonprofit corporation formed under the laws of the State of *(the applicable state)*, states that the Association shall obtain, maintain, and enforce policies of insurance as provided in the Declaration or the Bylaws of the Association.

B. Article *(insert here the association's specific paragraph number or letter pertaining to insurance provisions)* of the Declarations of Covenants, Conditions, & Restrictions of the Condominium Association prescribes the type of insurance and specifies the responsibilities of the Association and the owners to place and maintain in force at all times appropriate insurance to protect the owners, the Association, and its members.

C. It is the intent of the Board of Directors to:

1. Ensure that the Association has adequate coverage for property and liability insurance;
2. Ensure the continuing insurability of the Association at a reasonable price;
3. Prescribe a procedure for reporting and processing insurance claims.

D. The Declarations and Bylaws of the Association are silent regarding responsibility for the payment of the Association insurance policy deductible.

NOW THEREFORE, BE IT RESOLVED THAT the conditions, requirements, and procedures set forth below be adopted.

I. INSURANCE DEDUCTIBLE; OWNER AND TENANT INSURANCE

1.1 <u>Determination of Deductible; Notice.</u>

(a) Determination of Deductible by Board. The Board of Directors shall determine the amount of the deductible for property loss insurance policies and any other insurance policies required to be obtained by the Association as provided in the Declarations—*Article 16.1.(a)*—of the Association or applicable law. In determining the deductible under the policies, the Board shall take into consideration, among other factors, the availability, and cost and loss experience of the Association. In making the determination, the Board members shall exercise their reasonable business judgment.

Note: Many associations have established deductibles much higher than usual, e.g., anywhere from $10,000 to $20,000, in order to diminish an overabundant number of small claim losses against the association's policy.

(b) Notice. The Board of Directors shall give written notice to the owners of the amount of the deductible under the Association policies and any change in the deductible proposed in renewal or replacement insurance policies not more than ten (10) days after the

(continued)

Exhibit 10.2 *(Continued)*

effective date of the change. The notice shall be delivered to each unit or mailed to the mailing address of each unit or mailed to the mailing address designated in writing by the owners. The notice shall include the following notice in at least 12-point type that is either all capitals or boldface:

RESOLUTION

**NOTICE
CHANGE IN ASSOCIATION
INSURANCE COVERAGE**

THERE ARE CHANGES IN INSURANCE POLICIES CARRIED BY THE ASSOCIATION. YOU SHOULD IMMEDIATELY NOTIFY YOUR INSURANCE AGENT OF THE CHANGES SET FORTH IN THE ENCLOSED INFORMATION AND ASK YOUR AGENT TO DETERMINE IF CHANGES TO YOUR INSURANCE POLICIES ARE NECESSARY.

1.2. Responsibility for Insurance. The responsibility for insurance shall be as provided in this section.

(a) Owners' Property Insurance. Owners shall be responsible for obtaining and maintaining insurance policies insuring their units for any losses less than the deductible amount under the Association's polices and for insuring their own personal property for any loss or damage.

(b) Tenants. Tenants shall be responsible for insuring their own personal property for any loss or damage.

(c) Owner and Tenant Liability Insurance. Owners and tenants of all units shall obtain and maintain comprehensive liability policies having combined limits of not less than Three Hundred Thousand Dollars ($300,000) for each occurrence. The insurance shall provide coverage for, without limitation, the negligent acts of owners and tenants and their guests or other occupants of the units for damage to the general and limited common elements and other units and the personal property of the others located therein.

(d) Association. The Association shall have no responsibility to obtain or assist in obtaining property loss insurance for any owner or tenant for:

(1) Damage to a unit not covered by the Association's policy (because of the deductible amount or because the claim for loss or damage is one not normally covered by fire and property loss insurance policies with extended coverage endorsements); or
(2) For any damage or loss to the owner's or tenant's personal property.

1.3. Deductible.

(a) Damage Not Resulting from Negligence.

(1) Damage Affecting More Than One Unit. If a loss affects more than one unit, when there is no negligence by any party, the parties that have sustained damage (the Association, unit owners, or both), shall pay their proportionate shares of the Association deductible. The share shall be a percentage

Exhibit 10.2 ***(Continued)***

determined by dividing the damage to those portions of the building, the noncasualty maintenance of which is the responsibility of the party under the governing documents of the association, into the total of all building damage incurred in the loss.

(2) Damage Affecting One Unit. If the damage is confined to a single unit, the unit owner shall be responsible for the entire deductible of the master association policy.

(b) Damage Resulting From Negligence. If a loss affects more than one unit, the common elements, or a combination thereof, to the extent the damage is the result of the negligence of a party, the deductible shall be allocated to the negligent party.

(c) Owner Policy Deductible. Owners of damaged units shall be responsible for payment of their individual condominium unit owner policy deductible.

II. Duplicate Insurance Coverage. In the event of duplicate insurance coverage, the insurance policy obtained by the unit owners shall be considered the primary coverage.

III. Procedure for Claims Handling.

3.1 All claims against the Association's insurance shall be processed through and coordinated by the Board of Directors, or, if authorized, the Association's managing agent.

3.2 Charges of managing agents for handling claims shall be paid by the Association to the extent the deductible is paid by the Association; and by the owner to the extent the deductible is paid by the owner. The deductible is per occurrence. The Association shall, when possible, include the managing agent's insurance claims administrative services within the insurance claim, if a claim is filed.

3.3 The Association shall seek reimbursement for all expenses of processing the claim from an owner when the claim exists and the insurance does not cover all the costs based on the same percentage share as the deductible is allocated.

ATTEST:

________________________ ________________________

Date
Board of Directors

____

____

____

____

Source: Invest West Management, LLC, AMO

community and insurance carrier has different styles of coverage, and the checklist clearly designates the responsible party for insuring each area and paying any deductible.

Insurance Types

Associations need several types of insurance. These include property, comprehensive general liability, directors and officers liability, earthquake (if required), fidelity, flood, and workers' compensation. Each is discussed in the sections that follow; note, however, this is not intended to be an all-inclusive list.

Property Insurance. *Property insurance* indemnifies a person who has an interest in physical property for its loss or the loss of its income-producing abilities. The definition encompasses all lines of insurance written by property and inland marine insurers and can include certain kinds of insurance written by casualty insurers, e.g., burglary and plate glass coverage.

Property Coverage. Property insurance covers all real property and insurable improvements owned and maintained by the homeowners association. This may include the following:

- *Buildings.* Residential units, clubhouses, offices, guardhouses, restrooms, equipment rooms, etc.
- *Structures.* Arbors, trellises, cabanas, pools, play equipment, gates, walls, fencing, fountains, roadways, statues, walks, monuments, etc.
- *Other property.* Furnishings, computers, fine arts, valuable papers, accounts receivable, signs, trees and shrubs, etc.

Buildings can generally be included in property coverage in three ways. The governing documents usually dictate which of the following forms to use:

- *All-inclusive.* Most CC&Rs require this type of coverage. It includes property found in units that was initially installed in accordance with the association's original plans and specifications, or a replacement of like kind and quality. It also *includes improvements and betterments made at the expense of, or acquired by, the unit owner.* This can involve completed additions, fixtures, permanently installed machinery and equipment, fire extinguishing equipment, floor or wall coverings, cabinets, and appliances used for refrigeration, ventilation, cooking, dishwashing, laundering, etc. With this type of coverage, the unit owner only needs to insure his or her personal property for any part of the association deductible for which the unit is responsible.

Exhibit 10.3

Areas of Responsibility Checklist

**AREAS OF RESPONSIBILITY CHECKLIST
FOR MAINTENANCE & INSURANCE**

ASSOCIATION

1. **Exterior Siding & Trim**
   ~Repair, replace, paint, caulk
2. **Gutters & Downspouts**
   ~Repair, replace, paint, caulk, clean
3. **Roofs, Roof Flashing, & Decking**
   ~Repair, replace
4. **Perimeter Wall Studs & Insulation**
   ~Repair, replace
5. **Party Wall Studs**
   ~Repair, replace
6. **Building Ceiling & Floor Rafters**
   ~Repair, replace
7. **Unit Doors & Locks—Exterior**
   ~Paint, caulk, flash, exterior trim
8. **Windows & Screens**
   ~Paint, trim, caulk, flash
9. **Electrical**
   ~Electric panels, meters
   ~Exterior outlets & fixtures
   ~Wiring from meters to unit breakers
10. **Plumbing**
    ~Common supply & drain lines
    ~Central hot water heater
11. **Decks**
    ~Repair, replace, paint
12. **Hallways & Stairways**
    ~Repair, clean, paint
13. **Sidewalks & Steps—Common Area**
    ~Repair, replace, clean
14. **Insect & Pest Control**
    ~Unit exteriors: wood boring or stinging insects; animals
15. **Water & Smoke Damage**
    ~Damage to interior from common area source

(continued)

Exhibit 10.3 *(Continued)*

16. **Fireplace & Chimney**
~Replace chimney cap, exterior repairs

17. **Common Area Trees, Flowers, Plants, Shrubs**
~Maintain, remove, replace

18. **Elevator**
~Repair, replace, remodel

19. **Pool, Pool Deck, Furniture, & Equipment**
~Maintain, repair, replace, remodel

20. **Fences**
~Repair, replace, refinish

21. **Signage—Entry, Address, Street**
~Repair, replace, refinish

UNIT OWNER

1. **Perimeter Wall Interior Sheet Rock**
~Repair, replace

2. **Party Wall Sheet Rock**
~Repair, replace

3. **Unit Interior Wall Sheet Rock & Finish**
~Repair, replace

4. **Unit Interior Ceilings & Floors**
~Finish, sheetrock, insulation, subfloor

5. **Unit Fixtures & Finishes**
~Appliances, cabinets, plumbing fixtures
~Floor coverings, window treatments

6. **Unit Doors & Locks**
~Repair/replace door, door casing, & locks

7. **Windows & Screens**
~Repair, replace

8. **Plumbing**
~Supply/drain lines from connection with common unit water shutoff valves, interior fixtures, unit hot water heater

9. **Decks & Patios**
~Surface materials

10. **Insect & Pest Control**
~Unit interiors

11. **Water & Smoke Damage**
~Damage to unit interior from unit or neighbor source

Exhibit 10.3 ***(Continued)***

12. Fireplace & Chimney
~Clean, interior repairs

13. Electrical
~Unit electric wiring, switches, etc.

Source: Invest West Management, LLC, AMO

- *Standard features.* This type of coverage includes property contained in the units that was initially installed in accordance with the association's original plans and specifications or a replacement of like kind and quality. This coverage *does not include improvements or betterments.* Unit owners can insure improvements and betterments separately on a unit owner's policy.
- *Bare walls.* This coverage excludes property within the units and only covers the structures up to the interior drywall. Fixtures, cabinets, floor or wall coverings, etc. are not covered. With this coverage, a unit owner must insure all interior items (standard items or improvements) with his or her own policy.

Property Coverage Options. After deciding which form of property coverage to use, the association selects the options it needs. The following list details many of the options available and their purposes.

- *Blanket endorsement.* A single amount of insurance that can be used on all property insured without a limitation of coverage on one specific item.
- *Replacement cost coverage.* Replacement of the damaged property with no deduction for depreciation. Unlike *actual cash value*, replacement of like kind and quality is provided at current costs—even if those costs are greater than the cost of the original construction.
- *Extended replacement cost coverage.* Replacement cost coverage with a percentage added for inflation. Coverage is usually 120 to 125 percent of the policy limit.
- *Guaranteed replacement cost (GRC) coverage.* Replacement cost with no cap on the limit of the policy. GRC covers up to the limit of the loss—even if the loss exceeds the limits of coverage outlined in the

policy. The GRC has been the preferred policy for community associations because, with this policy, the community will never be underinsured. Not every insurance carrier offers the GRC.

- *All risk or special form insurance.* A policy that covers loss caused by any peril not specifically excluded. Normal exclusions are earthquakes, floods, pollution, latent defects, insects, and wear and tear.
- *Agreed amount endorsement.* This endorsement waives any coinsurance clause and eliminates the possibility of a coinsurance penalty if the property is not insured to value at the time of loss. The insured and carrier agree to insure the property to a certain stated amount.
- *Building ordinance coverage.* This coverage is generally excluded and must be added by endorsement. The coverage is broken up into three components:
    1. *Contingent liability.* This coverage is needed to rebuild the undamaged portion of a building when regulatory authorities condemn an entire building rather than replacing just the damaged portion.
    2. *Demolition.* This covers the cost of demolition and removal of debris of the undamaged portion of the building in the event that building ordinance or law requires demolition.
    3. *Increased cost of construction.* This covers the increased cost associated with reconstruction to meet current building codes.

Comprehensive and Commercial General Liability. In most jurisdictions, "comprehensive" general liability policies have been replaced by the newer "commercial" general liability forms, which include all the standard and optional coverage of the earlier forms. Both are discussed here for ease of comparison and understanding.

Liability insurance pays for and renders services on behalf of an insured for loss arising out of his or her responsibility to others imposed by law or assumed by contract. A *comprehensive general liability* or a *commercial general liability (CGL)* policy covers a variety of general liability exposures, including premises and operations (owner, landlord, and tenant or manufacturer and contractors); completed operations; products liability; and owners and contractor protection. Contractual liability and broad form coverage can be added to *comprehensive* general liability coverage. The latest *commercial* general liability forms include all sublines and provide broad coverage.

Primary Liability Coverage. CGL policies insure against third-party claims arising from alleged bodily injury or property damage to members of the public. The insurance company has the duty to defend the association against any claim that alleges injury or seeks damages, even if the association is negligent. The property management company is generally included as an *additional insured*—a person other than the named insured who is protected under the terms of the contract. Usually, additional insureds are added by endorsement or referred to in the wording of the definition of *insured* in the policy itself.

Coverage should include the following:

- *Host liquor liability.* Provides coverage for liability that may arise if the association sponsors events at which alcoholic beverages are consumed or served.
- *Nonowned or hired auto liability.* Provides coverage for the association against liability when a nonowned or hired vehicle is used for association business.
- *Independent contractors liability.* Protects the association from loss due to liability arising from operations of subcontractors.
- *Personal injury.* Extends bodily injury to include false arrest, imprisonment, malicious prosecution, libel, slander, defamation of character, invasion of privacy, and wrongful eviction and entry.
- *Contractual liability.* Provides liability protection for a legal obligation assumed under the terms of a contact.
- *Advertising liability.* Provides coverage against claims of libel, slander, defamation of character, infringement of copyright, invasion of privacy, etc. arising from an advertising program.
- *Medical payments.* Provides coverage for medical expenses of members of the public injured on the common property.
- *Cross liability.* Provides protection if an owner or member of the association sues the association for bodily injury damages occurring on common areas because of negligence on the part of another unit owner or the association.
- *Severability of interest.* Precludes the insurance company from denying liability because of negligent acts of the association or a unit owner.

Liability Limit. The *liability limit* is the maximum amount for which a liability insurance company provides protection under a particular policy. Condominium associations must examine the limits of their liability insurance to ensure that enough insurance is in place to protect individual condominium unit owners from sharing in large judgments.

Three types of liability limit are generally recognized for CGL policies: claims-made, general aggregate, and occurrence. The types of limits available for the older and newer forms of CGL policies vary slightly; they are indicated below:

- *Claims-made coverage.* A policy providing liability coverage only if a written claim is made during the policy period or any applicable extended reporting period. For example, a claim made in the current year could be charged against the current policy even if the injury or loss occurred many years in the past. If the policy has a retroactive date, an occurrence prior to that date is not covered. (Available for *commercial* general liability.)
- *General aggregate coverage.* This limit represents the most the insurance company will pay for any and all liability occurrences or losses under the policy during any policy year. (Available for *comprehensive* general liability.)
- *Occurrence coverage.* A policy form providing liability coverage only for injury or damage that occurs during the policy period, regardless of when the claim is actually made. For example, a claim made in the current policy year could be charged against a prior policy period; it may not be covered if it arises from an occurrence prior to the effective date of the policy. (Available for *both* CGL types.)

An umbrella or excess policy is commonly recommended to obtain higher limits. *Umbrella liability insurance* can also include general liability and directors and officers liability.

Directors and Officers Liability. *Directors and officers liability insurance* protects directors and officers against claims arising out of loss from alleged errors in judgment, breaches of duty, mismanagement, or wrongful acts. A *wrongful act* could be any breach of duty, neglect, error, misstatement, misleading statement, omission, or other act performed or wrongfully attempted by the association. This type of insurance also covers expenses incurred in defending lawsuits arising from alleged wrongful acts of the officers or directors. This must be mandatory coverage for the professional community management firm. Every management contract should insist on the association including its management agent as an additional insured on the property.

Directors and officers liability policies should cover the following:

- The association
- Directors and officers, past and present

- Employees
- Committee members
- Volunteers
- The manager or management company

Common exclusions from directors and officers liability policies include the following:

- Fraudulent or illegal acts
- Failure to maintain earthquake insurance
- Pollution
- Construction defects
- Bodily injury

Note: Policies differ in coverage and exclusions, so please read the policy for specific information.

Earthquake Insurance. Not every association needs coverage against earthquakes. However, if it is a requirement of the CC&Rs, unless a resolution to change such required coverage is made, it must be included in the association's insurance coverage. Usually this is categorized as being part of the *difference in conditions (DIC).*

If the association's documents require earthquake insurance, the association must purchase the coverage. If the documents do not require earthquake insurance, they are usually worded so the association *may* purchase it. In some planned developments, the association is not responsible for insuring the structures for any risk.

When earthquake coverage is taken, the deductible amount may be a negotiable item. This insurance usually carries a 5 to 10 percent deductible for each occurrence or by line of coverage.

Fidelity Insurance. *Fidelity insurance* is a type of surety that means the insurance company will reimburse an employer, the insured, for loss due to the dishonest acts of a covered employee. If the manager is a direct employee of the association, the association's fidelity coverage covers that employee. However, if the manager is an employee of a third-party management company, that company's fidelity coverage may cover that employee only for the management company's losses.

One way for the association's funds to be covered by fidelity insurance is for its policy to endorse the management company onto the policy. Some fidelity insurance policies allow this practice.

Coverage indemnifies the association for loss of money, securities, or any other property due to dishonest acts committed by an employee acting alone or in collusion with other persons with the intent to cause the association to sustain a loss. Examples of dishonesty include theft, larceny, embezzlement, and wrongful abstraction. Directors, officers, and management company employees are deemed employees of the association.

Limits are determined by the *Federal National Mortgage Association (FNMA)* or the governing document (CC&R) requirements, and they generally require a limit equal to three months' association fees plus reserves.

Flood Insurance. Lenders require homeowners in community associations in flood plains to obtain flood damage insurance through the *National Flood Insurance Program (NFIP)* or through their own sources of coverage. When flood insurance coverage is taken, the deductible may be a negotiable item. This insurance usually carries a 5 to 10 percent deductible by line of coverage.

Workers' Compensation Insurance. *Workers' compensation insurance* is an insurance policy that pays workers' compensation law benefits on behalf of the insured employer. It insures against claims for work-related injuries or diseases suffered by employees that are compensable by statute and/or imposed by law as damages.

According to state law, workers' compensation benefits must be paid to an employee by his or her employer without regard to liability. Payment is made in the case of injury, disability, or death as the result of occupational hazards. Coverage is provided for payment of medical expenses and reimbursement of lost wages. The association must determine the amount of insurance coverage and the terms of the coverage.

Coverage should be considered even if the association has no regular employees. Protection may be necessary if the association employs casual labor or hires an independent contractor with no insurance coverage. In addition, coverage may be needed for contractors who have let their policies lapse or have done work outside the scope of their contractual duties.

As mentioned before, there is indeed a high degree of liability involved in the management of community associations. This chapter has provided an overview of many legal and insurance aspects that affect the wellbeing of associations. A prudent manager will stay up-to-date on these issues and policies, maintaining appropriate expert and legal counsel when necessary. Proactively minimizing the risk involved in association management—for individuals sitting on the board as well as the professional manager—paves the way for a healthy, well-managed community.

Glossary

accounts payable (A/P) Monies due to others for services rendered or goods ordered and received.

accounts receivable (A/R) Monies due from others for services rendered or goods ordered and delivered.

Accredited Management Organization® (AMO®) A designation conferred by the Institute of Real Estate Management (IREM) on real estate management firms that are under the direction of a Certified Property Manager® (CPM®) and meet and comply with stipulated standards as to accounting procedures, performance, and the protection of funds entrusted to them.

Accredited Residential Manager® (ARM®) A professional certification conferred by the Institute of Real Estate Management (IREM) on individuals who meet specific standards of experience, ethics, and education.

accrual-basis accounting A method of accounting that involves entering amounts of income when they are earned and amounts of expense when they are incurred, even though the cash may not be received or paid; also called *accrual accounting*. All certified audits must use *accrual accounting*. Compare *cash-basis accounting*.

actual cash value (ACV) Insurance that pays a claim based on the purchase price of the item, minus an allowance for depreciation because of age and use. Compare *replacement cost coverage*.

additional insured A person other than the named insured who is protected under the terms of the contract.

agenda The outline or plan for a meeting, including matters to be acted or voted upon.

agreed amount endorsement An amendment that waives any coinsurance clause if the insured carries insurance in an agreed amount. The insurer then agrees to pay the face amount on the policy in the event of total loss of property covered or upon occurrence of a stated contingency.

all risk insurance A policy that covers losses caused by all perils except those specifically excluded in the policy contract. Also called *special form insurance* or *special property coverage.*

Americans with Disabilities Act (ADA) Enacted in 1990, the federal law that prohibits discrimination on the basis of disability. Of the Act's five sections, two are directly applicable to real estate managers: Title I (employment) prohibits discrimination in recruiting, hiring, promotions, compensation, training, and termination on the basis of physical or mental disability. If qualified applicants or employees who have a disability can perform the *essential functions* of a job, employers must make *reasonable accommodations* for them by improving access, restructuring jobs, adjusting work schedules, and the like. Title III requires all buildings that are open to public commerce to be made accessible to disabled people to the maximum extent possible by removal of architectural barriers in areas of public accommodation, provision of auxiliary aids and services to assist in communication, and modification of discriminatory policies, procedures, and practices. Title III affects all public areas of commercial properties and areas of residential properties that are open to the public.

annual budget A 12-month estimate of income and expenses; the financial plan of operation that the association adopts. The budget determines assessments, purchases, and savings strategies; it is a tool for measuring financial performance. Also called *operating budget.*

annual meeting A once-a-year mandatory assemblage of unit owners to conduct condominium or homeowners association business as required by the governing documents. The board gives its annual report to the members, elects a board of directors for the upcoming year, and presents the new budget for ratification, if necessary.

arbitration A conflict resolution process that is usually sanctioned and implemented by the local courts. Its decisions have a stipulated judgment as the final result. As with any legal process, it may have a negative effect on the association and should be a final resort in resolving issues.

architectural control committee (ACC) A volunteer committee that exists for the purpose of preserving the community's architectural integrity.

articles of incorporation The document that establishes the corporate structure for the community association; a certificate that establishes a homeowners association as a corporation under state law. These articles define the purpose and powers of the association. Also called *certificate of incorporation.*

assessments In community associations, these are amounts charged against each owner to fund the community's operation. Also called *dues*, *maintenance fees*, or *regular assessments.* See also *special assessments*; *individual assessments.*

asset Any item that has monetary value and is owned by a person or business, such as real property, cash, land, stocks, bonds, or equipment. Usually used in plural, *assets*, to identify the collection of entries on a balance sheet that represent the book values of various categories of items owned (e.g., *capital assets*, *current assets*) as of a given date.

assignment The transfer, in writing, of an interest in a bond, mortgage, lease, or other instrument. The transfer of one person's interest or right in a property (e.g., a lease) to another. Also, the document by which such an interest or right is transferred. Specifically, the document used to convey a leasehold is called an *assignment of lease.*

Association Management Specialist (AMS) A professional designation conferred on the manager who has demonstrated professional competence by having two years' experience managing the finances, administration, and facilities of at least one association.

audit An independent look at an association's financial records; usually occurs annually. Certified public accountants (CPAs) analyze the association's financial statements and provide assurance they are presented in accordance with *generally accepted accounting principles (GAAP).*

balance sheet A statement of the financial position of a person or a business (or community association) at a particular time, indicating assets, liabilities, and owner equity; provides a quick snapshot of a community's financial stability.

binder A tool used by the association manager; generally contains the current year's operations and "immediate access" information, designed for quick reference and to be taken to board meetings. The binder can be developed in an electronic format.

blanket endorsement A single amount of insurance that can be used on all the insured's property without limitation of coverage on one specific item.

blanket fidelity bond Insurance to cover the loss of money or of real or personal property when such loss is due to dishonesty of any employee of the company. Otherwise, a *fidelity bond* is usually obtained on an individual basis.

board of directors In a community association, the volunteer leadership elected to enforce the governing documents; a committee entrusted to represent the interest of all members in major financial or mechanical decisions. Also called *board of managers* or *board of trustees.*

breach of contract Failure to fulfill an obligation (as a mortgage or other contracted payment) when it is due. The nonperformance of a duty, such as those required in a lease or other contract. Also called *default.*

budget An itemized estimate of income and expenses over a specific time period for a particular property, project, or institution. The guide to an association's current and future financial operations; also called *financial plan.*

budget and finance committee An important advisory body of the association that works with the treasurer (usually a member), management agent, and board on all financial matters. This committee assists in preparing the annual budget for submission to the board of directors.

budget variance statement A type of financial statement that shows the differences between projected and actual amounts of income and expenses. Higher income and lower expenditures than expected constitute favorable variances, while lower income and higher expenditures are reported as unfavorable variances. Usually a component of the monthly management report sent to ownership.

Building Officials and Code Administrators (BOCA) International A non-profit organization that set up a model building code used widely in U.S. municipalities.

building ordinance coverage Insurance coverage purchased in addition to a fire and extended coverage policy to fully cover replacement cost of the structure (because rebuilding or repairs may have to conform with current building codes, increasing the cost of such work) and to meet any mortgage requirements that are in place.

business judgment rule A rule that serves to protect the decisions of the board when those decisions are not arbitrary or illogical. In legal cases, when the board has acted in good faith, exercised honest judgment, and acted in the best interests of the association, the courts will tend to treat the board the same as they would any other corporate director making a business decision for an organization.

bylaws Regulations that provide specific procedures for handling routine matters; secondary laws that govern a community association's internal affairs and deal with routine operational and administrative matters. Also called *code of regulations*.

capital expenditures Amounts spent on capital assets, such as major improvements, large equipment, additions to buildings, buildings themselves, and land.

capital replacement reserves Monies set aside in an investment tool for future major expenses (e.g., roof replacement, painting, asphalt sealing).

cardiopulmonary resuscitation (CPR) A basic emergency procedure for life support consisting of artificial respiration and manual external heart massage.

cash-basis accounting A method of accounting that recognizes income and expenses when money is actually received or paid; also called *cash accounting*. Compare *accrual-basis accounting*.

cash flow statement A report of the actual inflow and outflow of cash and its related sources and uses in a given accounting period; typically a 12-month spreadsheet showing a month-to-month picture of the flow of money through a property.

Certified Manager of Community Associations (CMCA) A professional designation conferred by the Community Associations Institute (CAI) on a manager who has demonstrated a fundamental knowledge in the management of community associations.

Certified Property Manager® (CPM®) The professional designation conferred by the Institute of Real Estate Management (IREM) on individuals who distinguish themselves in the areas of education, experience, and ethics in property management.

chart of accounts A classification or arrangement of account items by type of income or expense (e.g., rent advertising, insurance, maintenance), as well as assets and liabilities, accounts receivable, and accounts payable.

code of behavior A set of principles describing the behaviors that are commonly recognized and used to govern an organization; frequently outlined in a specific ethical code or a code of conduct for the members of the organization to follow. Such codes exist to guide interactions between individuals or within the group.

commercial general liability (CGL) insurance This inclusive policy provides broad protection against liability claims, including all standard and optional coverage of the earlier *comprehensive* general liability forms. Compare to *comprehensive general liability (CGL) insurance.*

common area Portion of the entire community association that is not defined in the declaration as belonging to an association member's individual unit, lot, parcel, or space; used by all of the unit owners, and all owners share the common operation and maintenance expenses. Also called *common elements.*

common elements Another name for the *common area* of a community association.

common interest development (CID) Another name for *community association.*

community association A type of housing that combines individual ownership of individual dwellings with shared ownership of the common elements by the entire group of community owners. Individual owners, through compulsory association membership, must share in the decisions affecting those areas of the association that are common to all who live in the community. Encompasses, among others, the planned unit development (PUD), condominium, cooperative, and homeowners association (HOA). Also known as a *common interest development (CID).*

Community Associations Institute (CAI) A professional trade association that offers courses and professional designations respected in the industry. This membership organization includes condominium and homeowners associations, cooperatives, and association-governed planned communities; individuals and firms that manage these types of properties; and other individuals and organizations who work with or provide services to community associations.

community building The use of strategies intended to create or enhance a sense of community among individuals who live in a particular area or have a common interest.

completed operations and products liability A type of insurance coverage purchased by contractors to protect themselves from liability arising from manufacturing defects after installation of fixtures, equipment, or mechanical items. Also called *completed products liability.*

compliance Fulfilling specified requirements as stipulated by law or the terms of a lease agreement.

comprehensive general liability (CGL) insurance An inclusive policy that provides broad protection against liability claims, and to which contractual liability and broad form coverage can be added. In most jurisdictions, these policies have been replaced by the newer *commercial* general liability forms. Compare to *commercial general liability (CGL) insurance.*

condemnation A declaration that a structure is unfit for use. The taking of private property for public use by governmental power of eminent domain, including payment of just compensation. Also, the official act to terminate the use of real property for nonconformance with governmental regulations or because of hazards to public health and safety.

condo-hotel A type of community association in which owners pay monthly assessments and units are rented out for a specific amount of time each year to outsiders. Also, this type of residential building or unit in such a building. See also *community association.*

condominium (condo) A multiple-unit structure in which the units and pro rata shares of the common area are owned individually; a unit in a condominium property. Also, the absolute ownership of an apartment or unit, generally in a multi-unit building, which is defined by a legal description of the air space the unit actually occupies plus an undivided interest in the common elements that are owned jointly with the other condominium unit owners. In mobile home parks or manufactured housing communities, outright ownership of an individual lot (including pad, utility connection, parking space, etc.) within a multiple lot part or community along with a prorated shared ownership of the common area and common facilities. See also *community association.*

conflict of interest A situation that arises when the private interests of an individual in a position of trust (such as a director) conflict with the interests of the association.

contingency cost The expense to cover any unknown condition (such as an accident) or any unforeseen expenditure. Included when estimating management fees to cover unexpected costs that arise as the job is in progress.

cooperative (co-op) An association in which individuals own shares of stock in a corporation that holds the title to a multiple-unit residential structure. A shareholder does not own a specific unit outright but has the right to occupy it as a co-owner of the cooperative association under a proprietary lease. Also, the building owned by such a corporation or an apartment in such a building. See also *community association.*

covenants committee A committee that may assist outside counsel in preliminary work on nonpayment of assessments, violations of association rules and regulations, and foreclosures. It is a judiciary for hearing cases involving violations or infractions of rules and reporting recommendations to the board. Though it may not be included in all communities' committee structures, utilizing a covenants committee carries great weight if legal enforcement and judgments of a punitive nature are necessary.

covenants, conditions, and restrictions (CC&Rs) Another name for *declaration.*

covered loss Any situation or loss for which an insurance company will pay benefits under a policy when such an event occurs.

current liabilities Economic liabilities (e.g., accounts payable, accrued interest not yet due) that arise in the conduct of business activity and must be met in a comparatively short time (usually within a one-year period).

custodial maintenance All policing and housekeeping functions as they relate to the common area. The day-to-day cleaning and other work that is essential to preserving the value of a property; also called *janitorial maintenance* or *housekeeping*.

declarant The person (usually the developer) under whose control the association exists for a defined initial period before it is transferred to the association members.

declaration The most important document the community association uses to govern itself. A legal document that establishes how everyone and everything is to operate within the organization; it commits land to community association use, creates a community association and serves as its constitutional law, defines the method of determining each unit owner's share of the common area, and includes restrictions and covenants. The declaration defines individual ownership rights as well as the association's rights. Also called the *deed of restrictions* or the *covenants, conditions, and restrictions (CC&Rs).*

deductible A specified amount the insured party must pay before the insurer pays on a claim.

deed of restrictions Another name for *declaration.*

deferred maintenance Maintenance issues that are scheduled for completion at a future date. Ideally these are tasks that are not urgent and can be performed at a more opportune time without increasing the severity of the problem. However, ordinary repairs that are deferred can eventually have negative effects if neglected for too long. Also, an amount needed for repairs, restoration, or rehabilitation of an asset (e.g., real property) but not yet expended. See also *preventive maintenance.*

Department of Housing and Urban Development (HUD) A department of the U.S. government that supervises the Federal Housing Administration (FHA) and a number of other agencies that administer various housing programs.

developer The individual or entity that invests in building a property and is responsible for construction and, when the development is a rental property, may also engage in marketing and leasing. The developer may also be the owner of the land, or the developer's investment may consist solely of time and expertise. Real estate development is often done on a speculative basis.

difference in conditions (DIC) A policy designed to fill in gaps in a business's commercial property insurance coverage; a separate contract that expands or supplements property insurance so as to cover on an all-risk basis, subject to certain exclusions.

directors and officers liability insurance Protection against financial loss arising out of alleged errors in judgment, breaches of duty, and wrongful acts of a board of directors and/or officers in carrying out their prescribed duties.

due process An established course for judicial proceedings designed to safeguard the legal rights of the individual. A minimal level of fairness that the courts insist be given to anyone before he or she is punished or fined.

dues Another name for *assessments.*

easements Legal rights afforded a person to use land owned by another person or business for a specific purpose. Easements may be granted by a deed or created as a result of actual use that was not prohibited.

emergency maintenance Unscheduled repairs that must be done immediately to prevent further damage or to minimize danger to life or property.

emergency maintenance plan The written guide for handling unexpected repairs and maintenance emergencies, to be kept by each board member and the management firm for easy access. The plan should include a list of critical telephone numbers and contact information for utility companies, plumbers, electricians, all other related contractors, and police and fire departments.

emergency procedures Procedures developed in order to minimize injury to people and damage to property in the event of natural or manmade disasters, usually including specific procedures for evacuating buildings.

endorsement An amendment to an insurance policy that provides or excludes specific coverage for a specific portion or element of a property, or makes additions or changes to the existing terms of a policy; also called a *rider.*

equity The value of real property in excess of debt. The interest or value that an owner has in real estate over and above the mortgage and other financial liens against it; outright ownership. In accounting, the excess of a firm's assets over its liabilities. See also *balance sheet.*

errors and omissions (E&O) insurance A form of liability insurance. In the case of the property manager, E&O insurance protects against liabilities resulting from honest mistakes and oversights (but provides no protection in cases of gross negligence). Sometimes called *professional liability insurance.*

exclusive common area Another name for *limited common area.*

executive summary A brief summation analysis of the physical assets of the property and the financial status of the community; provides the board with an overview of the community's reserve funding situation.

ex officio member A person who serves a committee by attending meetings and offering counsel, but does not have a vote in the committee's decisions.

expenses Any business-specific costs incurred in operating the community. For income tax purposes, costs that are currently deductible from income, as those for goods or services.

extended replacement cost coverage Insurance that includes *replacement cost coverage* plus an added percentage for inflation.

Fair Debt Collection Practices Act (FDCPA) A federal law that created a series of guidelines for debt collectors to follow. Designed to prevent collection agencies from harassing debtors, the law was later expanded to include any organization that collects consumer debt (including real estate managers). The law is governed and regulated by the Federal Trade Commission (FTC).

Fair Housing Act Alternate name for Title VIII of the Civil Rights Act of 1968, which prohibits housing discrimination on the basis of race, color, religion, and/or national origin in both rental and sales practices. The Act makes several types of activities illegal, including refusal to rent, discriminatory language or images in advertising, and denying the availability of units. The law is enforced by the U.S. Department of Housing and Urban Development (HUD).

Federal Housing Administration (FHA) A division of the U.S. Department of Housing and Urban Development (HUD) whose main activity is insuring residential mortgage loans from private lenders. The FHA does not lend money; nor does it plan or construct housing, but it does set standards for construction and loan underwriting.

Federal National Mortgage Association (FNMA) Often referred to as *Fannie Mae*, a U.S. government–sponsored private corporation that buys mortgages from banks and other lending institutions and sells them to investors to create a fund for mortgage lending.

fidelity insurance A type of surety to reimburse an insured employer for loss due to the dishonest acts of a covered employee.

fiduciary A person to whom property or power is entrusted for the benefit of another. One charged with a relationship of trust and confidence, as between a principal and agent, trustee and beneficiary, or attorney and client, when one party is legally empowered to act on behalf of another.

fiduciary relationship An agreement based on trust in which one person or group handles financial transactions for another.

financial plan Another name for *budget.*

floor plan An organizational design for situating employees in an office to attain maximum functionality. Also, architectural drawings showing the floor layout of a building and including precise room sizes and their interrelationships. The arrangement of the rooms of a single floor of a building, including walls, windows, and doors.

full management A plan for managing a community association that requests all the services a professional management company provides.

fund accounting A method of accounting and presentation in which assets and liabilities are grouped according to the purpose for which they are to be used. Fund accounting segregates association financial activities into operating funds and replacement funds.

general consent Another name for *unanimous consent.*

general ledger A formal record of all a community association's financial transactions, using the *chart of accounts* to identify the classification of each transaction. Accounts are transferred as final entries from the various journals to the general ledger, where they are posted as debits and credits and thus show the accumulated effects of transactions.

generally accepted accounting principles (GAAP) The principles used to establish accounting procedures; they help to establish uniformity in the financial statements that community associations receive and create.

goals Objectives in a plan of action to accomplish a vision.

governing documents The legally recognized and recorded paperwork that creates and controls the association. A collection of documents including the plat map, declaration, articles of incorporation, bylaws, rules and regulations, and policies and procedures.

guaranteed replacement cost (GRC) coverage Insurance that covers replacement costs with no cap on the policy limit.

heating, ventilation, and air conditioning (HVAC) systems Combinations of equipment and ductwork for producing, regulating, and distributing heat, refrigeration, and fresh air throughout buildings.

historical data Statistics or items of information that are over one year old.

homeowners association (HOA) An organization of homeowners in a condominium, cooperative, or housing subdivision whose major purpose is to maintain and provide for the rights of owners to have easement in the use of common areas. Homeownership is a requirement for membership. An HOA may, in some instances, be organized by the builder or developer of a condominium, cooperative, or planned unit development (PUD). Also called *planned development community*. See also *community association*.

horizontal property A term often used to refer to condominiums in Brazil.

Horizontal Property Act of 1958 Puerto Rico passed this act to define the ownership of real property under the condominium concept. The legislation was motivated by Puerto Rico's booming population, housing shortage, and scarce buildable property.

incorporated Formed into a legal corporation; can fall under the jurisdiction of the state corporation statutes.

indemnification Legal exemption from responsibility for a loss that may occur in the future or for a loss or damage already suffered. The condition of being indemnified. The action of indemnifying.

indemnify To exempt from incurred liabilities or penalties. To secure against harm, damage, or loss. Contracts and insurance policies usually include an *indemnification clause*.

individual assessments Monetary penalties imposed on a single owner. An individual assessment may be imposed for not paying regular assessments in a timely manner or to reimburse the association for any maintenance repairs that are the sole responsibility of one owner. Also called *personal assessments*. See also *assessments*; *special assessments*.

inspection An in-depth visit to a property to check on matters such as compliance issues, architectural control, and special project reviews.

Institute of Real Estate Management (IREM®) A professional trade association of individuals who meet established standards of experience, education, and ethics with the objective of continually improving their respective managerial skills by mutual education and exchange of ideas. The Institute is an affiliate of the NATIONAL ASSOCIATION OF REALTORS® (NAR), and is the only professional real estate management association serving both the multifamily and commercial real estate sectors. IREM offers courses and professional designations respected in the industry. See also *ACCREDITED MANAGEMENT ORGANIZATION® (AMO®)*; *ACCREDITED RESIDENTIAL MANAGER® (ARM®)*; *CERTIFIED PROPERTY MANAGER® (CPM®).*

insurable interest An interest in an insured person or thing that will support the issuance of an insurance policy.

insurance committee This may be a separate committee, or it may be combined with the budget and finance committee. Its function is to evaluate the insurance needs of the association, obtain bids from reputable sources that provide community association insurance, and review such policies each year to ensure the needs of the association are met.

landscape and grounds committee A committee that concentrates its efforts on overseeing all common areas and individual homeowners' grounds. This committee makes expense recommendations and works with the management agent to write specifications for landscape and grounds care. This committee is often referred to as the *outdoor maintenance committee.*

liability An obligation to do or to refrain from doing something. In legal terms, a duty or responsibility owed to another from which a claim may arise against an individual or a business. In accounting, a debt owed by an individual or a business. In a balance sheet, cash inflows and outflows are classified as assets and liabilities; see also *current liabilities*; *long-term liabilities.* In insurance, legal responsibility for bodily injury or damage to another person's property caused by negligence.

liability limit The maximum amount for which a liability insurer will provide protection on a single claim.

libel Defamation that maliciously or damagingly misrepresents by written or printed words.

lien The claim of one person upon the property of another to secure the satisfaction of a debt or obligation. In a homeowners association, a lien can be placed on the property, possibly leading to foreclosure, if a property owner fails to abide by the governing regulations.

limited common area That portion of the community association that is defined in the declaration as devoted to the exclusive use of one or more members but not to all of them. Also called *exclusive use common area* or *limited common elements.*

limited common elements Another name for *limited common area.*

long-term liabilities In accounting, obligations whose maturity dates are more than a year from the date on the balance sheet. In finance, debts whose due dates are more than ten years in the future; *long-term debt.*

lot A distinct portion of land; an individually owned portion of a homeowners association, typically consisting of a piece of land and everything on it.

maintenance administrators Specialized staff hired by management firms to supervise and coordinate maintenance operations. They receive requests, create work orders, contact vendors for repairs, determine the best response to maintenance issues, and oversee the execution of maintenance jobs.

maintenance committee This committee is responsible for overseeing the interior and structural portions of the common area. Periodic inspection of the common elements may be necessary in addition to reviewing work specifications and estimates for contractual work. This committee often works closely with a management agent in inspecting and checking work projects.

maintenance fees Another name for *assessments*.

management agreement A contractual arrangement between the owner(s) of a property and the designated managing agent, describing the duties and establishing the authority of the agent and detailing the responsibilities, rights, and obligations of both agent and owner(s).

marina condominium A type of community association in which purchasers buy the moorage slip for their boat and pay assessment fees to maintain the common elements, such as docks, moorage covers, electrical and sewage hook-ups, and building facilities. See also *community association*.

mediation committee A volunteer member body created by the association board to assist in solving conflicts within the community. This committee establishes a nonlegal means for solving disputes; it may have a board director as a liaison committee member.

Megan's Law Federal legislation enacted in 1996 mandating that every state provide some level of community notification when a sex offender moves to a new address. The law requires disclosure to the public of the presence of convicted sex offenders (names and addresses), but does not address the responsibility of a property owner to a tenant regarding this disclosure.

member-at-large An association's bylaws may provide for this additional board position, allowing the board to divide its responsibilities.

menu-driven services Services provided by the management company whereby a community association can choose what services will benefit its particular association from a list of offerings. See also *menu of services*.

menu of services A format for providing management services that illustrates various administrative and/or supervisory capabilities offered and the cost to the community, allowing clients to pick and choose which services they use. See also *menu-driven services*.

minutes An official record of a meeting's proceedings. Minutes document the operations of an association's board meetings, annual meetings, and special meetings. They record the decisions made and provide a public record for present and future association members. The secretary is usually responsible for overseeing the recording and writing of minutes.

mission statement A summary that describes the aims, values, and overall plan of an organization; identifies the association's purpose.

mixed-use condominium A type of community association in which commercial, retail, and residential entities can all be members and are combined in a single facility. Also, such a structure or facility. See also *community association*.

modified accrual/cash basis accounting A business accounting method in which items that repeat at regular intervals (e.g., utilities) are accounted on a cash basis, while those requiring accumulation of funds toward a large dollar payout (e.g., insurance and real estate taxes) are accounted on an accrual basis; sometimes also called *modified cash-accrual system*.

morays Ethics that prevail by means of an unwritten code; responsibilities that each successful board should consider. In defining itself as a community leadership group, the board must contemplate certain practices and "morays of business."

motions Formal proposals put to the vote under parliamentary procedure. Items on which action must be taken.

multi-use association An association that has both commercial and residential members.

mutual benefit corporation This nonprofit corporation is formed solely for the benefit of its members. If a dispute arises regarding the operations of the corporation, the members must resolve the dispute. Not all community associations choose incorporation; however, for the benefit of the members, incorporation is highly recommended.

National Flood Insurance Program (NFIP) A federal program created by Congress in 1968 to make flood insurance available in communities that enact and enforce satisfactory floodplain management regulations.

National Housing Act The first significant housing legislation in the United States, this 1934 act created the Federal Housing Administration (FHA).

National Register of Historic Places A federal list, authorized under the National Historic Preservation Act of 1966, established to record and preserve buildings of architectural and historic significance. Such registration places restrictions on the rehabilitation or restoration of designated buildings.

newsletter/communications committee A committee that provides a vital link in the network of communications within an association. The committee typically publishes a newsletter on a regular basis.

official records Collection of an association's authoritative documents; can include notices of mailings, meeting minutes, membership lists, association correspondence, and the association history.

on-site management A plan for the management of a community association whereby the community hires on-site personnel to administer the needs of the association. Compare *self-management*; *professional management*.

operating budget Another name for *annual budget*.

overhead The cost of doing business; general operating expenses of a business (e.g., wages, insurance, utilities, taxes). The fixed expense needed to keep the doors open while managing a community association.

parcel number On a plat map, a number that identifies the specific subdivision lot or metes and bounds parcel.

parliamentary procedure Established rules of parliamentary law and unwritten rules of courtesy used to facilitate the transaction of business in deliberative assemblies. Some states and some associations' governing documents require the use of parliamentary procedure in association meetings.

personal assessments Another name for *individual assessments.*

planned development community Another name for *homeowners association.*

planned unit development (PUD) A type of development that usually includes a mixture of open space, single-family homes, townhouses, condominiums or cooperatives, rental units, and recreational and commercial facilities within a defined area under a specific zoning arrangement. Generally, PUDs are large in scale and built in several phases over a number of years. Typically, all infrastructure for the site is constructed before the improvements are built. Also, a *zoning* classification that allows flexibility in the design of a subdivision, usually setting an overall density limit which allows clustering of units to provide for common open space. See also *community association.*

plat map The drawings that illustrate how a property is divided into units or lots. The map shows the exact location of all property boundaries, unit boundaries, and common area locations. Also known as the *recorded map*, *subdivision map*, *condominium plan*, *site plan*, *plan*, and *parcel map.*

premises liability An area of law that holds property owners or managers responsible for injuries sustained by others on their property, including slip and fall incidents and other injuries resulting from hazards, defects, or poor maintenance.

premium The amount paid periodically by an insured party to obtain and retain specific insurance coverage.

preventive maintenance A program of regularly scheduled inspection and care that allows potential problems to be prevented or at least detected and solved before major repairs are needed. See also *deferred maintenance.*

principle of indemnity A requirement that, when a loss occurs, an individual should be restored to his or her approximate previous financial condition. Consequently, the policyholder is not allowed to profit by insurance.

Professional Community Association Manager (PCAM) A professional designation conferred by the Community Associations Institute (CAI) on individuals who have met certain minimum requirements as to experience, education, and participation in the profession of association management. This designation requires extensive educational and management experience as well as the completion of a case study.

professional management A plan for the management of a community association whereby a community contracts with a professional management company to oversee the management for them. Compare *self-management*; *on-site management*.

profit The amount of money gained in a business transaction after deducting all the expenses; the surplus earned when the price received for a good or service exceeds the cost of producing it. A key element in determining the value of a business.

profit and loss statement A summary of the revenues and expenses of a community association for a particular period of time, generally one year; also called *operating statement*.

proof of notice affidavit A document signed to verify that mail has gone out through the U.S. Post Office on a given date.

property damage insurance A type of insurance protecting against liability for damage to or destruction of others' property that may result from occurrences in or about a specified property, or because of the insured party's negligent action or inaction, and for which the insured is legally liable. Also called *property damage liability insurance*.

property insurance A policy that protects the insured against direct or indirect loss arising out of damage, destruction, or other loss of real or personal property.

protected classes Groups, usually minorities in the population, specifically protected against discrimination under the U.S. Civil Rights Act of 1964 and later amendments to that law. Protected classes include race, religion, color, national origin, and sex; in regard to housing, familial status and disability are also protected classes. Other protected classes may be created under state and local laws. See also *Fair Housing Act*.

proxy A person authorized to act for another; an agent or substitute.

public offering statement A document prepared by the declarant for the first sale of each unit. Its purpose is to provide information for new buyers so they can make informed decisions about their purchases. It includes information about the rights and obligations of unit owners. The requirements for public offering statements differ from state to state.

quorum The number of members required in attendance to transact business legally. Business cannot be conducted at a meeting unless a quorum is present.

regular assessments Another name for *assessments*.

replacement cost coverage Insurance to replace or restore a building or its contents to its pre-existing condition and appearance with no deduction for depreciation. Compare *actual cash value (ACV)*.

request for proposal (RFP) Written specifications for services to be provided by a bidder, often including the scope of work and details of design and use and asking for specifics regarding materials, labor, pricing, delivery, and payment.

reserve plan The document that identifies all common area maintenance components and establishes a funding plan to address their necessary maintenance. An analysis of the common area components that are expected to wear out in 3 to 30 years is conducted (often by a professional company), and the reserve plan is the written report that results. Also called *reserve study*.

reserves Funds set aside on a continuing basis for future expenditures; monies set aside to allow the association to meet nonrecurring and/or major expenses, as required in the governing documents (and in most states).

reserve study Another name for *reserve plan*.

resort association A type of community association in which individual owners, through purchase, own the right to use of the resort for specific periods of times. Also called *timeshare* or *vacation ownership association*. See also *community association*.

revenues The flow of funds into a community (e.g., cash, receipts, rent).

review A check of the association's financial statements. The auditor interviews board members, the professional manager, and others involved with operations in order to assess the association's financial procedures, compare the current financial statements with the previous year's statements, and provide a report or opinion of the association's financial health. Reviews are less expensive to conduct than audits. See also *audit*.

risk management Procedures to minimize the adverse effects of a (financial) loss by identifying potential sources of loss, measuring the likely impact of such losses, and implementing controls to minimize losses when they occur. In insurance, the process of controlling risks and managing losses.

rules and regulations Guidelines for tenants or owners that outline requirements specific to rent payment, tenant maintenance responsibilities, and the like. Specifics are usually incorporated in the lease, either as a specific provision or as a rider, and they vary by property type. The rules and regulations give further definition to a community association's declaration and bylaws.

rules and regulations committee This committee provides consistency and continuity to existing rules and regulations and makes recommendations to the board to update regulations as needed. This committee is often an adjunct to, and under the control of, the covenants committee. Also called *bylaws committee*.

seasonal maintenance Routine upkeep that is necessary at the same time every year, such as pruning, mulching, watering, gutter cleaning, snow removal, caulking, and weather-stripping.

self-management A plan for the management of a community association whereby the members carry out policy decisions and administer the affairs of the association. Compare *on-site management*; *professional management*.

sick association A property that is fiscally or physically destined to fail, often with very little working capital and high capital expense. If the members are unwilling to make the necessary financial commitment, this situation should preclude contract commencement.

site visit A cursory visit, usually consisting of a drive-through looking only for any obvious association problems or needs. It requires much less time than an inspection.

social and recreational committee A committee assigned to build community relations. Plans social events like cookouts, pool parties, tours, card clubs, and holiday celebrations to generate a friendly atmosphere and camaraderie within the association.

special assessments Amounts charged to each owner for the purpose of meeting a specific community need; generally one-time or short-term payments. The governing documents include a provision for imposing special assessments. See also *assessments*; *individual assessments*.

standing committees These groups recommend changes in and implementation of policies; they do not establish policy—that is the board's responsibility. The board creates standing committees to take care of the association's recurring needs.

strategic planning Determines where an organization is going over the next one to ten years, how it will get there, and how it will know if it gets there. The board uses the strategic plan as a road map to the community's future.

strategic planning meeting A time for the board president (or chairperson) along with all directors and committee volunteers to meet and discuss the community's governance processes. A meeting spent strategically planning and accomplishing a list of goals to benefit the community.

team approach An organizational approach used by some community association management companies whereby the community association manager, bookkeeper, assistant manager, and various support personnel are assigned to all the same properties. They work together as a collective team for the associations under their oversight.

tort Damage, injury, or a wrongful act done willfully, negligently, or in circumstances involving strict liability, but not involving breach of contract, that results in injury to another's person, property, reputation, or the like, and for which the injured party is entitled to compensation.

toxic leadership A poor leadership style characterized by negative traits and tactics, such as arrogance, quick reprisal, rigid commitment to an idealized goal, micromanaging, bullying, threatening, and yelling. Toxic leaders sap strength from their associations, instill fear in employees and volunteers, and paralyze organizations.

umbrella liability insurance A policy that provides liability coverage above and beyond the limits of a basic liability policy.

unanimous consent If no one in a meeting objects to an action, the president simply states that the action is approved, and the secretary records it in the minutes. Also called *general consent*.

vehicle-related injury insurance A type of insurance that protects the association against claims if a vehicle is used on the association premises.

vision A plan for the future that describes where the members want to see themselves or the association in a specified amount of time.

voice over Internet protocol (VoIP) Technology used to transmit the voice in digital form as an audio stream, rather than relying on traditional telephone lines. The system also routes incoming calls. A VoIP network is now being explored to combine voice and data networks into one common communication network.

welcoming committee A group established to make the moving transition pleasant and informative for new residents. The committee informs new residents about community governance and vital community information; it also often functions much like a social committee in planning activities to bring neighbors together. A member of the welcoming committee should visit all new residents, possibly providing them with information about shops in the area, a map of neighborhood schools and churches, and a list of other homeowners.

workers' compensation insurance A type of insurance that, by law, must be carried by an employer to cover the expenses that arise from employee sicknesses and injuries that occur in the course of employment, usually including medical and disability benefits and lost wages.

Index